D1570096

The Florida Seminoles
and the New Deal

1933–1942

The Florida Seminoles and the New Deal

1933-1942

Harry A. Kersey, Jr.

Florida Atlantic University Press
Boca Raton

E
99
S28 K47
1989

5624548

Copyright © 1989 by the Board of Regents of the
State of Florida
All rights reserved
Printed in the United States of America on acid-free paper ∞

Library of Congress Cataloging-in-Publication Data

Kersey, Harry A., 1935–
  The Florida Seminoles and the New Deal, 1933–1942.
  Bibliography: p.
  Includes index.
  1. Seminole Indians—Government relations.   2. New
Deal, 1933–1939—Florida.   3. Indians of North America—
Florida—Government relations.   I. Title.
E99.S28K47   1989   323.1'197   88–31032
ISBN 0–8130–0928–6 (alk. paper)

The Florida Atlantic University Press is a member of University Presses of Florida. UPF is the central agency for scholarly publishing of the State of Florida's university system, producing books selected for publication by the faculty editorial committees of Florida's nine public universities: Florida A&M University (Tallahassee), Florida Atlantic University (Boca Raton), Florida International University (Miami), Florida State University (Tallahassee), University of Central Florida (Orlando), University of Florida (Gainesville), University of North Florida (Jacksonville), University of South Florida (Tampa), University of West Florida (Pensacola).

Orders for books published by all member presses should be addressed to University Presses of Florida, 15 NW 15th Street, Gainesville, FL 32603.

56018

*This book is dedicated
to my mother, Margaret,
and
to the memory of my father,
Harry A. Kersey*

Contents

Illustrations

Come Light the Fire and Sing the Song

Towering bald cypress trees threaten to engulf the small clearing deep in the Big Cypress Swamp. Its scattering of thatched-roofed structures perched on the edge of a marshy pond, the Seminole camp is a reminder of another, simpler time. As a lowering sun brings the first hint of evening, several generations of Indian women gather beneath the shelter of a thatched-roofed *chiki* to sew, talk, and prepare their meal. Palm logs which nourish the blazing fire fan out from its center like the spokes of a giant rimless wheel. One of the women adjusts the logs, moving them to and fro, to control the heat of the fire beneath a low iron cooking grate. It is a time for closeness, a time for sharing, but above all a time for learning.

The ageless, invariant rituals of camp life are patiently explained to the outsider visiting among them:

"Seminole women tend the fire. Fire is a central symbol of hearth and home for Seminole women with rules and restrictions regarding its use." The words are intoned softly in precisely modulated English by a beloved granddaughter.

The cant continues but now in the deeply accented English still spoken by many of her mother's generation: "I was taught that you have four logs going to your fire meaning Four Corners of Earth. Each clan has a different meaning for the four logs and how to take care of their camp, their home, and how to raise the children, and this goes back a long way."

The grandmother's low voice is barely audible as she speaks in *i-laponki*, that exquisitely subtle tonal language of her people which whites call Mikasuki: "A woman's place is by the fire. It's up to each woman to control her own life and carry out the cooking. . . . When a woman grows old it is her place to have a home and have a fire going. A Seminole woman must never stop teaching what she has learned in childhood so that she will know how to continue to be a Seminole." Almost ninety years of Florida sun have modeled the old woman's face into mahogany ravines, and the glow of the campfire highlights her cloudy, nearly sightless eyes. She wears the traditional Seminole garb—an elaborate patchwork skirt topped by a solid blouse and cape of bright purple, plus the inevitable strands of colored glass beads—while her hair is kept in the "old way," pulled up in a knot on the top of the head. Her hands move incessantly, the long slender fingers clasping and unclasping in a palsied cadence with the conversation.

"Medicine or singing can be used to protect the fire in the home." The old woman begins to sing softly, her hands beckoning urgently toward the leaping flame. In hushed tones it is explained that she is summoning an animal spirit to protect the fire. Such conjuring is essential to the spiritual medicine that the women of their clan have practiced for generations.

"You must always pick your first camp, start the fire, and sing the song. This will be your first home and it will be protected."

So spoke Susie Billie, venerated as a medicine woman on the Big Cypress Reservation and grand matriarch of the Panther clan in that region. She sat quietly in the family camp surrounded by the Panther women, including great-granddaughters, and with a serene wisdom passed along the secret of family continuity and survival for her people: Seminoles must understand their place in the order of things and observe the old ways.

"If you put your fire out when you go to the next camp, it will be there when you return. You don't see ashes, you don't see the flame, but it is there because you used the medicine before you left. Use this song and medicine to keep your family together. I'm teaching this to my children and grandchildren, I want them to have the knowledge."

By performing this timeless rite of cultural transmission, as recorded in the video documentary "Four Corners of Earth,"[1] Susie Billie personified the cultural persistence of the Seminoles in the face of adversity. Born around the turn of the century, she had lived through several rapid and traumatic transitions in Seminole culture: from the hunting-trapping-trading era, through the privation of the Great Depression, then near-termination of federal protection, and ultimately the organization of her tribe as a corporate entity. More than the renowned medicine men, she and the other women had been day-to-day reservoirs of strength and conservators of those folkways that bind a people together long after archaic forms of religious and political organization have disappeared. Primarily through their efforts the unique Seminole culture did not fade away despite enormous pressures from the outside world.

Thus, cultural persistence is necessarily a central theme in any study of the Seminoles during the Great Depression and New Deal.

In a symbolic way, Susie Billie's admonition to keep the fire blazing—in the spiritual sense—by retaining a strong core of values and observing rituals also expresses the important theme of personal identity. Although throughout the 1930s most Seminoles retained a strong sense of their "Indianness," particularly the reclusive Mikasuki-speaking traditionalists who remained in the Everglades, some elements were culturally less cohesive. Uprooted from their traditional campsites and hunting grounds, and forced to seek employment in the wage-labor market, many Seminole families maintained a marginal existence on the periphery of white settlements. Others voluntarily took up semipermanent residence in commercial "tourist villages" for at least a part of the year. As a general rule, the closer the proximity and more intense the contact with whites, the greater the likelihood of a breakdown in traditional values. Drunkenness, promiscuity, illegitimacy were rampant where small enclaves of Seminoles were cut off from the support of their traditional clan and kinship system even though in the wild the Indian camps were often widely separated from each other.

The Great Depression had a differential impact on the Florida Seminoles, and therein lies the third major theme of this study: cultural adaptability. For the Indians who maintained their traditional life-style at camps deep in the Everglades and Big Cypress Swamp the economic collapse that afflicted the nation went relatively unnoticed until the late 1930s. They subsisted by hunting, trapping, and fishing and secured a modest cash income by displaying wild animals and selling handicrafts to tourists passing along the Tamiami Trail during the winter season. For the most part they were a tight-knit, introverted group with little use for the outside world. It was only when the bottom fell out of the economy again after 1937 that a number of them considered relocating to the Big Cypress Reservation where employment was available, and even then it took a severe religious rift within the group to impel such a move. By contrast, from 1933 onward many homeless and unemployed Indians, primarily Muskogee-speaking Cow Creeks from north of Lake Okeechobee, rallied to the federal trust lands where they could find at least part-time employment. Initially they came to the small Dania Reservation where they could make a camp or live with relatives temporarily while working for a few months, then later settled on the Brighton Reservation as the government's employment relief programs shifted to the rural settings.

The Indians' New Deal was midwifed by the enigmatic John Collier, a charismatic reformer turned abrasive bureaucrat, who served as President Franklin Roosevelt's Commissioner of Indian Affairs from 1933 to 1945. His major achievement was securing passage of the Indian Reorganization Act in 1934, which paved the way for modern tribal economic and political self-determination. More immediately, though, he marshaled the resources of New Deal relief and employment agencies to benefit American Indians. So with the advent of a Civilian Conservation Corps there was also created a CCC–Indian Division; in a similar manner CWA, WPA, NRA, and other programs were also extended to the reservations. Numerous projects in water management, range fencing, pasture revegetation, road and bridge building, and telephone line installation funded by these programs not only provided employment for Indians but also added substantially to the value of their landholdings. Ultimately, the Seminoles reached a point where they could successfully enter the cattle business, thus paving the way for limited self-governance as well as a degree of personal financial independence for some. Other advances were the establishment of a handicraft guild, the opening of day schools, and improvements in the living conditions on the reservations. However, it was not until 1957—twenty-two years after a small number of them had voted for inclusion under the Indian Reorganization Act—that the Florida Seminoles received their tribal constitution and a corporate charter from the federal government.

Congress's vote to end funding for the CCC-ID in 1942 signaled the end of the Indian New Deal; it had fallen victim to a combination of factors. During Roosevelt's second term, conservative Republicans and southern Democrats who never cared for the New Deal voted with colleagues from western states with huge tribal populations to dismantle Indian programs. John Collier, who had alienated a broad cross section of legislators, increasingly became the focus of their attack and ultimately forced President Roosevelt to accept his resignation. Finally, World War II absorbed the energies and resources of the nation, and all but the most essential programs were cut back or eliminated.

As the Seminole Agency scaled back its programs for the duration of the war, the Seminole people did not drift away from the reservations as many other tribes did. There was no great exodus for urban centers to participate in war production, nor did their young men register for the draft or join the military in any great number. For the most part, the Seminoles were content to remain in place, working in government jobs on the reservations or as agricultural labor nearby, slowly building their cattle herds, and enjoying a security they had not known in earlier decades of this century. To that extent the Indian New Deal and federal programs succeeded, not by accelerating social and economic assimilation but by allowing the Seminoles to develop at their own tribally determined pace. When the time was right, the Seminole and Miccosukee tribes would move dramatically into the forefront as models of economic and political success among American Indians.

Because many readers may be unfamiliar with the history of the Florida Indian tribes, a brief discussion of some concepts and terminology that might cause confusion is in order. Even those who are widely read in this field often remark on the bewildering array of spellings and synonyms that confront experienced researcher and novice alike. For example, both *Mikasuki* and *Miccosukee* commonly appear in the literature to identify both the tribal entity and the language. Historically, the favored anthropological-linguistic usage has been *Mikasuki*, identifying both the ethnic group and its variant of the Hitchiti language. Until recently only a lake in northern Florida bore the spelling *Miccosukee*. When the modern Miccosukee Tribe of Indians in Florida received federal recognition in 1962, it adopted that older spelling. Since this study deals with a time period prior to the formation of the Miccosukee Tribe, the spelling *Mikasuki* has been used throughout. Another confusion might arise when various quoted sources refer to the Cow Creek Seminoles, meaning those who spoke the *Muskogee* or *Creek* language. I prefer the usage *Muskogee-Seminole* to distinguish this ethnolinguistic subdivision of the tribe. Actually, the term Cow Creeks as applied to all Muskogee speakers is misleading, since their camps were spread throughout the region north of Lake Okeechobee. In the 1880s the ethnologist Clay MacCauley had located only two northern bands of Seminoles, one of them having camps on Cow Creek; that settlement survived into this century and the term was apparently extended to include all Muskogee-Seminoles. For the most part, though, the terms are used interchangeably. A third problem pertains to the proper spelling of anglicized Seminole and Mikasuki surnames. It seems that no two commentators in the 1930s agreed on the spelling for family names such as Tommie(y) and Billie(y). Unless otherwise noted, the spellings used are those that appear on the 1942 census roll of the Seminole Agency.

This work is the second phase in a continuing study of the Florida Seminoles in the twentieth century. It takes up where the first volume, *Pelts, Plumes, and Hides: White Traders among the Seminole Indians, 1870–1930,* left off, and it concludes with the Seminoles about to confront the crisis generated by federal termination policy during the 1950s. Much of the material incorporated into this study first appeared in articles written for journals such as the *Florida Historical Quarterly, Florida Anthropologist,* and *Tequesta,* and the *Journal of American Indian Education.* It was also my good fortune to serve as editor of J. L. Glenn's *My*

Work among the Florida Seminoles, the memoir of a federal Indian agent in Florida during the New Deal era. The basic research was conducted primarily at the National Archives in Washington, D.C., the Stirling Library of Yale University, and collections of the Florida Historical Society, Fort Lauderdale Historical Society, and the Florida State Museum Oral History Archives. Financial support at various stages of the research was provided by grants from the American Association for State and Local History, the American Philosophical Society, and the D'Arcy McNickle Center for the History of the American Indian at the Newberry Library. The author was also the recipient of a faculty research grant from the Florida Atlantic University Division of Sponsored Research.

It is an unfortunate reality that most published and archival materials on the Indian New Deal have been produced by non-Indians, and the information is filtered through a distinct ethnocentric bias. Until recent years there had been no systematic effort to gather oral history accounts from the tribal people who actually lived through that era in Florida. In focusing on the Indian New Deal in Florida, I have relied heavily on the words of the Seminoles themselves, taken from a variety of documents and taped interviews with elders who were participants in the CWA, CCC-ID, or other federal programs, and thereby adding a uniquely Indian perspective to the narrative.

All historians accrue an intellectual debt to scholars who have preceded them in a field, and I claim no exception. Anyone working on ethnohistory of the postremoval Florida Seminoles must necessarily begin with an examination of the cultural context framed by William C. Sturtevant and the late Charles Fairbanks. Other writers such as James Covington, James Buswell, Merwyn Garbarino, Ethel Freeman, R. T. King, Kenneth Philp, and Patsy West, to name but a few, have provided narrowly focused studies on various aspects of modern Seminole culture which proved particularly useful. I readily concede my general admiration for the efforts of these scholars who have added greatly to our knowledge of the Florida Indians.

On a more personal level, it would be impossible to acknowledge everyone who played an important role in seeing this project through to completion; thus I am reluctant to single out a few for fear of alienating many. Nevertheless, some individuals have offered special support and encouragement which kept the work on course. That ubiquitous factotum of Florida history, Samuel Proctor, editor of the *Florida Historical Quarterly* and director of the Doris Duke Southeastern Indian Oral History Program, has provided a constant stimulus to collect Seminole oral data and publish the results. It would have been impossible to complete research without the excellent support services provided by the Florida

Atlantic University Library, especially acquisitions director Zita Cael. I also owe an incalculable debt to Margaret Walker, a consummate professional librarian who provided invaluable assistance throughout every phase of the research and writing. Colleagues in several departments have been exceptionally supportive, while a few generous individuals including John Childrey, Donald Curl, Julian Rice, Henry Schubert, and Thelma Spangler read and critiqued portions of the manuscript in its initial stages; their suggestions have vastly improved the final product. My patient wife, inured over many years to being a sounding board for innumerable variations on Seminole tribal history, offered her usual consistent encouragement for the work. Of course, I alone assume responsibility for any shortcomings of the book.

Finally, a word of appreciation for my friends the Seminoles and Miccosukees. As a native Floridian I grew up among—but not of—the Indian people; to a white youngster they were fascinating, exciting, exotic, yet somewhat distant and aloof. Such perceptions changed as I began to work on the reservations and interacted with the people and their leaders. Over the last twenty years Indians have welcomed me into their homes, communities, political gatherings, churches, and even the Green Corn Dance. Through this constant process of interaction many close and lasting friendships have been established with tribal members. In recognition of this relationship, during the past decade it has been my privilege to serve as one of the five nontribal members of the Florida Governor's Council on Indian Affairs, appointed by three successive state administrations at the request of the Seminole Tribe. In return, I have attempted to offer honest advice and counsel when requested, assisted the tribes in those limited ways available to academics, and committed myself to producing sympathetic yet scholarly portrayals of their culture and history. I hope this volume will be considered a reaffirmation of that commitment.

1

Florida Seminoles at the Crossroads

The Great Depression of the 1930s, following as it did the exuberant prosperity and unrestrained financial excesses of the Roaring Twenties, caught millions of Americans both economically and psychologically unprepared to deal with privations. The earlier collapse of a wildly speculative Florida land boom accentuated by disastrous hurricanes in 1926 and 1928 had wrecked the state's economy well in advance of the 1929 stock market crash. In Florida as elsewhere throughout the nation, ethnic and linguistic minority groups suffered disproportionately high rates of unemployment and economic hardship during the depression. One of the few ethnic groups in the state not adversely affected immediately, if only because its members were already dangerously close to the poverty level, was the Seminole Tribe of Indians.

The first quarter of this century had witnessed a dramatic decline in the fortunes of Florida's Indian minority. As late as 1900, a few hundred Seminoles still maintained their independent existence in the wilderness of the lower peninsula. The tribe was divided into two linguistic groups: the camps located north of Lake Okeechobee spoke the Muskogee or Creek language, while those in the Everglades–Big Cypress region and along the lower east coast retained a Hitchiti language called Mikasuki. Although divided by language, all Seminoles shared a common cultural core encompassing social and political organization, clan membership, and religious beliefs. They resided in widely dispersed extended-family camps, conducted subsistence farming on the rich hammocks, and peregrinated freely while hunting and trapping in the region between Lake Okeechobee and the Ten Thousand Islands. They also engaged in a profitable reciprocal trading relationship with white merchants throughout the region.[1] The trading houses that operated at locations on the periphery of the Everglades—the best known and most active were Frank Stranahan's at Fort Lauderdale, Bill Brickell's at Miami, George Storter's on Allen River, Smallwood's Store on Chokoloskee Island, and Brown's

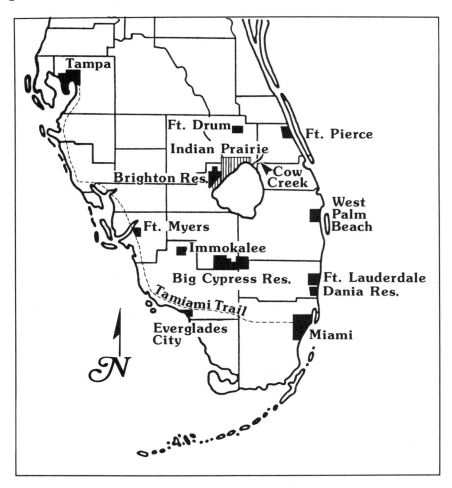

"Boat Landing" in the Big Cypress—absorbed a large volume of bird plumes, alligator hides, otter pelts, and other items that the Indians brought in from their hunting grounds. These valuable commodities were in great demand by the international fashion industry, so the Indian trade in Florida thrived from the 1870s through the first decade of the twentieth century. As long as the Seminoles retained unrestricted access to the wetlands of South Florida and game remained plentiful and profitable, they showed no inclination to change their traditional lifestyle. The tribe vigorously rejected all overtures by government agents and missionaries that would have led it to a more settled reservation-bound existence. Within less than two decades, however, the conditions that had supported this cultural pattern were radically altered, and the Seminole people found themselves confronting a social and economic crisis of major proportions from which they had not begun to recover when the depression arrived.

The first calamity to befall the Seminoles was the rapid demise of the hunting and trapping base of their economy. After 1906 the State of Florida embarked upon a program to drain the Everglades, a key element in Governor Napoleon Bonaparte Broward's scheme to convert the entire wetlands area south of Lake Okeechobee into a vast agricultural production center. The drainage canals that were cut from Lake Okeechobee to the Atlantic Ocean radically lowered the water table of the Everglades with disastrous effects on the region's wildlife population. It became increasingly difficult for Indian and white hunters to take alligator hides and otter pelts in profitable numbers for shipment to northern markets. In addition, the federal Lacey Law of 1900, as well as the Florida statute of 1901, ostensibly outlawed the lucrative traffic in domestic bird plumes.[2] Even so, it was a New York law of 1910, passed under prodding from the National Audubon Society, that ultimately denied plumes to the fashion industry of this country. With the onset of World War I and the loss of European markets, the plume and hide trade virtually collapsed. Ironically, this sudden termination of demand for Seminole products occurred at a time when they were becoming increasingly dependent upon participation in a cash economy.

A collateral pressure was being exerted on the Seminoles by the rapid growth of population in South Florida. This growth was precipitated by the frenetic expansion of railroad systems for the millionaire developer Henry M. Flagler and his chief rival, Henry B. Plant. By 1896 the Florida East Coast Railway had extended its tracks to Miami, while the Plant System offered easy access to the lower west coast of the peninsula. Each arriving train brought more settlers to the new towns that grew up along the railroads' rights-of-way. Soon, new farms, groves, and ranches were pushing inland from both coasts. The Indians quickly found themselves being systematically displaced from traditional campsites and hunting grounds to which they, of course, held no legal title. The Florida land boom of the 1920s greatly accelerated this process of forced relocation. Fortunately, the government officials charged with supervision of the Seminole Indians had foreseen such an eventuality and as early as the 1890s had begun acquiring parcels of Florida land as federal reservations. These periodic accumulations, plus the parcels set aside for the Seminoles by President William H. Taft's Executive Order of June 28, 1911, amounted to over 26,000 acres in four South Florida counties.[3] Many of the Seminole people eventually turned to these enclaves as the Great Depression worsened.

A more subtle yet equally important change occurred in the nature of Indian-white relationships with the passing of the Florida frontier. In the egalitarian "contact communities" that grew up around the trading posts in the late nineteenth century, Indians and whites had interacted on the basis of various relationships involving friendship, hospitality, education, and medical and legal assistance, as well as trade. Bonds of mutual trust were forged between many Seminoles and whites who appreciated the Indians' basic values of honesty and sharing and treated them with respect and dignity. For the most part, Indians were accorded a high degree of social parity within the frontier settlements; they became accepted participants at social and religious functions and returned the hospitality when whites ventured into their Everglades domain. Moreover, the interaction actually led to a strengthening of Seminole culture. An anthropologist familiar with the Seminole culture of that era found that "through these mutual trust relationships, the Indians added to the 'maintenance input' of their social system by resuming after the war and removal period the food and hardware trade without yielding appreciably any other aspects of the carefully guarded boundary-maintenance system of their basic culture."[4] Over time this easy relationship disappeared when Seminoles no longer played a functional role in community life. Rather, they became cultural anomalies, curiously dressed strangers living beyond the pale who occasionally came into town to sell a few deerskins or huckleberries. There was no longer a strong bond of empathy—sympathy perhaps, but no true understanding and acceptance of Indians as people.

The Seminole malaise was a constant source of concern to both public and private observers familiar with the Florida situation. In 1912 the commissioner of Indian affairs notified Senator Duncan U. Fletcher of Florida that "during the past year the tanneries have stopped the purchase of alligator skins, so now a crisis is approaching, as at least 75 per cent of the Indian's income is derived from that source."[5] By 1913, Dr. William J. Godden, for eight years an Episcopal medical missionary in the Big Cypress, had devised a plan for an agricultural project that would teach the Indians to support themselves, noting, "this they do now by hunting the alligator and otter and selling their hides, but the hunting season will soon be a thing of the past, as a means of livelihood."[6] His descriptions of Indian distress due to a paucity of game in the Everglades so alarmed a group of Fort Myers residents that they formed the Seminole Indian Association in 1913 as a private society committed to

*L. A. Spencer (courtesy Fort
Lauderdale Historical Society)*

providing support for the Indian people through both direct financial aid and political action. This organization became nearly moribund during the next twenty years but would reorganize vigorously during the depression era.

Although the market for pelts and hides recovered somewhat following World War I, with rising prices reflecting the scarcity of game, the Seminoles were never again a major factor in this trade. The greatest volume of game was taken by white hunters using more modern equipment and better techniques than the Indians. Writing in 1921, government agent Lucien A. Spencer found that "the year just closing has been a season of distress for many of the Seminoles. There was no demand for fur or alligator hides, the only two things they depend on to obtain money with which to buy the necessities of life other than those which they obtain through hunting. A certain amount of illness has been caused by undernourishment among the children, and an unbalanced ration containing too much meat among the adults. It was also necessary to furnish certain of the older Indians provisions in order to prevent famine conditions."[7] Spencer was undoubtedly one of the few people knowledgeable enough about the overall condition of the Florida Indians during the 1920s to comment competently, and he would spend the better part of two decades working to stabilize their eroding position.

In January 1900 the Rev. Lucien A. Spencer, an Episcopal priest, arrived in Florida to serve as dean of St. Luke's Cathedral in Orlando. There he was associated with the Rt. Rev. William Crane Gray, Episcopal bishop of the Missionary Jurisdiction of Southern Florida, who had undertaken a mission effort among the Florida Seminoles in the 1890s. Spencer was no stranger to Indian work, having served as a missionary among the Chippewa at the Whiskey Bay Reservation in Michigan in 1897. He quickly became involved in promoting mission work at various locations throughout the Big Cypress region and constantly sought to improve the Indians' condition. Eventually he felt that the only effective way to reach this goal was to leave the ministry and become a government official. He would later recount to a congressional committee, "I entered the service of the Indian Office the 1st day of March, 1913. . . . I had always been very much interested in the Indians and was continuing to look after them here and I urged the Government to do something for them. Finally they said they would start in if I would take charge here. That was how I came to the work."[8] Although he was commonly referred to as the Indian agent, Spencer's official title during his fifteen years of service was "Special Commissioner to the Seminole Indians."

Spencer established the Seminole Agency headquarters in Miami, where he operated with no staff and a minimal budget. The best he could do was visit as many of the Indian camps as possible and deal with emergency situations. In his first annual report the new agent noted that the Seminoles were living in twenty-nine camps spread over a territory of 900 square miles. This situation presented tremendous transportation difficulties; for example, for him to reach camps in the Big Cypress it was necessary to take a launch up one of the canals to Lake Okeechobee, cross the lake, descend the Caloosahatchee to Fort Myers, and then make the long journey inland by ox cart. Nevertheless, Spencer persevered in making contacts and was soon accepted and trusted by many Seminoles. Within four months of assuming his post, he was required to conduct a census of the tribe. He compiled the most accurate figures on the postremoval Seminole population in Florida that had been produced in this century. The Seminole population, including blacks living with the tribe, was placed at 567 persons. A census enumeration was repeated annually by June 30 throughout the remaining years of Spencer's tenure.

Few older Seminoles living in the 1980s remembered Spencer or his work. Frank Cypress recalled Spencer only as the "government worker which our people believed was going to send Indians to school, so at our camp we really didn't get involved with him."[9] The octogenarian Abraham Clay, when asked if any of the agents stood out, said, "Yes, there was a boss, Spencer. I know him, he overlooked [oversaw] the Indian people and assisted them with their problems."[10] Susie Billie, although close to ninety years of age, recalled that she had no direct contact with the government agent. When asked if he helped the Indian people, she ventured, "He might have. I really don't know, but not us personally. I'm sure he helped because he moved around and did a lot. There was also a woman called Old White Woman. She took me to a doctor in Miami several times."[11] This reference was apparently to one of the Public Health Service nurses who served during a later period, for another informant confirmed that his camp had received such service: "Yes, there was Miss [Charlotte] Conrad. Indians called her Old White Lady. She wore white uniform and that's why they called her that name. She made home visits even if it was muddy and her car would get stuck, she still visited people."[12] Over the years it was inevitable that Spencer, who could be paternalistic and arbitrary, would incur the enmity of some Seminoles. At least three letters ostensibly sent by Florida Indians condemning the agent's actions were received in the office of the commissioner of Indian affairs; one was signed only with X's affixed to handprinted names; the other two came from Spencer's tribal nemesis, Tony Tommie.[13]

In the fall of 1916, Spencer was called to active duty as a chaplain with the rank of captain in the Florida National Guard unit serving on the Mexican border in pursuit of the bandit Pancho Villa. During his absence the agency was temporarily administered by Inspector W. S. Coleman of the Indian Office. Captain Spencer returned to Florida in March 1917; however, the following month the United States entered World War I, and his regiment was activated as part of the American Expeditionary Forces sent to France. Faced with the uncertainties of wartime, Spencer resigned from the Indian work in August 1917. His replacement, F. E. Brandon, moved the Seminole Agency headquarters to Fort Myers to be closer to the majority of the Indians. When Spencer was released from active military service in November 1919, Brandon insisted that he resume the post of special commissioner.

The Seminole Agency headquarters remained in Fort Myers for the next six years. But Indian Office officials continually questioned where it should be located in order to provide services most efficiently to the widespread Seminole campsites. Also, there was a growing awareness that the Mikasuki-speaking Seminoles and the Muskogee or Creek-speaking elements should be treated as distinct polities rather than as a single tribe. In a *Special Report of the Florida Seminole Agency*, issued by the U.S. Senate in 1921, Spencer reported that "the population of the Florida Seminoles is made up of two distinct tribes speaking different languages and having little in common. The northern tribe, locally known as the Cow Creeks, numbering 115, speak the Muskhogean language, while the southern tribe, known locally as the Big Cypress Indians, with a population of 339, speak a dialect language known as Miccosukee."[14] The issue of a location for a headquarters was ultimately resolved when the Dania Reservation opened in 1926.

During Spencer's absence, his replacements, Coleman and Brandon, had moved forward with a plan to develop the so-called Hendry County Reservation. This wild, desolate 17,000-acre tract was the largest available parcel that could feasibly be fenced and stocked as a permanent home for the Seminoles. The agents expected to entice the Indians living in the Big Cypress to resettle on the new reservation, where the government could supply them with cattle and hogs and teach them industrial skills. The Seminole Agency headquarters was to be located there, along with a store and a hospital offering the medical services of a doctor and nurse. It was not a new idea. Similar schemes had been proposed for the Seminoles in the past, particularly by Dr. J. E. Brecht, who served as Seminole agent in 1892–99, and by the missionary Dr. Godden in 1913. The plan for an industrial station was consistent with the nineteenth-century Christian reform movement goals of detribalizing and assimilating the American Indian, which the U.S. Indian Office still strongly supported. However, the planners had not reckoned with the intransigence of the Mikasuki-speaking Seminoles, who steadfastly refused to settle on government land, or the parsimony of the Indian Office, which failed to fund the project adequately. Spencer undertook the project with his customary vigor, but it never got off the ground. Although over twenty miles of fence was put in, several buildings constructed, and a caretaker hired, funds were never appropriated to purchase cattle. Only a few hogs were placed on the range and most of those were eaten by panthers. No Indian families ever moved onto the land. Finally, a number of influential Seminoles asked the Indian Office to abandon this failure and use the money to support sick and indigent Indians, thus freeing their families to seek employment. This proposal was adopted at a Washington conference, and the Hendry County Reservation proejct was shut down on 30 June 1926.[15]

The preceding year had been a time of peak stress for the small group of Seminole families living on the east coast in the vicinity of Fort Lauderdale. Since 1901 there had been Indian camps on the north fork of the New River, where they relocated following the breakup of the large Pine Island settlement.[16] It was the height of the land boom, and even the marginal lands on the outskirts of the city where the Indians

Ivy Stranahan in the 1960s (courtesy Fort Lauderdale Historical Society)

camped were being reclaimed by owners anxious to sell at a profit. The only place where these dispirited and dispossessed Seminoles could legally be settled was a 360-acre government parcel set aside by the 1911 Executive Order, located four miles west of the town of Dania in Broward County. In order to facilitate their transition to reservation life, Spencer enlisted the assistance of Mrs. Frank Stranahan, a long-time resident of the area who was known and trusted by the Indians. Spencer, still located in Fort Myers, had also telegraphed Tony Tommie, the only Seminole to have attended public school and a self-proclaimed leader of the east coast group, asking him to lead his people to the government land. However, Tony, for reasons of his own, departed for the Big Cypress without taking any part in the relocation process. That left it up to the indefatigable Mrs. Stranahan; she loaded a group of the Indians in her Model T Ford, drove them over deeply rutted sand roads to the new site, and with some difficulty convinced Annie Tommie and the others to take up residence on the high and dry oak-covered property that had long been known to the Seminoles as "Big City Island."[17]

Ivy Cromartie Stranahan, a strong-willed and independent Florida frontier woman, befriended the Seminoles when she was young and spent over sixty years of her life working in their behalf.[18] She was a native Floridian, born at White Springs on the Suwanee River in 1880. Her farming family had gradually migrated down the peninsula, finally settling in Dade County. At age eighteen she was hired as a teacher and sent to the tiny hamlet on New River that was to become Fort Lauderdale. In 1900, she quit teaching and married Frank Stranahan, a man many years her senior, who operated the New River ferry and an overnight camp for stagecoach passengers traveling along the east coast. His most lucrative business, however, came from the trading post where he bought pelts, plumes, and hides from the Seminoles who poled their canoes down the New River from the Everglades. Theirs was a childless marriage, so Ivy soon turned her interest to teaching Indian youngsters who accompanied their parents to the trading post how to read and write English. In later years she drove to the nearby Seminole camps, conducting impromptu classes from the running board of her Model T for all who wished to attend. It was she who worked with Spencer to have Tony Tommie admitted to the Fort Lauderdale public school in 1915, and the Stranahans offered constant support for the agent's efforts.

As early as 1916, Mrs. Stranahan had gained a statewide forum when she assumed the post of chairman of the Indian Welfare Committee for the Florida Federation of Women's Clubs.[19] Nationwide, the state federations would become a major factor in the movement to reform government Indian policy during the 1920s, and Ivy Stranahan maintained close contacts with the leadership of national Indian welfare groups such as the American Indian Defense Association as well as with the Florida congressional delegation. She established a particularly close relationship with one Florida senator, Duncan U. Fletcher, and frequently corresponded with him on matters of concern to the Seminoles. Fletcher, in turn, reportedly promised to take no action affecting the Indians in Florida without first consulting Mrs. Stranahan. Theirs remained a potent alliance until Fletcher's death in 1936.

The same Washington conference that ended the Hendry County Reservation project also authorized the opening of "a camp for sick and indigent Indians" at Dania. So in response to Mrs. Stranahan's urging that he come to the east coast to supervise the newly resettled families, Spencer decided to move the headquarters for the Seminole Agency there as well. Under his direction, ten one-room cottages and a small administration building were erected in 1926, just in time to have them completely demolished by the great hurricane of September 18.[20] During the following month the assistant commissioner of Indian affairs, E. B. Merritt, came to Florida to survey the damage at Dania and other camps throughout the Everglades; the Indian Office then appropriated $6,000 for Florida Seminole rehabilitation.[21] Within nine months the rebuilt reservation consisted of a large administration building containing offices,

Headquarters building, Dania Reservation (courtesy National Archives)

superintendent's quarters, and teacher's quarters; an electric pumping plant sufficient for all camp needs; a four-vehicle garage; ten two-room Indian cottages; a school building; an infirmary; and a laundry with bath and toilets.[22] The idea of developing Dania primarily as a refuge for sick and indigent Indians was quickly put aside, as the ten cottages were immediately occupied by the Tommies, the Osceolas, and the Jumpers; meanwhile other Indian families took over buildings formerly belonging to white squatters on the government tract. The Dania Reservation, which served as home for the east coast families, officially became the new Seminole Agency headquarters on 1 July 1927.

The long-range goal was to attract as many Indian families as possible to the Dania Reservation, where they could receive educational and health care services and have an opportunity to learn industrial skills—an idea that did not die easily among Indian Office bureaucrats. Thirty-five acres of the reservation were cleared and planted in crops by Indian laborers under the direction of a government farmer, John Marshall, who was also Spencer's son-in-law. Seminoles were employed three days a week at $2.50 for an eight-hour day. In 1929, Spencer reported that "the lands at this unit are being subdivided into five acre tracts (which are sufficient for any one family) and the Indians are given employment at the Agency sufficient to furnish them with the necessary food and clothing, providing they spend the remainder of the week clearing their own tracts."[23] Apparently only a few Seminole families took advantage of this opportunity, preferring instead to work for the government as occasional laborers. In this manner the Seminoles living at the Dania Reservation were introduced to wage labor well in advance of New Deal employment schemes.

One major difficulty that the Seminole agent encountered was ensuring that sick or infirm Indians received proper medical attention. Because the camps were scattered over such great distances, it would have been virtually impossible for an agency physician to care for the numerous cases. All medical problems were treated by the nearest white physician and paid for at the current prices charged to non-Indian patients. The small infirmary at Dania offered an alternative between leaving sick Indians in the camps unattended and hospitalizing the most serious cases. At least one doctor from the town of Hollywood was willing to visit the reservation patients for $5, while some physicians charged triple that amount to visit the outlying camps—if they would come at all. During fiscal year 1930, a total of $3,897.22 was spent on the health needs of the Florida Seminoles, ranging from $1,153.45 for physicians' services to $85 for burials.[24] Regarding the latter, the dedicated Spencer once responded to an investigator's inquiry about who paid for the Indian funeral expenses by saying, "If I have the money in my fund, all right. I won't fight about it, I will pay from my own personal funds, if necessary."[25] The burial expenses ranged from $10 for children to $50 for some adult Indians who died away from the reservations, with most of the cost going for caskets.

Spencer was also insistent that the schooling of Indian youngsters should have as high a priority as industrial training. For nearly a quarter of a century volunteers such as Mrs. Stranahan had been providing sporadic informal sessions in the camps, but now there was an opportunity for regular formal instruction. In 1927 the school session was held for the first time in a one-room structure in the Indian housing area. The first teacher was an Indian woman, Mrs. Lena King, the wife of a Creek Baptist minister from Oklahoma who was doing missionary work among the Seminoles. Opening day was not without its complications. "On the Sunday preceding" the agent reported, "Tony Tommie, a self-styled chief of all the Seminoles, and certain white friends professing great friendship for and interest in these Indians visited the camp in my absence and impressed upon the Indians that the children would all have to submit to vaccination. Thereupon all the Indians fled from the camp except one family and the school opened with but three pupils."[26] Ironically, only twelve years earlier Spencer had praised Tony's educational efforts as the first Indian pupil in the local public schools!

Enrollment had recovered significantly by the end of the year; however, there were twenty-five desks available, and Spencer was determined that more Seminole children should receive an education. He continually attempted to persuade families with young children who lived in the outlying areas to move to Dania. When he was rebuffed in this effort by some headmen, the agent proved tough and resourceful; in 1927 he reported, "The Indian Town camp which I was preparing to move here refused to come on account of the above interference, and I promptly cut off their ration supply. At the end of three weeks of starvation they moved here and placed their children in the school."[27] The school opened for a second year in 1928 with Mrs. John Marshall, Spencer's daughter, as the teacher. She had filled in when the teacher initially assigned became ill; nonetheless, two months of the short six-month term were lost. The school was still considered an experiment with instruction limited to the first-grade level. The report of a citizen's committee that inspected it in 1929 described the facilities as "a small day school for Indian children . . . maintained despite a tribal law forbidding school attendance. 14 children are enrolled. They are all in the first grade and spoke no English when enrolled. They are quick to memorize but slow to reason. School hours are as follows: 9:00 to 11:30 classes. 11:30 to 1:00 luncheon. 1:00 to 2:30 classes. 2:30 to 5:00 gardening. 6:00 to 7:00 night classes for adults. . . . All pupils are very much interested in school work and take a special pride in word tests in English pronunciation. The small children seem bright and happy and maintain a good standard of school deportment with no suggestion nor evidence of fear or over-exercised authority on the part of the teacher."[28] Although the committee was perhaps overly laudatory and optimistic in its appraisal, the report had inadvertently identified an early "community day school," which integrated intellectual and practical skills while it attempted to strengthen local concern by involving all age groups. This was a forerunner of the tribal day school model introduced under the leadership of "Deweyan" progressive educators brought into the Indian Office during the reform period that began in the late 1920s and extended through the New Deal.

Actually, the 1920s was a decade of monumental reassessment and reorientation not only in education but in every aspect of American Indian policy. It was the time when a new coalition of Progressive Era reformers, intellectuals, social scientists, women's groups, and aggressive Indian leaders coalesced in opposition to further extension of federal intrusion into the affairs of tribal peoples. These "New Reformers" believed that the narrow assimilationist policies of the federal government were shortsighted and did not take into account the persistence of Indian cultures. What they particularly objected to was the large-scale erosion of Indian lands and civil liberties that peaked with the General Allotment Act of 1887.[29] This legislation, commonly known as the Dawes Act, set in motion a process for dividing tribal lands into individual holdings. It was the first stage in a policy, jointly promoted throughout the last half of the nineteenth century by Christian reformers and the federal Indian Office, to detribalize the Indians and set them on the road to assimilation into the mainstream of American life. Similarly, there were attacks through legislation and bureaucratic policy on the structure of traditional tribal leadership, Indian religious practices, the new Native American Church, and even Indian modes of dress, adornment, and hair style.

The initial issue around which these New Reformers rallied was their opposition to the Bursum Bill of 1921. This legislation, introduced by Senator H. O. Bursum of New Mexico, would have affirmed non-Indian claims to thousands of acres of Pueblo lands. He was supported in this effort by Albert B. Fall, secretary of the interior in the Harding Administration, himself a former senator from New Mexico who seriously questioned Indian rights to lands that had been set aside in the past by Executive Order. After nearly two years of bitter confrontation in Washington, the Bursum bill failed to pass. Then in 1923, Secretary Fall resigned in disgrace over the scandalous Teapot Dome oil reserve fraud, for which he was ultimately imprisoned; soon thereafter a Pueblo Lands Board Act passed, and a "Committee of 100" prominent citizens was appointed to make recommendations on Indian policy. Those favoring the revamping of federal Indian affairs seemed to have carried the day. Yet, the assimilationist forces were still active and powerful and had influence in Congress. This was clearly seen in the passage of the 1924 Indian Citizenship Act, which conferred full citizenship on all Indians born within the territorial limits of the United States.[30] In essence, the law grants Indians a type of dual citizenship, although its implications were unclear. For example, it left unresolved the question of citizenship for Indians within states that still set their own voting qualifications. Although the legislation expressly held that this new status in no way infringed upon the Indians' rights to property and other benefits deriving from tribal membership, many Indians feared that it was a pretext by which the federal government might sever its historical political relationship with the tribes.

In 1928 the privately funded Institute for Government Research issued a report titled *The Problem of Indian Administration*, popularly known as the Meriam Report for its director, Lewis Meriam.[31] This document, the result of an extensive and intensive study of Indian health, education, economic conditions, law, and the federal administration of Indian affairs, was critical of both the Indian Office and Congress. It was hailed by the leaders of such diverse groups as the missionary-oriented Indian Rights Association and the newer, more militant American Indian Defense Association, which claimed that it pointed the way to a much-needed overhaul of the Indian affairs system. The Hoover Administration, which came to office in 1929, brought with it a strong commitment to revamping Indian affairs along lines suggested by the Meriam Report. The appointment of Charles J. Rhoads as commissioner of Indian affairs and J. Henry Scattergood as assistant commissioner was a positive sign of that commitment.[32] Both men were Quakers known for their humanitarian efforts in Europe following World War I. They had had lengthy associations with philanthropic organizations working in behalf of Indians; Rhoads was a former president of the Indian Rights Association. Their appointments were strongly endorsed as a step in the direction of bringing a moral, humane aspect to Indian administration at the national level.

The period between March 1929 and early 1930 was a "honeymoon period" for the new administration at the Indian Office, during which all elements with a vested interest in Indian policy cooperated in proposing new legislation and promulgating new programs. Even so, between the assimilationists and the cultural pluralists there remained underlying philosophical tensions that were never fully resolved and would ultimately cause the uneasy coalition to dissolve; for the moment, however, they worked together. Although the Hoover administration never fully achieved its goals for the reform of Indian policy—in fact, the preeminent reformer John Collier referred to the era as a "false dawn" for the American Indian—it laid the groundwork for sweeping changes made during the New Deal.[33] During this period policy decisions began to be made in light of comprehensive studies such as the Meriam Report, as well as some less publicized landmark works such as the *Report of Advisors on Irrigation on Indian Lands* (1928) and *Law and Order on Indian Reservations of the Northwest* (1929). In this context of renewed interest in the conditions of Indian tribes, two significant studies of the Florida Seminoles were initiated.

In 1931 the U.S. Senate issued *Survey of the Seminole Indians of Florida*,[34] sponsored by Senator Fletcher. It was a report made the previous year on conditions among the Seminoles by Roy Nash, who was employed as a troubleshooter for the Indian Office with the title "special commissioner to negotiate with Indians" and who reported directly to Commissioner of Indian Affairs Charles J. Rhoads. Nash spent several months in Florida gathering data for the report, which provided the most

comprehensive view of the Seminoles since Clay MacCauley's survey for
the Smithsonian Institution half a century earlier. It is unclear what precipitated this special study, although interestingly the vice-president of
the United States, Charles Curtis, wrote to Rhoads noting that friends
in Florida had informed him that the situation among the Seminoles
needed investigation. "They claim," he wrote, "that whiskey is being introduced and girls are being debauched, and many things are taking
place that should be looked into,"[35] and he requested that a good special
agent or inspector be sent to look into the matter. Rhoads replied to
Curtis assuring him that "at the present time, a thorough survey is being
made of the conditions among the Seminoles; and we have, therefore,
sent a copy of your letter to the Agency with instructions to forward it
to the man making the survey so that he can give special attention to
the conditions which your correspondent mentions."[36] Accordingly,
Nash was ordered to investigate these specific matters and embody them
in his report.

When Senator Fletcher inquired about the qualifications of the official
the Indian Office was sending to Florida, Commissioner Rhoads declared that Roy Nash had impressive credentials for such a task. He was
a trained social worker, writer, and explorer who for several years had
served as executive secretary of the NAACP. Following service in World
War I as an officer of artillery, he spent three years making a social survey of the rural population of Brazil, which was largely Indian. His book
The Conquest of Brazil won international acclaim and was included in the
League of Nations' list of recommended readings.[37]

The Nash Report touched on every aspect of tribal life, gave candid
appraisals of policies and programs, and concluded by offering suggestions for possible directions that Indian Office efforts might take. He
was especially critical of the educational program, finding that "the
Dania School goes on in 1930 with seven or eight pupils. The net result
of all this education, formal and informal, is perhaps four Seminoles who
can carry on a conversation in fairly fluent English; three who can write
an understandable though ungrammatical letter and keep simple accounts." He was equally concerned about the declining socioeconomic
status of the Seminoles and asked rhetorically, "What progress have
Seminoles made in half a century? They have been driven into the most
inhospitable swamps in Florida. They have been robbed of all security
and possessions. They have been forced to abandon their cattle. They
have been driven from groves and fields to which their only title was
that of creator. With diminishing game, their economic position has become increasingly insecure. Tribal organization and authority have suffered a progressive decay. Long and rightly regarded as one of the most

moral groups in the world, there is observable a definite drift toward promiscuity. Education has made no mark upon their minds. Syphilis and gonorrhea have made their appearance. The children of warriors have become drunkards and beggars."[38] He shared Spencer's concern that many Indians had taken up residence in commercial tourist camps at Miami and St. Petersburg, where they were engaged in the "demoralizing employment" of being placed on public display like wild beasts. Although Nash painted a dismal picture, he still felt that there was hope if proper action could be taken quickly.

The first of his recommendations was that a man of "vigorous physique" be appointed as Indian agent, for only such a person could effectively get around in the Florida swamplands. Spencer had died in the spring of 1930 while accompanying a federal census enumerator on the Hendry County Reservation. An Indian informant provided details that imply that Spencer probably died of a heart attack: "His car got stuck and he was pushing it, and during the strain he got short of breath, turned pale, and some people got some canvas down. He lay down on it and died."[39] With Spencer's passing the Seminoles lost an agent and friend who was widely respected in Florida and in Washington.

Nash recognized that it would take time for a new person to establish the personal rapport so essential to working effectively in the camps, and he suggested that few tangible results should be expected for at least two years. The major function of the new agent should be to further the economic position of the Seminoles; thus his second recommendation was to continue moving as many Seminoles as possible onto federal lands where they could be guaranteed permanent occupancy, to develop a trading post to deal in furs and handicrafts, and to promote development of a cattle program on the Hendry County Reservation.

The Nash Report undoubtedly provided a realistic profile of the Florida Seminoles at a crucial period in their history. Nevertheless, coming as it did within a year of the stock market crash of 1929, this commentator could not gauge the impact that the depression years would have on the Seminoles so he made no mention of the need for special governmental programs to sustain the Indians during hard times. Rather, he echoed much of the conventional Hoover administration self-help rhetoric extolling the virtues of gathering the Seminoles on reservation land and transforming them into self-sufficient cattlemen and farmers. Roy Nash was a perceptive and humane individual, typical of his day. He had accepted the assimilationist imperative espoused by the Indian Office: the American Indian could only survive by abandoning tribalism as quickly as possible.

To his credit, though, Nash realized that assimilation could only be accomplished at the expense of traditional tribal values, and he decried that reality. Like many others, he was seeking a way to lessen the immediate acculturational impact on the American Indian. He asked, "Ought we, then, attempt to make a 'white man' out of the Seminole as rapidly as possible, inasmuch as absorption is his ultimate fate?" His answer was "emphatically no. There is something infinitely precious, vastly worth cherishing in this remnant of primitive culture persisting into the 20th century surrounded by industrial civilization. The metamorphosis will come fast enough, do what we will. And the transition from a good Indian to a poor white man is going to be a thing painful to look upon— progress stumbling along by-paths of tribal disorganization, moral degeneration, and the disintegration of personality. . . . Let us help the Seminole maintain his unique qualities and virtues; let us help him stand on his own feet with dignity in the presence of the civilization in which he is destined to blend; and let us always keep open avenues by which the transition from a primitive hunter to a unit in a society based on private property and the wage system can be accomplished gradually and with ease. But let us never, in pursuit of the desirable, lose sight of the actual."[40]

During the same period that Roy Nash conducted his intensive survey of the Florida Seminoles for the Indian Office, the U.S. Senate was engaged in its own wide-ranging investigation of Indian affairs throughout the nation. The Senate felt compelled to act because of a spate of critical reports appearing on Indian issues as well as the lobbying efforts of militant reform groups; even so, during the 1920s it was the first sign of major congressional interest in changing the status of the American Indian. An investigating subcommittee for this purpose had been authorized in 1928 by a Senate resolution.[41] The findings and recommendations of the subcommittee were published in several sections under the title *Survey of Conditions of the Indians in the United States*. Section 16 dealt with the Florida Seminoles; it included both statistical information and the transcript of a subcommittee hearing held on March 31, 1930, at the Dania Reservation.[42] Only two of the five members on the subcommittee gathering information were present at the Florida hearing, but they were among the most powerful figures considering Indian legislation during that era. The session was chaired by Senator Lynn J. Frazier of North Dakota, chairman of the Senate Committee on Indian Affairs and a consistent critic of the Indian Office, and Senator Elmer Thomas of Oklahoma was also in attendance. Both men represented states with large Indian populations and were strongly committed to the assimilation of the tribes. The tenor of their questions revealed an interest in promulgating those federal programs that promoted similar trends

among the Seminoles. On the whole, most of the substantive information that the hearing brought to light concerning the Seminoles was also
included in the Nash Report. It is highly unlikely, though, that the members of the Senate Committee on Indian Affairs were aware of the existence of the Nash Report until it was printed the following year.

Among the persons testifying at the Dania hearing were Mrs. Frank
Stranahan and Spencer, both of whose statements were printed in their
entirety in the final report. Mrs. Stranahan provided a detailed account
of her efforts to get the east coast families to settle on the Dania Reservation and expressed the belief that real progress had been made with the
group there; however, when Senator Frazier asked her opinion on why
more Indians had not chosen to move to federal lands, she replied somewhat prophetically, "They are not yet really agreed that it is the thing
to do, to go on a reservation. They just haven't been educated up to it,
and they don't want their freedom confined or restricted. It is my opinion that as long as they can get along in the Everglades they are going
to remain there. There are tracts of land set aside in the Everglades, as
you all know, and if the Everglades ever becomes limited to this particular reservation, then I think they will do as they did before—go on it."
Hers was essentially the scenario that unfolded throughout the 1930s:
as conditions deteriorated the Seminoles gravitated to government lands
seeking security and employment. Several of the Seminoles residing at
the Dania Reservation also made brief appearances before the subcommittee and answered questions. Most had a limited grasp of English and
occasionally needed Spencer to interpret what the senators were asking;
nevertheless, they presented an interesting contrast between old and
new ways. A taciturn Willie Jumper limited his answers to most questions
about the spare Indian life-style to a simple "Yes, sir" or "No, sir"; but
in response to the chairman's inquiry concerning his injured hand, replied "I broke my wrist cranking a Ford car." Jim Gopher then revealed
how the transplanted Seminoles still perceived the new reservation
home in terms more appropriate to their wilderness existence. When
asked if he had a garden, Gopher answered, "He [Spencer] gave me
land, with a pump for the spring." The interchanges could also become
disconcerting; when Naha Tiger, who was visiting from the Cow Creek
settlement, was asked whether his children had ever attended school, his
reply was, "No they have never gone to school." Senator Frazier then
asked if he would like to send his boys and girls to school, and Naha
responded "I have no children living. These children [his adopted fam-
ily] are orphan children."[43] The slightly bemused senators had no further questions.

Lucien Spencer, testifying less than a month prior to his death, was asked, "What are you trying to accomplish down here for these Indians?" His reply must have warmed the hearts of Frazier and Thomas, for it embodied the goals which assimilationists held dear: "My idea," he told them, "is to get the Indians started in some self-supporting business so that Government won't have to drop one cent on them. . . . We have 62 now that are self-supporting with their families." He then spelled out the obstacles that lay in the way of achieving Seminole economic independence, primarily that the small budget the Indian Office provided did not allow him to stock and fence the reservation or hire Indians on a regular basis, finding that "the Indians have lost confidence because the promises made to them have been broken so often in the past 20 years. . . . We are living from hand to mouth. I can't urge my recommendation too strongly that we be given a herd of cattle to start with. In ten years we would become self-supporting all around. . . . In fairness and justice to the Indians, I think that ought to be done, and I believe the Government is morally obligated to see that it is done."[44]

Despite Spencer's impassioned pleas, almost a decade was to pass before the Washington bureaucracy deigned to place a cattle herd on Seminole land, while additional allocations of funds to improve employment opportunities on the reservations came only with the advent of New Deal relief programs. Although numerous studies were conducted, with thousands of pages written about the impoverished nature of Indian life in America, conditions did not seem to improve. Even with the stresses placed on the national economy by the depression, the Hoover administration did manage to raise appropriations for the Indian Office from $15 million in 1928 to $28 million in 1931.[45] Unfortunately, little of it ever trickled down to the Florida Indians.

By 1931, the Florida Seminoles had reached a crossroads where their continued existence as a viable tribal entity was in doubt. Several factors had combined to severely erode the already fragile cultural linkages that bound them together as a people. There was also a real danger that some Indians might be absorbed into that amorphous ethnic mix of urban and rural poor spawned by the dislocations of the depression years. The creation of urban Indian communities as a result of federal resettlement programs was still decades in the future, and even then the new polities would be Pan-Indian rather than tribal in orientation. The immediate problem for the Seminole people, of course, was economic survival. With the full impact of the Great Depression beginning to be felt throughout the land, the economy ground to a halt. For more than a year any hope of pouring significant funds into development projects for the Seminoles would be impossible; meanwhile families living on the reservation learned to make do with what the government could provide. Those Indians not ensconced on federal land would have to fend for themselves.

Moreover, it had become increasingly obvious that the Florida Seminoles were divided into at least three major socioeconomic factions. The "progressive" reservation families who settled at Dania in the late 1920s, ultimately accepting employment and schooling, would be emulated by others who migrated to the rural reservations throughout the 1930s seeking security and employment. The second element formed a pool of paripatetic agricultural wage-laborers who moved about South Florida, living temporarily on or near the farms and groves where they were employed. There was also a small contingent that spent at least part of each year working in the commercial camps of Miami and other tourist-oriented cities. The makeup of this growing wage-labor constituency cut across linguistic groups, clan lines, and even ceremonial busk group membership. The third and largest group was comprised of those "traditional" families who remained in their wilderness camps throughout the depression. Such diversity would make it difficult to achieve social or political cohesiveness among the depression-era Seminoles.

Another obstacle confronting the Seminoles was the total lack of a tribal governmental structure to represent them with federal and state authorities. When the Senate subcommittee conducted hearings on the Indian reservations between 1928 and 1930, the members were astounded to learn that most American Indian tribes lacked any semblance of a formal organization to express their wishes or to deal in their behalf. In many cases the senators recommended that tribes immediately form local councils, thereby somewhat presaging the impetus to organize the tribes that would come during the Indian New Deal. That would work if there was a high degree of homogeneity among the tribal members on a given reservation; it was less feasible where reservations were occupied by different tribes, or the tribes were highly factionalized. In the case of the Seminoles, only a minute fraction of their number was living permanently on federal land at the outset of the Great Depression; furthermore, most Seminoles had no interest in creating a formal tribal government. As late as the 1930s, Christian missionaries had made few converts among the Florida Indians, and there was still widespread participation in the Green Corn Dance. The ceremonial busk groups headed by medicine men and councils of elders thus remained the primary political membership group for all but a handful of the Seminoles.[46]

The years of Lucien Spencer's administration had been devoted to laying a foundation that would ensure the future social and economic stability of the Florida Seminoles; the work was incomplete at the time of his death. That task was to become more complicated during the devastating depression that occupied the government. Only the selection of a strong and capable successor to Spencer, coupled with infusions of federal relief and employment funds, could see the Seminoles through the difficult days to come. Ultimately, though, the key to Seminole survival would be the strength and resilience of the people themselves—traits they had developed over two centuries of nearly constant struggle in Florida.

2

The Depression Descends

The years 1930–32 witnessed the cataclysmic conclusion of Hoover's New Era. A rapid winding down of the international economy triggered widespread unemployment that eventually reached fifteen million persons in the United States and plunged the nation into terrible despair. Ultimately, this national miasma affected the Florida Indians, who found themselves increasingly shut out of an ever-shrinking employment market. Denied their traditional hunting and trapping income, reduced to menial agricultural wage labor, or eking out a meager existence in their Everglades camps, a large number of the Seminole population suffered real deprivation. The Office of Indian Affairs saw its appropriations decimated and its ability to provide assistance to the tribes severely curtailed; officials at the local agency level did the best they could with limited funds and occasionally proved incredibly resourceful in finding economic alternatives prior to the New Deal.

The individual selected to serve as agent for the Florida Seminoles during those difficult early depression years was James Lafayette Glenn. A thirty-nine-year-old Texan, Glenn was a graduate of Trinity University and the Lane Theological Seminary in Ohio. In 1924 he brought his family to Everglades City, the governmental and commercial center of newly formed Collier County, where he had accepted a position in the community church. In addition to his pastoral duties and civic activities, Glenn also served briefly as editor of the local newspaper in what was essentially a company town, which placed him in close association with D. Graham Copeland, chief engineer and director of Collier Corporation operations in Everglades City. Moreover, the young minister's work had apparently not gone unnoticed by Barron Collier, the multimillionaire developer who was opening up the southwest frontier of Florida. So when it was thought that Lucien Spencer was going to resign as Seminole agent in 1928, Collier wrote in support of Glenn for the position.[1] This effort proved to be premature, but when Spencer died two years

*James L. Glenn (courtesy Fort
Lauderdale Historical Society)*

later the Collier interests again urged Glenn's selection.

Glenn had frequent opportunities to contact the Seminoles, for the families who maintained their camps at nearby Turner River regularly came into Everglades City. He befriended one of the headmen of the small Mikasuki-speaking band and through that contact initiated an "open air school" for the Indian youngsters. Years later he recalled, "Josie Billie worked out an understanding with the several families concerned whereby I could run out from the Town of Everglades, where I was then employed, and set up this class."[2] Glenn and his wife went to this settlement several times each month to teach the rudiments of reading and writing.

Because he was greatly concerned with the welfare of the Seminoles, Glenn feared that a cross-state highway known as the Tamiami Trail, completed in 1928, would become a disruptive influence on their culture by opening up the heart of Indian country to outsiders. That same year, he and a colleague visited the camp of Billy Fewel, a well-known Seminole elder who lived deep within the Big Cypress. Of this place he wrote: "This is one of the most beautiful Indian homes that I have ever known. Here lived Billy Fewl and his son-in-law, Wilson Cypress. Billy was perhaps a hundred years old when I first visited him. He had been a re-

sourceful man, and led his people during a most difficult period of read-
justment, and was one of the older men who had the respect of this
whole group. . . . He was a gracious host and at meal time shared some
of his daughter's biscuits. The home is built on a high spot of land and
is surrounded with guava and banana trees. He wanted us to sleep on
one of these catch-all tables that is part of every Indian home. . . . It had
been very hot through the day, for the glades were dry, and the rock
formation absorbed the sun's rays and cooked the lower atmosphere
with heat. But night brought a cool breeze from the distant Atlantic, and
the Indian people in the home gathered about their campfire and
laughed and talked until almost midnight."³ The photographs and written narrative of this visit to "Californee Camp" encapsulated a congenial
vignette of traditional Seminole camp life that was rapidly changing. Interestingly, Glenn's visit predated by two years Nash's detailed if unflattering description of this same camp; moreover, the Nash Report was
presented without any visual documentation.

The last official function that Roy Nash performed during his sojourn
in Florida was to recommend a replacement for the deceased Lucien A.
Spencer. After examining the records of the ten candidates being considered for the post, he wrote to Commissioner Rhoads: "In the course
of my survey I have formed certain impressions of the various local men
who desire to succeed the late Capt. Spencer. . . . I unhesitatingly affirm,
Dr. [John C.] Gifford having eliminated himself, notwithstanding my
ministerial prejudice, that Rev. Glenn is the only resident of Florida to
be considered for the position." Although Nash expressed some reservations about recommending another preacher as Indian agent in light of
the reform trends of the day, he went on to spell out how Glenn had
been involved with the Indians during his four years in Everglades City
and reiterated that Collier County was really the center of Florida Indian country. Furthermore, he found that the power structure was receptive to having Seminoles as active participants in social and economic
life: "Collier County is a one-man affair, which in this case is a circum-
stance all in the Indian's favor. I have never met Barron Collier, but I
have had several conversations with Mr. D. Graham Copeland, who
manages Mr. Collier's Florida interests, and I know him to be an executive of the highest type whose generous interest in the Seminoles is entirely above the suspicion of any motive other than the uplift of a lowly
people. . . . His ability to put the influence of the Collier County's representatives at Tallahassee, of the Collier County sheriff, of the Southwest
Mounted Police, squarely behind the Seminole Indian Agent, I do not
question; his willingness to put that influence behind Rev. Glenn is
stated in his letter transmitted herewith."⁴ Because of this strong local

Billy Fewel, J. L. Glenn, and Wilson Cypress (courtesy Fort Lauderdale Historical Society)

support, and the fact that Dania was on the east coast 100 miles distant from over half of the Seminoles, Nash recommended in his final report that the Seminole Agency be relocated to Collier County.

Evidently this endorsement plus recommendations from such prominent Floridians carried great weight with the Indian Office, for Nash was authorized to approach Glenn about accepting the position. Following a brief meeting with Commissioner Rhoads and Assistant Commissioner Scattergood in Washington during March, Glenn was approved for the Seminole post; on April 10, 1931 he was appointed special commissioner to negotiate with the Florida Indians at an annual salary of $2,900.[5] During this stay in the national capital, Nash introduced the new agent to two influential members of the Florida congressional delegation, Senator Duncan Fletcher and Congresswoman Ruth Bryan Owen, both of whom would take an active interest in Seminole affairs during his tenure. Shortly thereafter Glenn returned to Florida and moved his family into the upstairs living quarters of the two-story headquarters building at the Dania Reservation. At that time the Indian community was still relatively isolated, being about four miles west of the small coastal town of Dania, and therefore had to be self-sufficient in terms of power generation, water supply, telephone lines, and the like. Also, it presented a long trip over poor roads for Mrs. Glenn, who continued to work for several years as a public school teacher in Broward County.

One of the agent's first moves was to engage a new staff for the Seminole Agency. Although he had great personal admiration for Spencer, whom he had known for some time, Glenn disagreed with the nepotistic practice of employing his daughter as teacher in the Indian day school and her husband as the government farmer. For the teaching position he requested, and received, the appointment of an experienced civil service employee. A carpenter who lived in the town of Dania was hired as the all-purpose farm laborer. To complete the turnover, a new caretaker was employed for the still virtually deserted Hendry County Reservation. In addition, the Washington office had assigned a deputy special officer for suppression of the whiskey trade with Indians. Throughout this period Glenn had no office staff or bookkeeper and was forced to serve as his own disbursing agent. Even so, the agent was expected to provide a wide variety of services for the Seminole people, and these demands would increase throughout the depression years.

Glenn was appalled by the institutional drabness and physical inadequacies of the Indian housing area at Dania and resolved that it should be rebuilt to make it more habitable and hospitable; he believed that it should be a community where the Seminoles would want to live rather than a federal slum. Admittedly, he was also uneasy about living in the "big house" while his charges occupied small, cramped, one-room cottages that the agent likened to "dog huts." Although the accommodations were far from luxurious, and the government employees paid for their quarters, Glenn felt that it was a mistake to combine several functions into a single structure, "for the reason that it had the appearance that the white employees were spending everything on themselves. The Indians, themselves, were quick to feel this, and the hundreds of tourists who visited the Agency would believe nothing else." This uneasiness was reinforced by the comment of one young Indian girl who, even after the agent had renovated the abandoned squatter's shack in which her family lived, still resented the disparity in living conditions. According to the agent, "She was naughty one day and I said, 'Betty Mae, you must not treat us that way, we have built you a nice home.' She answered, 'You no build upstairs.' In other words the white employee had the best home in which to live."[6]

To alleviate this situation, Glenn exercised a good deal of ingenuity. A building fund of only $800 had been allocated to the agency, but he had Washington's permission to use it for renovating the Indian homes. In November 1932, it was learned that some racetrack barns in the nearby town of Pompano were being sold, and each of these structures contained about 50,000 feet of lumber. He purchased one of the barns for $60, had it dismantled and the lumber brought to the reservation, then employed Seminoles as unskilled laborers in the renovation project. As he recalled, "We moved these cottages about a hollow square, and made each into a building eighteen feet by twenty-four feet."[7] The refurbished houses now had a bedroom ten by eighteen feet and a roofed porch fourteen by eighteen feet; furthermore, the thatch-covered porches were meant to give the Indian families an open space to utilize that was similar to the chiki platforms that they had known in the Everglades. Glenn knew that the Seminoles were accustomed to gathering on platforms for meal and leisure time or for virtually any other function, and to his credit he took this into account when trying to improve the housing area. Each home had a large landscaped yard, and they were set far enough apart to give a feeling of independence to the occupants. The infirmary and school building were also moved into positions facing the large quadrangle, while the community bathing facility was improved with the addition of a solar heating unit to afford a continuous supply of hot water. A concrete sidewalk connected all sides of the quadrangle, the center of which was reached via a rock road. The entire living area was then enclosed with a high hedge of Australian pines.

While the revitalized housing was undeniably an aesthetic and hygienic improvement over Spencer's "Ten Little Indian Shacks" sitting in a row and baking in a shadeless field, it nevertheless pointed up a major short-coming of Indian administration that still existed during that period. Both Spencer and Glenn were benevolently paternalistic agents who provided what they thought the Seminoles needed, usually without any attempt to consult the Indians themselves. In this instance, though, it is likely that any facilities provided by the federal government would have been acceptable to the nearly destitute Seminoles who moved to Dania. In fact, one of the Seminole men who appeared before the Senate subcommittee hearing there in 1930, asked what the government could do to improve the situation, replied with pathetic candor, "I don't know, [I'll take] anything."[8] He did not question the underlying assimilationist motivation of the Indian Office representatives. It thus became a case of fostering acculturation not so much by the use of coercion as through co-option. After all, those Seminoles who were most resistant to any change in their life-style did not move to federal reservations until much later during the depression era; some ardent traditionalists would never make that move.

Like his predecessor, Glenn was committed to encouraging the Seminoles to take up industrial pursuits, primarily those connected with farming and stock raising, so that they might become more economically independent. In the annual report for 1932 he wrote, "this economic transition is inevitable. The Indian is going to fit himself into a new industrial world. The best the Government can hope to do is to guide him in this change, and save at least a part of the tribe for wholesome trades. Such an endeavor is constructive citizenship building."[9] To this end, Indians were employed as day labor working their own reservation plots under the supervision of the government farmer; over $1,800 of the agency budget was expended for this purpose in 1932, which was triple the amount spent the preceding year. The agent was a great devotee of self-help, and he got the Indians living at Dania to plant a crop of beans, which harvested out at 178 hampers with a gross value of $326.85. With the profits the Indians bought a small herd of range cattle which were grazed on 320 fenced but unimproved acres. They also raised calves, which were given to them by local dairymen. "Thus," he concluded, "the Indians' natural interest in stock is revived and encouraged." There was also money to purchase a brooder and incubator to improve the flock of chickens kept by the Seminole women and to buy a milk goat for every Indian schoolchild. Glenn was particularly partial to the goat as a milk source because "it is easily transported on the running board of an automobile, and can survive on a scant food supply."[10] It was reported that the Seminole families soon became quite attached to "Bell," "Bernice," "Silkie," and the rest of their goats.

Indian houses at Dania prior to restoration by Glenn (courtesy National Archives)

One of the Dania houses rebuilt by Glenn (courtesy Fort Lauderdale Historical Society)

When the Seminoles settled into a sedentary reservation life-style at Dania, it provided an excellent opportunity for religious groups to launch a missionizing effort among them. However, since early in this century the only denomination to have any success in reaching the Florida Seminoles had been the Creek and Seminole Baptists from Oklahoma.[11] They began in 1907 when Andrew J. Brown, a Seminole missionary from Wewoka, Oklahoma, went among the Seminole camps twenty-two miles south of Jupiter in the vicinity of Indiantown and preached his first sermon from an ox-drawn wagon. Two years later Brown and a group of native preachers returned for a second missionary visit to Florida; upon returning they reported favorably to their native Baptist church on the possibility of opening a permanent missionary work among the Florida Seminoles. By 1912 the Indian Baptist Church ran into financial difficulties and turned the mission work over to the large twenty-six-church Creek, Seminole, and Wichita Association, which sent its first missionary that year. Due to historical animosities and acculturational differences the native missionaries who came to Florida prior to the 1920s were not cordially received by their Florida relatives; they generally remained for six months, then returned to Oklahoma. The Rev. Willie King, a Creek Indian from Wetumka, Oklahoma, was the fifth missionary sent to Florida by the association, and the first to remain for a period of years.[12] He came originally in the 1920s accompanying his wife who was a Christian assisting with the mission work, but they returned to Oklahoma after three years. Following his wife's death Willie converted to Christianity, became a minister, and returned to Florida where he served as a resident missionary until 1945.

By 1932, King was living at the Dania Reservation on a plot of land that Indian Baptists in Oklahoma had purchased from the government.[13] At this mission station he preached to a few Indians who were interested in the "Black Book," as they called the Bible. A small frame church building was erected, and services were held each Sunday morning and on Wednesday evenings. Virtually the only Seminoles who attended were women and children, and church records reveal that there were only eleven converts. Nevertheless, the First Seminole Indian Baptist Church was organized as a full-time church on June 6, 1936.[14] The two deacons selected by the new congregation were Willy Jumper and Jimmie Gopher, the latter a former medicine man. These two old men were probably the earliest Seminole male converts to Christianity, although it is unclear whether they were ever baptized, and one church history claims that the first Seminole male was not baptized until 1944. Despite King's best efforts, Seminole resistance to Christianity remained strong, and the Dania church's membership was static for the next seven years.

The missionary received a minimal financial stipend of $50 per month from the association in Oklahoma, and although the Florida Baptist Convention supplemented his salary by $25 per month beginning in 1934, he always needed additional income.[15] Agent Glenn frequently employed King in the capacity of interpreter and intermediary, especially among the Muskogee-speaking Cow Creeks, calling him "one of the most faithful and helpful men I had in all the Service."[16] Although King did not make many converts among the Seminoles during the 1930s, he was constantly witnessing to the camps by working on the Indians' behalf in a number of ways. He was always on the move tending the sick, settling family disputes, helping with livestock, advising on financial matters, and negotiating with local authorities when a Seminole ran afoul of the law. His patient and devoted work paved the way for the large number of conversions to take place during the next decade. In 1938 much of the financial support for King's work was assumed by the Home Mission Board of the Southern Baptist Convention; also, at the same time he shifted the focus of his activities almost exclusively to the Cow Creeks living on the Brighton Reservation and in the region north of Lake Okeechobee.[17] He considered this a more fertile mission field because he spoke the Muskogee language and understood the people better than the Mikasukis at Dania. As a consequence, after 1940 King was able to preach at the Dania church only about one Sunday a month. The few Christian Seminoles at Dania were mostly left to their own devices, and attendance declined until there were only seven members. Then in 1943 a dynamic young Oklahoma Indian missionary, the Rev. Stanley Smith, arrived to assist King, and he made his headquarters at the Dania Reservation. That would mark the beginning of a turbulent era in which Seminole conversions to Christianity accelerated dramatically.

Although the introduction of Christianity had been an assimilationist article of faith among the Indian Office bureaucracy for many decades prior to the New Deal—likely the reason why reservation land was sold to the Baptists for a mission to begin with—Spencer, despite his clerical background, was not overly supportive of the Indian missionaries. He respected the Seminole beliefs and was suspicious of the Oklahoma Indians who came among them only briefly each year; in 1929 he commented, "I am willing to confess that I am very lukewarm to missionary activities and will continue to be so until I meet a missionary that is willing to take the Indian's native religion as a foundation and build it up to our ideal, instead of destroying his faith and leaving him nothing in return."[18] Glenn was less skeptical about the Baptist missionary effort; of course, he had a close working relationship with the resident missionary, Willie King, and often called upon him to help promote government policies. Although he was careful to distance himself from any overt involvement in the missionary work on the reservation, the agent did indirectly reinforce Seminole religiosity by involving them in his own off-hours ministry. Glenn occasionally filled the pulpit at local churches, and one of the Seminole women remembered, "We used to go out and sometimes he preached at night. We used to go sing for him. I remember that—Indian songs, Christian songs."[19] Over time the Seminole youngsters and adults continued to make frequent singing appearances at churches in the Fort Lauderdale area; white Christians, in turn, visited the Indian church, and that further accelerated the assimilation process.

All things considered, Glenn was convinced that good progress had been made in moving the Dania Reservation families along the path of rational, incremental acculturation. They were living in vastly improved housing which even retained an aspect of their culture as evinced by the thatch-covered porches; never mind that the living area now exuded the geometric formality of a small white neighborhood rather than the casualness of the Everglades camps. The Seminole men were adapting to day labor, farming, and herding—although it is questionable whether the Indian really had a natural interest in stock raising. The women and children seemed to be more receptive to the domestic tasks such as gardening and keeping small stock. Certainly the availability of an infirmary where less than critically ill Seminoles could recuperate in the presence of their families was a positive aspect of reservation life. The day school continued to function, although enrollment had remained relatively static for five years. The Baptist church provided yet another stabilizing influence in the inexorable transformation of the Seminoles.

The agent's overarching concern, of course, was that only a minute number of Seminoles were involved in this process. The census of 1932 had enumerated 562 members of the tribe, but fewer than a fifth of that number made their permanent residence at the Dania Reservation. The rest were scattered throughout South Florida, earning a living as best they could and having limited contact with the Indian Office officials; this created immense difficulties in reaching sick or injured Indians and in enforcing the liquor laws. Even so, in 1932 a total of over 1,000 visits to physicians were reported for a population of less than 600 Indians, while the special deputy, Walter B. Lewis, brought forty-two liquor law violation cases before the courts and got twenty-nine convictions. Such efforts took a great toll on the stamina of both men; Glenn by his own account occasionally put in eighty-hour work weeks. It was not uncommon for him to travel several hundred miles and drive half the night over bone-jarring unpaved roads to reach sick Indians and get them to a hospital. Ultimately, in frustration he would write, "The welfare and progress of the Seminole, the efficiency and thoroughness of the Indian Service in Florida require the centralization of the holdings of land for these Indians."[20] Thereafter, most of his energies were expended in attempting to secure one or two large tracts of land upon which to settle the Seminoles and center the federal programs in their behalf. As Glenn would find out, it is one thing to obtain land for a reservation and another to change Indian attitudes about settling on the property and taking up industrial pursuits.

How did the Seminoles respond to these federal programs? There have been numerous studies of Seminole cultural adaptation during this era, most written by non-Indians. In none of these accounts was there a systematic attempt to present an Indian perspective on the events of the time or to have them recount their own tales of survival. With the passing of time there were fewer and fewer surviving Seminoles who were adults during the Great Depression, and the oral tradition from that period was in danger of being lost. In 1983, coinciding with the fiftieth anniversary of the inauguration of New Deal programs for Indian peoples, a project was initiated to gather oral history accounts of the depression and New Deal era from the surviving Seminole elders. As chance would have it, most of the informants came from that element of the tribe that had remained off the reservations throughout most of the 1930s. What emerged from these interviews was the fact that these elders, both Creek- and Mikasuki-speaking, shared a number of common characteristics. The most striking of these was their spirit of independence and total self-reliance. Most of the Seminole people did not live on federal land at the outset of the Great Depression, and most families were not inclined to do so. Neither did they look to the federal government as a source of employment, education, or even medical services except in cases of extreme emergency. Most of the Florida Indians still shunned anything having to do with the U.S. government, a position reinforced by the fact that only two generations separated them from the traumatic period of the Seminole Wars and removal from Florida, and it would take many years before these attitudes were modified significantly. In fact, most Seminoles of the depression era would have preferred to remain at their traditional camps deep in the Everglades and pine woods, carrying on the old ways, and maintaining only limited contact with the outside world of the white man. This cultural conservatism was a Seminole hallmark, particularly among the Mikasuki-speaking elements.

The Seminole elder's keen sense of identity with a unique time/place context may be sensed in the following excerpts. In the first, Albert Billie describes his life before moving to what is now the Big Cypress Reservation: "When young man [I] lived out here, not sure [where]. Lived out in forest of cypress trees. Farmed out there. Most of the people during that time have died. My sister died and I'm not sure how long I'll live. My mother said, 'When I go you must live and join with other people.' Not long after that she got very ill and died, not sure of the year." When asked where his family had lived during the 1920s, old Frank Cypress simply replied, "I was told I was born in the clearing where the big lake lays."[21] Similarly, most of the elders tied events to particular occurrences in their lives, or to specific places, rather than to chronological dates. Such people do not take easily to the regimentation and limitations of the white man's ways.

The Seminole camps were still amazingly self-sufficient places half a century ago. Materials to make the thatched-roof, all-purpose chikis were readily available, and only a small plot of hammock land for subsistence farming was required to sustain an extended family group. In their small gardens the Indians could easily grow corn, pumpkins, sweet potatoes, cow peas, and sugarcane. Many campsites had stands of bananas, guava, lime, and sour orange trees, and a variety of berries were plentiful in season. The women kept herds of hogs which foraged near the camps. A hunter could easily bag deer, bear, turkey, duck, curlew, turtle, alligator, and manatee to provide meat. Fish were always available for spearing in the shallow waters of the Everglades or could be caught conventionally in the lakes and rivers. The staple food of the Seminole camp was *sofkee,* a gruel derived from hominy grits, often enhanced with chunks of dried meat and eaten with a communal spoon. The sofkee pot was continuously on the fire in most camps, and the inhabitants ate on an irregular schedule as their work allowed. Despite this relative abundance of food, the Seminoles still needed hard cash to buy grits, coffee, salt, sugar, baking powder, and canned goods, as well as clothing, camp hardware, rifles and ammunition, and the ever-present sewing machine. In short, they were rapidly becoming a cash-dependent and less autonomous people.

As their meager cash flow dried up during the depression, the Seminoles became more peripatetic in their search for employment. In the early years only a few of them would come to the Seminole Agency seeking assistance—these included both unaccompanied males as well as entire family units, and they stayed for only short periods of time. A much larger number of Indian families moved about South Florida engaging in seasonal agricultural work. Still another segment of the Seminole population took up residence in commercial tourist villages for at least part of the year, returning to their camps periodically and during the off season. Even those families that occupied Everglades camps and remained in place throughout the 1930s often ventured into urban centers such as Miami to visit their kinfolk at the commercial villages and sold their own handicrafts and food products to tourists. This increased mobility exposed the Seminoles to both the best and worst elements in white society, and some elders claimed it had a corrupting influence on the younger generation. Certainly with this degree of fragmentation the warp and woof of traditional Seminole values would be severely strained as never before, and in some instances the old ways disappeared completely.

Agricultural labor was by far the most common source of employment for the Seminoles throughout the depression. In his final annual report written in 1929, Spencer found that "very little employment is open to these Indians due to the fact that they speak very little English and cannot be made to understand what is wanted of them. Some truckers hire the women at the time of harvesting crops."[22] The following year Roy Nash expanded on the topic, noting: "In the winter and early spring when garden truck is to be harvested the Seminoles make fair wages for perhaps 45 days a year. They receive $2 a day for picking tomatoes and eggplant; picking beans at 20 to 30 cents a bushel pays them $4 to $5 a day. Children generally help their parents and receive no individual wages."[23] Although Glenn was primarily interested in having the Seminoles become self-employed farmers on government land, he was quite aware of their active role in the migratory labor market. Years later in a memoir he recalled that "Indian women have found work on a nearby farm and have fitted into the industry about them. They are picking peppers, and I am told that they were more careful in handling the vines than either white or Negro labor. Like so much farm work, they are employed only a few weeks of the year, but it does help them provide for their homes."[24] It is noteworthy that this period signaled the entry of many Seminoles into the wage-labor economy, when formerly they had been almost exclusively entrepreneurial.

Harvesting crops was just one aspect of the annual economic cycle that the off-reservation Seminoles developed out of necessity during the depression years. The account of eighty-five-year-old Susie Billie, the venerated "medicine woman" from the Big Cypress region, was typical: "I lived around here, grew up here. Employment was scarce. People hunted, killed raccoons, killed deer, made moccasins and sold them to buy groceries. Ate berries and whatever else could be found or hunted. There was a lot of hunger. If you didn't go looking, or was lazy, if you couldn't help yourself, you would go hungry. . . . There was men who found employment for people, but the pay was very cheap back then. There was farm labor. When of age to work in fields you could use money for clothing and food. . . . A day's work pay was $1.50." Another octogenarian, Abraham Clay, still living alone in his camp near Ocho-pee, recalled earning money by "picking tomatoes, cutting wood, build-ing railroad tracks and various other jobs [such as] cattle fence making . . . [also] looked for alligators, raccoons, otters and hides to sell." When asked if his people traveled to different locations seeking work, Willie Tiger answered emphatically, "Yes, Indiantown, Fort Pierce, Vero Beach, yes we traveled and lived in those areas where work was available. Picking oranges and various other farm labor."[25] Evidently some Indian families lived on the farms where they worked or made temporary camps nearby. In one instance an interpreter inquiring about this aspect of Seminole life, inadvertently learned a bit of her own family's history when a relative recounted, "Oh yes, your mother would go there when she was little. So she was our only child at the time. But she was born past Deep Lake, a place called the big carved tree. On the other side was a cypress forest. We moved there; people there were camping dur-ing tomato picking time and that's where your mother was born."[26]

Inevitably, worsening economic conditions had led a few Seminole families to take up semipermanent residence on farms in the vicinity of Lake Okeechobee by 1930. Nash found that eight or ten Indians "live in an old house on the farm of a friendly white man, Mr. Clarence Summerlin; they come and go, working for him when he has work for them, hunting and berrying as the mood strikes them, a distinctly transi-tional type. . . . Dan Parker houses his family in an old barn and makes a precarious living as a casual laborer. . . . Mrs. Ella Montgomery . . . by the gift of a Ford car persuaded the family of Charlie Cypress to aban-don his home in the Big Cypress and build a camp adjoining Mrs. Montgomery's home at Loxahatchee Farms, 10 miles west of Palm Beach."[27] Although Nash was probably correct in his assessment that these Seminoles were exceptions for that time, several elderly Indian in-formants reported living on farms prior to settling on federal land. The practice of settling in at farms for protracted periods of time may have become more widespread as the depression worsened.

Obviously, many Seminoles were still engaged in hunting and trap-ping to raise cash as late as the 1930s. It is well documented that the heyday of the Indian trade in pelts, plumes, and hides had long since passed, having peaked around the turn of the century. As Nash pointed out, "The Indian is a minority factor in the Florida fur trade," having been displaced by white hunters who used better equipment and were better organized to take the remaining game. Even so, the hide buyers were an important source of revenue for the Indians. When queried about this, Frank Cypress responded, "Yes, when tomatoes weren't in season we hunted alligators. The gators weren't too abundant either, but when we find a few and kill and sell those. . . . Raccoons were sold in La Belle for $1.00 apiece. Sometimes even 75 cents or 50 cents." Willie Frank also remembered that, "around 1930–1936, we did sell hides and pelts, raccoons, otters, alligators as a source of income."[28] Another source of wages for Seminoles during the winter months was to serve as hunting guides for white sportsmen in the Everglades, but, practically speaking, it was limited to a few well-known Indian hunters and produced irregular income at best.

There had been commercial "tourist villages" operating as Florida attractions since the time of World War I, primarily in Miami and St. Petersburg, then later at Silver Springs near Ocala in the central part of the state. In 1917 the Coppinger's Tropical Garden on the Miami River hired two Seminole families to set up a village inside the park.[29] Soon thereafter another village opened at the Musa Isle Grove, also located on the river, and was greatly expanded by 1919. Ten years later Spencer told the Senate investigating subcommittee that there were about thirty-five living at Musa Isle and about twenty-five at the Tropical Gardens; moreover, he offered the opinion that "the two amusement parks there are very detrimental to our work and we haven't enough money to prevent that. I pay an Indian $2.50 a day to work eight hours clearing land on the reservation. They pay him $2.50 a day to sit down and make a show of himself."[30]

One study of these attractions showed that it appeared that the early employees of both tourist attractions were mostly Mikasuki-speaking Seminoles from the Broward County area, including the family of the old matriarch, Annie Tommie.[31] Annie's family was among the original group of Seminoles that had been persuaded by Mrs. Stranahan to relocate to the Dania Reservation, and her sons played a prominent role in tribal affairs. Evidently this Indian family also retained a long-term connection with the Musa Isle establishment, for her son, Tony Tommie, was listed as one of the headmen there prior to 1940.

The Indians who lived within these villages were not on static display; rather, they engaged in activities typical of Seminole camp life such as cooking, sewing patchwork garments, or carving canoes and the like. Nevertheless, there were two activities that all tourists wanted to see:

WRESTLING PIT
DANGER
DO NOT SIT ON WALL
MUSA ISLE INDIAN VILLAGE
M........FLA.

BY TIGER, SEMINOLE INDIAN, PREPARES TO WRESTLE WITH ALLIGATOR AT AN INDIAN VILLAGE. TOUR

OURIST FLOR

Musa Isle Indian Village (courtesy Fort Lauderdale Historical Society)

alligator wrestling and an Indian wedding. The irrepressible Tony Tommie, not content to be a passive "show Indian," took a leading role in the activities staged for tourists and visiting dignitaries. Moreover, the City of Miami promoted both attractions by taking notable guests there to witness special events such as the weddings. In 1926 the *Miami News* described in detail one such wedding, that of Tony Tommie and Edna John, staged before a capacity crowd at Musa Isle. John Osceola performed the "ceremony," and the crowd flung coins and bills to the bridal pair. According to long-time employees at the attraction, the couple had been married long before the public ceremony, but some members of the Tommie family deny that the couple ever married. In either case, spectacles such as this led Glenn to complain, "This is neither Indian nor a wedding, and the people of Miami know it, and even some of the tourists know it."[32] Despite such criticisms the staged weddings continued to be popular with tourists. For this reason the efforts of government agents and reformers who tried to have the commercial villages shut down never received a cordial reception from the Miami city fathers, whose basic reasoning was that no one forced the Seminoles to live there.

Commercial villages drew Glenn's ire; like Spencer and Nash before him, he found them to be demeaning to the Seminole participants who were exploited for economic gain. There was also evidence that the Indians often contracted venereal and other contagious diseases during their residence in these camps. As long as such places were allowed to exist as an alternative to employment, the process of getting the Seminoles into proper industrial pursuits on the reservations would be prolonged. The federal officers were undeniably upset that a number of the Seminoles preferred the tourist village setting to relocating to the Seminole Agency, which may account for the intensity with which they reviled the tourist villages. In his 1935 report, Glenn gave his version of how the commercial village operators had preyed on the gullibility of the Seminoles and white tourists alike for their own profit. The ballyhoo of these show places featured the Indian as an unconquered, unrelenting, and implacable enemy of the ways of the white man, especially of the white man's government. The management was represented as the great benefactor and the government and its agent as the chief malfactors of the tribe. The Seminole was flattered at being accorded the status of an unconquered man. Past wrongs inclined him to believe the charges against the government and to confide in the management of these show places. White tourists were amazed to see a people "who had conquered the American government," were disgusted with the Indians' lack of sanitation, and knew enough of the government's past treatment of the Seminoles to accept the charges of current mistreatment. "It was not known,"

Glenn wrote, "by either the tourist or the Indian that the management in one case stated frankly that any solution of the Florida Indian problem would ruin his business. The injustice, distress, poverty, ignorance and disease of the tribe are the materials which boom such business. Day after day for more than a decade the Miami Indians have listened to a type of ballahoo which has had for its purpose the promotion and propagation of the Indian's bitterness toward the things of the government, and an effective blockade of the government's attempt to extend a program of justice and equity to their people."[33]

However, Patsy West's study based on extensive interviews with Seminoles who actually lived there lends a kindlier aspect to life in the commercial villages. Certainly the Indians went there of their own free will, and it has been suggested that the life-style was not too different from what they had known in the Everglades except that they were getting paid to let tourists see them performing everyday tasks. In addition, the trading posts and craft shops operating in the villages provided an outlet for Seminole-made goods from which they derived additional income. Granted that the operators of the villages reaped the greatest profits, most Seminoles evidently did not view them as oppressors to the same extent that non-Indian reformers did. Most important, according to West, these villages provided a transitional environment in which some Seminoles could earn a living while preserving many elements of traditional culture, such as speaking the Mikasuki language, building and maintaining chikis, cooking over an open fire, and producing handicrafts.[34] The villages generally provided safe enclaves in an urban setting from which the Indians could make gradual contacts with the outside world, although the unfortunate trade-off was that it often brought them into contact with violence, venereal diseases, and bootleg whiskey.

Informants among the Seminole elders generally confirm West's thesis that some families viewed the commercial villages as acceptable economic alternatives during the depression years. When questioned about visiting the Miami tourist attractions, Albert Billie confided, "My brother and I went there because Indians were living at a place called Indian Village. Three villages, one called Musa Isle. These three villages would visit each other. . . . People [tourists] would come in buses and they charged them. They had alligators and wrestled them, and they paid to watch. Others stayed at Miami and we lived at Silver Springs. . . . During the winters they would come get us to stay there, then leave when winter was about over." More detail on the third Miami area tourist village was furnished by Buffalo Tiger: "Back in 1926, I was old enough to remember this particular time, there is a village in Hialeah, and my uncle, his name is Willie Willie, established a nice little village; not too many

Corey Osceola at Musa Isle (courtesy Fort Lauderdale Historical Society)

people live around there that time. I am talking about [the] public. . . .
My uncle established that and we lived there about a couple of years I
believe. [The] 1926 hurricane blew everything down but during that
time we were out here to do our hunting, and we have villages out here.
I do not mean tourist villages. This is our home and we were out here
hunting and our village [was] there. [There were] some of the families
that lived in it with my uncle and the village [had] blown down and instead of rebuilding again, he made a choice. He was going to go to a
reservation. He went to [Dania], so they came back to the Glades."[35] Buffalo Tiger's family obviously never lived on a reservation, and during
his youth they constantly moved back and forth between their camp in
the Everglades and the Miami tourist villages. Many other informants
also reported visiting these villages briefly, or even for "a season," but
never considered them a permanent home.

The tale of Willie Willie's involvement with the Miami tourist attractions is one that Glenn offered as a tragic example of how unscrupulous
whites had taken advantage of the Indians. In the same annual report
in which he vilified the tourist village operators, he noted that "about
two decades ago an aggressive young Indian who owned and operated
a store in Ft. Lauderdale conceived of the plan of charging an admission
to white tourists who visited his camp. He prospered, and later enlarged
his trade by moving his business to Miami. He became so successful that
white men robbed him of his establishment."[36] When Glenn first learned
of the old Indian, he was living unattended and impoverished in a dilap-
idated shack on the Dania Reservation. However, the colorful Willie had
once been a wealthy man who spent his money freely on fast cars and
married a non-Indian wife. He and his father, Charlie Willie, had
opened a store near the New River where they bought produce directly
from other Indians and sold it to the market at a profit; however, his
fortunes soared after he erected a palmetto thatch fence around his
store grounds, moved a few Seminole families there, and began charging an admission fee to tourists. It was so successful that he moved the
operation to Miami and resettled his people at the Musa Isle attraction
around 1919. It was not long before he entered a business partnership
with several white persons, including a Mrs. Mayo and Egbert L. "Bert"
Lasher, a man reputed to have a criminal record. By 1923 Lasher had
somehow gained control of the Musa Isle show village and Willie Willie
was forced out of the business.[37] It was at that time that he moved to
Hialeah and opened the village that Buffalo Tiger described as being
destroyed by the 1926 hurricane.

Following this disaster Willie Willie moved to the newly opened reservation at Dania; an entrepreneur to the end, he kept some alligators

penned at his home and sold curios to tourists until he contracted tuber-
culosis and could work no longer. The old Indian passed away at Dania
in June 1929, and his brothers, who were antagonistic toward his non-
Seminole wife, killed the alligators and destroyed the rest of the personal property that had been accumulated, claiming that it belonged to
Willie and not to his wife. In 1930 Willie's surviving spouse, Elizabeth
Willie Willie, lying terminally ill in a New York hospital, brought charges
against Lasher, claiming that he had taken her husband's business with-
compensation. Her claim was brought to the attention of Congress-
woman Ruth Bryan Owen of Miami, who urged Commissioner Rhoads's
office to check into the matter.[38] This move led to investigations by the
Department of Justice and Federal Bureau of Investigation, which un-
earthed a great deal of circumstantial evidence that Willie Willie was
probably defrauded out of his business. However, since the alleged fraud
had not taken place on an Indian reservation, an assistant U.S. attorney
issued the opinion that it was not a federal offense and the case was
closed.[39]

Glenn was incensed that "Willie Willie, who founded a fifty-thousand-
dollar industry, died a pauper in a miserable white man's hovel." He
took some delight in the fact that evidently the publicity surrounding
a federal investigation, coupled with the declining economic conditions,
had led to the downfall of Lasher's business venture. The Seminole
Agency report for 1932, without mentioning anyone by name, announced, "the bankruptcy of one of the outstanding white characters
who has exploited the Indians for years. His dominance over a small
group of these Indians has been strained. He has endeavored to re-
establish himself but is meeting considerable difficulty." In his memoirs,
however, Glenn, in identifying one photograph of a commercial village,
recalled, "The picture shown . . . is not Musa Isle, but it is another such
village that Lasher built after we put enough heat on him to dispos-
sess him of Willie Willie's old camp."[40] Despite the pressures exerted by
government officials such as Glenn, a number of Seminoles continued to live and work at the commercial tourist villages throughout the
depression.

Not all of the tourist-related exploitation of the Indians took place in
commercial villages. It was not uncommon for Seminoles to attend the
opening of new business enterprises to provide local color, and a group
created a display at the annual Florida State Fair. There was a small colony of Seminoles at the World's Fair of 1933 held in Chicago, and such
environments always led to problems; for example, the agent reported
that, "two women broke faith with their homes in an infatuation with

some dirty white vultures, and an Indian man deserted his two children and wife for an Indian girl who already had an illegitimate child."[41] Closer to home in South Florida, Glenn was distressed over information that the Cypress Indians had turned their last Green Corn Dance into the semblance of the white man's show and admitted spectators for fifty cents each. In addition, some Indian families had begun to set up their own roadside exhibitions to attract tourists. They were located primarily along U.S. Highway 41, the Tamiami Trail, where it crossed the Everglades between Miami and Naples. These tended to be squalid little places, often consisting of just a family shelter and a few caged animals kept in unsanitary conditions. There were, however, at least two large compounds, one owned by Ingraham Billie and the other belonging to Chesnut Billie, which contained several chikis, animal cages, and an alligator pit, the whole surrounded by a thatched fence.[42] When the tourists stopped to view the animals or perhaps to buy some of the handicrafts on display, the Indian children would beg for coins or ask to have their picture taken for money. Glenn felt that the Seminole families who had sunk to this level of despair were among the most pathetic victims of the Great Depression. He was especially concerned for the children and vowed a renewed commitment to obtaining a large usable tract of land on which all of these Indians could live in dignity and adequately support themselves.

Meanwhile, an increasing number of Seminole families were beginning to suffer real economic distress. The early depression years had not been noticeably difficult for those Seminoles who were already living at a marginal subsistence level. A few old, infirm Indians and widows with dependent children were brought to Dania where they received monthly grocery allowances or other direct subsidies. But by 1933, as the depression tightened its grip, the need for direct aid increased dramatically. Eventually the federal relief programs initiated by the Hoover administration filtered down to the Indian reservations. Nevertheless, Glenn, who shared the views of President Hoover that self-help was preferable to government assistance, wrote, "Through the last year the Seminole Indians have had all the relief that might be absorbed without injury to the tribe. The Agency has furnished the sick, aged and other dependents with groceries to the amount of $1571. From ten to fifteen percent of the population have benefitted from these supplies."[43] Assistance came from both the public and private sectors. The U.S. Army had supplied the Indians with surplus breeches, overcoats, shoes, shirts, and leggings, while the Red Cross provided 2,000 yards of cloth as well as overalls, jumpers, sweaters, blankets, and infant garments. The agent himself was associated in the Seminoles' memory with the dispensation of this largess; one woman volunteered, "I remember he gave my grandmother ten dollars a week, or somebody give ten dollars a week, the government or something. Ten dollars a week to buy groceries, and they got a truck and went back and forth to Dania on Saturdays to get groceries."[44]

This dole led Glenn to declare that there was something fundamentally flawed with a system that provided more abundantly for relief than for industrial reestablishment of the tribe which would benefit it in the long run. He was proud of the effort that had been devoted to building up the industrial program of the Seminole Agency, with over 500 work days provided for Indian labor even though there was no special allocation of funds for that purpose. "For more than half the year," he wrote, "every Seminole who asked for employment was given work. Handling stock, driving trucks and tractors, farming, carpenter work and painting are some of the trades in which they have engaged. Thus the program serves as an industrial training school preparing these people to take their place in America's larger economic system."[45]

Glenn's annual reports were laced with economic assimilationist rhetoric which assumed that Indians would inevitably be absorbed into the mainstream of the national economy. Interestingly, this theme was also common to the New Deal employment, training, and revolving credit programs which sought to prepare Indians for economic independence. The fundamental difference was that the architects of New Deal Indian policy offered tribes an alternative: to develop economically within their own corporate structures. Glenn certainly could not be classified as a philosophical New Dealer in most respects—he was particularly opposed to Indian self-determination in educational and governmental matters, where he felt the Seminoles were not prepared to make informed decisions—but he did subscribe to that aspect of federal policy that would prepare the Indian for economic self-sufficiency. Supposedly, Indians who had received job training in federal programs could then choose either to remain on the reservations and work for their tribal enterprises or to seek employment in the outside world. However, it remains a debatable question whether many Indians throughout the nation developed either the skill levels or work habits and attitudes necessary to enter and compete successfully in the off-reservation job market.

On October 17, 1933, the Seminole agent signed and submitted his annual report for the preceding fiscal year. To that point the emergency relief projects generated by legislation passed during the first hundred days of Roosevelt's New Deal had not yet had an impact on the Seminole Agency. The agent was still attempting to provide a broad range of services for a widely dispersed Seminole population with a budget that had not increased appreciably in over two years. The most immediate need, however, was to create Indian jobs. It was well known that the Congress had appropriated funds for newly created federal relief agencies, and these in turn allocated large sums to the Indian Office which administered all tribal programs. Glenn had begun to despair that his small jurisdiction might be overlooked by the Washington bureaucrats who would oversee the distribution of funds for reservation projects. Therefore on June 2, he wrote directly to the new commissioner of Indian affairs, John Collier, requesting a reforestation project at the Dania Reservation; the request was denied. The commissioner responded that "after a careful consideration of the Seminole situation including a conference with Mr. Roy Nash, former Field Representative to the Commissioner, who is quite familiar with those lands, the conclusion has been reached that it will not be desirable to undertake any work under the Emergency Conservation Act at your jurisdiction." Naturally, Glenn was disappointed with this decision but remained undaunted; if anything he became more tenacious in his pursuit of funding. In October he sent forward another proposal for a labor project that was promoted as being "of mutual benefit to the nation's unemployed classes and our Indians."[46] It put forth the unique proposition that since the Seminoles were not in need of relief in any large way during the winter months, when hunting would enable them to subsist, other classes of unemployed persons, including Negroes, might be engaged in clearing reservation lands. What he had proposed was no less than the establishment of a potentially multiracial Emergency Conservation Work camp at the Dania Reservation. This time Glenn evidently struck the right note for he received an immediate response; Commissioner John Collier was intrigued by his proposal and set the administrative wheels in motion to discern whether such an arrangement was legal and, if so, how it could be funded. At long last it seemed that the Indian New Deal was on its way to the Florida Seminoles.

3

A New Deal
for the Seminoles

The election of Franklin D. Roosevelt as president of the United States in 1932 signaled a fundamental change in the social and governmental philosophy of the nation. Whereas Herbert Hoover had counted on the operation of a free enterprise system, minimal infusions of federal funds to create wealth that would trickle down to the lower classes, along with private charity and a self-help spirit to bring the nation out of the Great Depression, the new president was committed to using the full force of the federal government to improve the lives of all American citizens— including native Americans. Immediately following his inauguration in March 1933, Roosevelt introduced a legislative package known as the New Deal, which was to provide for the economic and social rehabilitation of the nation.

To assure that the full benefits of the New Deal would be extended to American Indian tribes, the Roosevelt administration looked to a thorough overhaul of federal Indian policy and new leadership for the Office of Indian Affairs. These changes would necessitate the appointment of an innovative, dynamic, and dedicated commissioner of Indian affairs who could work with Congress, Indian groups, and private associations in the context of the New Deal. Ideally, the new appointee would be a nationally prominent reform figure with a strong commitment to the American Indian, and there could be no connection with recent regimes at the Indian Office which had tried, but failed, to resolve the problems of Indian administration.

President Roosevelt would be strongly influenced in his final selection by the preference of Secretary of the Interior Harold L. Ickes, in whose department the Indian Office was located. Prior to entering the cabinet Ickes was a prominent Chicago lawyer and a leading figure in Republican party politics. Both he and his wife were active in the Indian rights movement; they owned a summer home in Arizona, and Anna W. Ickes had written extensively on Indian topics. In fact, for a brief time during

the tumultuous days of the early New Deal, Ickes himself had been considered for the post of Indian commissioner and was supported by such
leading Indian activists as Lewis Meriam, Nathan Margold, and John
Collier, but he opted instead for a cabinet post: "I had been thinking
matters over, and while I was still willing to be Commissioner of Indian
Affairs, it didn't altogether appeal to me . . . I just might as well try to
become Secretary of the Interior. It would be no more painful or fatal
to be hung for a secretary than for a commissioner." Moreover, he
noted, "It was clear . . . that Collier himself would like to be Indian Commissioner, although he was perfectly genuine in his offer to me of support."[1] Ickes strongly urged Roosevelt to appoint John Collier, undoubtedly the most charismatic figure to emerge from the Indian rights
movement during the preceding decade, to be commissioner of Indian
affairs.

Collier was a liberal reformer of the Progressive Era genre, thoroughly committed to improvement of the human condition and preser-
vation of social institutions. A native southerner from a prominent At-
lanta family, he had studied in Europe and at Columbia University and
then had become a social worker in the immigrant slums of eastern cities. These experiences framed his worldview; he developed a great appreciation of cultural and ethnic diversity and a keen awareness of the
difficulty in achieving a functioning social consensus. His initial contacts
with the Indians of the Southwest in the 1920s led him to believe that
they had achieved a degree of social integration that was lacking elsewhere, and he took up the defense of their fragile culture against as-
saults from both Christian reformers and the federal bureaucracy. His
became a constant, fractious, and critical voice raised against federal Indian policies aimed at stifling native cultures. As executive director of
the American Indian Defense Association, which he founded in 1923
following a stint as research agent for the General Federation of
Women's Clubs' Indian Welfare Committee, Collier frequently appeared
before hostile congressional committees to testify in behalf of tribal land,
mineral, and water rights and to defend Indian religious freedom. In
this role he was described as a "brilliant, impatient, caustic, and dedicated
man."[2] Despite the objection of some politicians who still smarted from
Collier's stinging denunciations of past federal policies, the Senate approved his nomination and he was sworn into office on April 21, 1933.[3]

The new commissioner moved immediately to protect tribal economic
and social interests. Orders were issued to halt any further allotment or
sale of Indian lands, while field agents were notified to allow Indians
complete freedom of religious practice. He also enlisted several of the
finest legal minds in the country to draft new legislation to guarantee

Indian sovereignty, promote self-government, and encourage the establishment of tribal business corporations. This legislation became the
Wheeler-Howard Act of 1934, the basic document of the Indian New
Deal. However, Collier did not wait for the legislation to pass to begin
attacking Indian economic problems. Because of the severely limited Indian Office budget, he effectively drew upon existing New Deal employment and assistance programs—especially Civil Works Administration,
Emergency Conservation Work, and Resettlement Administration—for
the benefit of the Indians.

The most important of these programs for the long-term rehabilitation of the American Indian was Emergency Conservation Work, signed
into law by the president in March 1933. It was a federal effort to employ young men between the ages of eighteen and twenty-five, whose
families were on relief, in forestry, prevention of soil erosion, and flood
control projects designated by the Department of the Interior. They
lived in military-style camps supervised by the War Department, received free quarters and meals, health services, some education, and a
small salary—most of which had to be remitted to their families. Because
of its strong emphasis on conservation projects the agency was given the
colorfully alliterative nickname "Civilian Conservation Corps," which
became its official title in 1937. Collier was convinced that the general
objectives of this program could be adapted to the needs of Indians. According to official records, "work on Indian reservations was included
from the beginning. Activities within the Office of Indian Affairs had
been handled briefly by the Forestry Division. On May 23, 1933, a separate Indian Emergency Conservation Work Division (IECW) was established. It was headed by a director and included several field districts.
When the Emergency Conservation Work became the Civilian Conservation Corps in 1937, the name of the Indian unit was changed to the
Civilian Conservation Corps–Indian Division (CCC-ID)."[4] Daniel E.
Murphy, a career Indian Office official, was the director of both the
IECW and the CCC-ID throughout their existence from 1933 to 1942.
During this time approximately $72 million was expended, and over
85,000 Indians participated as enrollees at camps established in seven-
teen states.

It was within this administrative network that Collier attempted to fit
the proposal from the Seminole Agency. There was a rapid round of
correspondence between officials at the state and national level before
the issue was resolved. Initially, Collier approached the Forestry Division
of the Department of Agriculture concerning the feasibility of establishing a CCC camp at the Dania Reservation, only to learn that funds had

been totally committed for the coming enrollment period. The assistant commissioner, William Zimmerman, also wrote to the director of the Civil Works Administration, Harry Hopkins, seeking his assistance in securing CWA funding. Ultimately, on November 23, 1933, the first New Deal project was approved for the Seminole Agency.[5]

Collier's office in Washington telegraphed authorization for Glenn to hire a clerk, a supervisor, and two skilled and five unskilled workers. The Seminole agent was to act as a deputy disbursing officer to the Florida Civil Works Program, which actually paid for the work. This project was drastically downscaled from the original proposal for employing sixty men to work on the reservation, but it was a beginning. The Indian men were set to work clearing palmettoes from an area on the north side of the reservation that was to become a campsite for Seminoles who visited Dania while seeking employment. The workers were instructed to cut the tops off the palmetto plants which were often head-high, then grub up their roots; this work had to be done carefully as the thickets were infested with rattlesnakes. The workmen also built rock driveways and laid sidewalks in the housing area. The white skilled labor was used to build a second small building to house sick Indians and to construct an addition to the school building for dining and cooking. The Indian and white employees labored well together, and Glenn believed that the Seminoles proved themselves to be excellent workers. Some progressed into the semiskilled category and were able to do finish work on the concrete walkways. The CWA project continued until February 15, 1934, and with rotation a total of forty whites and Indians had been given work.[6] Evidently a multiracial CWA project was abandoned.

As with so many New Deal programs, the CWA project contained more than a little make-work for the Indian employees. Several weeks were spent in clearing an Indian campsite on a portion of the federal land located near Miles City in Collier County. The Indian laborers were taken daily by truck from their homes at Dania, thereby subjecting them to a round-trip of several hours' duration in an open vehicle. The former Indian commissioner, Charles Rhoads, had accepted the suggestion of Roy Nash to relocate the Seminole Agency in the southwestern Florida region; thus in 1932 Glenn was preparing to move the headquarters to a four-section tract of government land near Miles City. With the change of national administrations, this move was postponed, and in 1933 the Washington office informed the agent that there were no funds for rebuilding the headquarters facilities at that location.[7] Therefore the efforts to clear this land as part of the CWA project could be justified only by claiming that it seemed advisable to have Seminole families in the region form settlements on more "elevated grounds"—even though the land was never occupied!

Washington had also directed that some of the CWA funds should be used to provide "work for women such as garment and quilt making."[8] Accordingly, a number of the women were put to work for several weeks sewing quilts and clothes for needy members of the tribe. It was assumed that this project—the only one formed specifically for Seminole women—would have economic value because they would learn a new vocation. However, Seminole women were already highly proficient at garment making, particularly sewing the patchwork that was sold commercially, and the making of quilts would have no lasting value because there was a limited market for such goods in the sultry climate of South Florida.

An Indian Emergency Conservation Work project for the Seminole Agency was approved on January 22, 1934, when a sum of $3,000 was allocated for "productive work of the greatest permanent value."[9] In this case the objective was to clear the Dania Reservation of its palmetto growth and timber felled during the 1926 hurricane. Five Indian laborers began to clear the densely matted roots with axes and hoes, but this method proved so slow and ineffective that only two acres were cleared in the first week. Glenn then rigged a pair of Fordson tractors to a plow to pull stumps and trained Indian drivers to operate the machinery. This job could be tough and dangerous, but some Seminoles proved particularly adept at it; as Glenn described the situation, "[another tractor] had the power and the weight to do the work required of it, but Andrew Jackson had one of the Fordsons, and he soon discovered that his machine had neither, and it also had the dangerous trick of turning itself upside down. If Indians have any claim to being good horsemen, Andrew was the best rider of a pitching tractor that ever sat a Fordson. He rode all over that machine and made it do its maximum work in spite of its wicked habits. He knew how to use the momentum of the weight of the machine to make it work for him, and he knew the exact split second when this momentum was used up and he had to release his clutch or be pinned under the thing."[10] Throughout the project the other Fordson tractor was operated with nearly equal skill by Robert Osceola.

The unreliable and underpowered Fordson tractors were not sufficient to overcome Florida's palmetto scrub, so the agent had to look elsewhere for another power source. After seven days of searching he found what he needed. A capitalist had invested a fortune in a Florida farm that did not pay, and he was selling his equipment for what it would bring. Glenn purchased a five-ton Holt tractor for $200 and a seven-foot road grader for $125; he bolted the plow to the grader table and used the tractor to pull the grader. The new outfit used fifteen gallons of gasoline a day where both Fordsons had consumed only twenty, but it provided the power necessary to clear the land. Josie Jumper learned to operate the Holt tractor expertly, and Glenn recalled admiringly, "He ran this machine for more than a year, and although it was a man-killing job he got as much work out of it as any white man anywhere. . . . Josie was never more delighted than when he tied this tractor to a large pine stump, and watched it drag the great roots out of the soil."[11]

At the end of the year over 140 acres had been cleared and planted in grasses having high food value for pasturage. The Indian workmen also fenced the land and constructed a telephone system for the Seminole Agency. A photograph of this 1934 land clearing project at the Dania Reservation was included in the "Final Report of the Indian Emergency Conservation Work and Civilian Conservation Corps–Indian Division Program, 1933–1942."[12] Most important, 1,075 man-labor days of employment were provided for the Seminole people, and it could be reported that "the Emergency Conservation program has enabled many families to purchase food and clothing for dependent members of the household." Although encouraging, the program's results could not be seen as a signal that all was well with every segment of the Indian community, for the agent went on to note that "again the FERA [Federal Emergency Relief Administration] has given a considerable amount of commodities to those in need. In many cases there were indigent Indians who were unable to look to any relative for assistance. Those people received direct relief from the regular Agency funds. A total of $1752.11 was invested in food for the members of the tribe."[13]

Within a few weeks after this IECW project began, the agent reported that Indians from every section of the state came to Dania seeking employment. His report may have been overstating the case. Although at times there were more than 150 men, women, and children camped at Dania, the number actually employed rarely exceeded fifty at any time. The final report of the CCC-ID reveals that between June 1933 and June 1942 ninety-two Indians and seven whites were employed in the projects at the Seminole Agency,[14] approximately 30 percent of the adult Seminole population of that day. The IECW enrollees received thirty dollars a month, plus food, lodging, and medical attention. Those providing their own food and lodging received an additional sixty cents for each day worked. However, the agents were in complete charge of the projects and often reduced the hours in order to distribute the funds among as many Indians as possible. As for limited hours at the Seminole Agency, Glenn was only complying with an explicit Collier directive.

The Indian labor was honest and diligent. When any member of the crew failed to live up to Indian labor standards the Seminoles, themselves, made the complaint to those in charge. Every man was expected to do a reasonable amount of work for each day.[15]

An official CCC camp never operated at the Dania Reservation, and no systematic program of job training had been arranged. Even though a small number of Seminoles did learn to operate heavy equipment such as the infamous Fordson and Holt tractors, most of the Indians engaged in unskilled labor. When questioned about their experiences working for the Indian Emergency Conservation Work program, most of the Seminole elders could recall the difficult but economically sustaining work. Asked if he ever went to Dania seeking work, Albert Billie responded, "Yes, I did, in 1934. Doing cleaning up reservation. I don't know the name of program." Although he did not go to Dania himself, Jimmie Cypress recalled that, "[the] first time my dad worked with government was with Mr. Glenn, a superintendent around 1930. During that time we lived in Immokalee. . . . He helped Dania Reservation get established and more developed, like clearing land." Another informant who worked in the CCC-ID program was Willie Tiger, who said, "yes, I did for a short time, around five months doing land clearing work, pulling up palmetto bush roots. Then taking the roots and stacking them up in piles to haul away." The oldest member of the group, Abraham Clay, remembered, "yes, I did a little bit of work there [Dania] clearing the land. Making small farm fields. There wasn't too much farm work. The pay was small, too. We worked at different jobs . . . about six dollars a week. Low pay."[16]

With no government CCC camp facilities available to the Seminoles, housing was at a premium, and entire families crowded in with their relatives. A hodgepodge of tents, lean-tos, and chikis became a makeshift village on the recently cleared campground. It presented a potential health problem because of the lack of adequate clean water and sanitary facilities. The agent enlisted the help of the Florida Public Health Service in policing the camps, and a public health nurse was assigned to visit the Seminole Agency on a regular basis. But one observer was moved to write, "My feeling is that the new nurse looks on our situation as a hopeless task, perhaps she will see her way when she recovers from the shock!"[17] Nevertheless, the average number of medical services for the 580 members of the tribe ran more than 100 a month, up from an average of 84 a month the previous year. This increase was attributed in part to an epidemic of measles which was particularly severe among the Indians crowded into the Seminole Agency. Glenn surmised that perhaps more than 100 Seminoles had the measles but only 62 reported for treatment to the Indian Office contract physicians.

The major reason for the growing incidence of Seminole medical problems, Glenn contended, was that they knew nothing of the cause of contagious diseases, and virtually everything in their daily camp routine made them susceptible to contracting and spreading illnesses. "His deepest fears are still lodged in the possible fatal magic of his medicine men. If he eats the young corn before it is consecrated at the Annual Green Corn Dance, or if he kills the opossum, the eagle, the frog, the snake, or the rabbit it will 'make him sick.' On the other hand, if he blows his breath on his hand and recites prescribed incantations, his herbs are endowed with the mystical curative powers. . . . Matters of personal hygiene and personal sanitation are not objects of concern to him. The members of a given family and all the guests of a household eat from a common spoon, and drink from a common cup. Pots, dishes, and foods are ravished by flies, and are almost never scalded. Water is taken from shallow holes, and is not always safe. The refuse from the body may contaminate the soil about the camp, and infest, and re-infest the Indian men, women, and children with hook worm. The malaria mosquito is not avoided, and patients suffering from contagious diseases are inadequately isolated from members of the tribe. Capes and sleeves are used for handkerchieves, and the clothing is never boiled. Teeth are not brushed, and the body is infrequently bathed. Foods contaminated with dirt, or even meats that have grown unsafe are eaten without fear, for in all of these things the Seminole entertains no conviction that they may and do cause illness and death."[18] The agent realized that this appraisal was brutally candid and unflattering and would cause some "friends of the Indian" to raise a howl of protest that he was insensitive to their culture; however, he maintained that his goal was to improve the health and sanitation conditions of the Indians, not to undermine or interfere in their religious beliefs in the magical curative powers of the medicine men. He hoped that in the near future, with the assistance of the public health nurse, a program of preventive medicine and sanitation could be initiated among the Indian people.

Despite the persistence of poverty and growing health problems, Glenn, always the optimist, could write at the end of 1934, "The New Deal affords many needful things to this remnant. The new land program, together with the plans for the rehabilitation of the tribe, should solve in large measure one of the most distressing social problems of the nation."[19] Unfortunately, the nation was just entering the midpoint of the Great Depression, and there would be many more years of hardship

for the Seminoles despite the federal programs designed for their benefit. Moreover, Glenn was correct in his assessment that an Indian agent
would never satisfy everyone. There were certainly individuals and
groups in Florida who either disliked the agent, disagreed with the objectives of federal Indian policies, believed that the federal government
was not doing enough for the Seminoles, or subscribed to some combination of these factors. Highly vocal critics began to emerge in 1934 and
were not reluctant to press their complaints with Commissioner Collier
via correspondence and statements in the press.

The first discordant note concerning Glenn's activities came from the
most unlikely of sources: Mrs. Frank Stranahan in Fort Lauderdale. She
always dealt with the Indians on a high moral and ethical plane to gain
their trust, and, although she was a devout Seventh Day Adventist, she
never overtly attempted to convert them to Christianity. As chairman
of the Florida Federation of Women's Clubs' Indian Welfare Division she
consistently supported the efforts of Spencer and Glenn, both of whom
were ministers but also nonproselytizers, to improve the social and economic conditions of the Seminoles. Therefore it attracted attention
when she wrote to Commissioner Collier to complain that the agent, ostensibly on orders from Washington, deducted housing charges or rent
from Seminoles working to clear land at the reservation. The Indians
came to her for aid because they had been told that if they settled on
the reservation they could always live there; now they were being asked
to pay. She then recounted, "I took these Indians to the reservation in
my own car, and I pledged them my word (with Mr. Spencer back of
me) that this land would always be their home. No Government Agent
or official could have gotten them located, and it has taken 30 yrs of
friendly dealings and always keeping my word with them to manage it.
Now, today they come to me to know what it means. I have told them
that I think everything is all right, for them to go back and go to work,
that I would write—that you did not understand and I know you will 'fix
it' all right." She urged the commissioner to prompt action, saying, "I
believe you will understand that to hesitate in not waving this regulation
for even one pay day will work havock in the minds of these wild shirtail
Indians who are just beginning to feel friendly and willing to do a part
in our, or your program. I sincerely beg of you to suspend this regulation until something can be worked out satisfactorily for the future.
Please wire me."[20]

On the same day that she wrote to Collier, Mrs. Stranahan also wrote
to her close friend Senator Fletcher. She reiterated essentially the same
information and implored him to intervene: "I have written Com. Collier quite fully, and if you are in Washington please contact him—or all

our Indians or their Indians are gone."[21] With this not too subtle urging, Fletcher made his interest in the affair known to the Indian Office. A response was soon forthcoming from Collier, explaining to Fletcher that Mrs. Stranahan had already been contacted and the matter would be taken care of immediately. A.C. Monahan, assistant to the commissioner, replied to Mrs. Stranahan; he blamed the misunderstanding on a misinterpretation by Glenn and included a copy of Collier's telegram: "Indians on Emergency Conservation Work not required to pay for quarters unless living Government buildings Stop Not required to pay for quarters in buildings specifically erected for use of Indians free and heretofore occupied by them."[22] This reply satisfied Mrs. Stranahan's immediate concern, although in subsequent correspondence she would request the return of a special deputy to quell the outrageous liquor situation among the Indians. In earlier days Ivy Stranahan had become a strident temperance advocate who fought to keep bootleg whiskey dealers away from Seminole camps. So strong were these sentiments that her husband was not allowed to sell any product in his store that had an alcohol base, such as vanilla extract, which the Indians might imbibe. The complaint about housing charges was a simple matter, easily disposed of by the Washington office but an embarrassment nevertheless, especially since an influential U.S. senator had become involved in the affair. It did, however, mark Glenn as one of the field agents who went by the book and perhaps overreacted to official directives.

A more persistent condemnation of the work at the Seminole Agency was leveled by W. Stanley Hanson, the long-time secretary of the Seminole Indian Association. The son of a pioneer doctor, Hanson had grown up hunting and camping with the Seminoles who frequently visited his family's home in Fort Myers. He learned to speak the difficult Mikasuki language and regularly attended their Green Corn Dance and councils at the invitation of the medicine men. In 1913 he was a founding officer of the association, which organized to support Dr. W. J. Godden's missionary efforts among the Big Cypress camps.[23] When Godden died the following year the association lost most of its inspiration and purpose as a society, although individuals such as Hanson sustained a vigorous personal involvement with the tribe. Whenever members of the Big Cypress band needed an intermediary with the outside world, they often spoke through Stanley Hanson rather than government officials. Although he worked primarily with the Mikasuki-speakers, Hanson was also well known among the Cow Creek band north of Lake Okeechobee. For two decades he traveled about the state at his own expense attending to the needs of Indians in the name of the association, and he rarely missed an opportunity to criticize federal inattention to the Seminoles. As the nation entered the depression, Hanson felt that interest had to be rekindled if the work was to continue. A committee was established to revitalize the Seminole Indian Association, and a reorganizational meeting was held at Tampa in September 1933. Only ten members of the original board of directors were still living, and Hanson was but one of two surviving officers. A new slate of officers and directors was chosen by the society, which retained Hanson as its secretary.

Throughout the 1930s the Seminole Indian Association operated with great enthusiasm and a modest budget. Hanson covered thousands of miles each year, speaking to educational and civic groups and drumming up economic support for the Seminoles. He was often accompanied at these sessions by members of the tribe. A major goal of the association was to promote a Seminole handicrafts industry and to register an official trademark to protect it from cheap imported articles being sold as genuine Indian crafts. To this end it supported the work of Deaconess Harriet Bedell, an Episcopal missionary, in developing a nascent cottage industry among Seminole families living near her mission station south of the Tamiami Trail. But this support did not imply association endorsement of her missionizing activities; Hanson was a zealous advocate of retaining traditional tribal beliefs and rituals in their pristine form, and he vigorously opposed missionaries and government agents whom he suspected of undercutting the old ways. The secretary also pursued with vigor any adverse actions by local law officers and courts and monitored the work of the Indian agents headquartered at Dania Reservation. In numerous instances he undercut the role of the agents by bringing groceries or transporting sick Indians to hospitals or doctors, although the Seminole Agency was legally responsible for their bills, then garnered visibility by publicly accusing the federal officers of not performing their duty. Such interference would ultimately bring Hanson into a direct confrontation with John Collier and Harold Ickes over the application of federal policies to the Florida Seminoles.

It was well known that Hanson had sought the appointment as Indian agent which went to J. L. Glenn but was deemed unsuitable for the post; thus the animosity between the two men was exacerbated. In his appraisal of the candidates Roy Nash had prophetically written of Hanson, "The man has lived for fifteen years in the hope of succeeding Capt. Spencer as Seminole Agent, and, I fear, is likely to prove a thorn in the side of anyone else who may be appointed." In his memoir Glenn told of disarming an Indian who was angry with him: "He had a pistol in his hand. I said, 'What is it, Charlie? Had not you better give me that gun?' He handed me the gun and replied, 'Mr. H., he say you lie *ojus* [plenty].' Mr. H. was our famous fanatic of Ft. Myers. I suspect that Mr. H. had not planned for Charlie to give the gun to me in that way." In another place he told of a rape case involving a Seminole girl: "This raising hell in the Indian work is a science as fully developed as the science of smoke screening an army or a task force of the navy. The more hell that is created, the more is covered up the motives and character of those who do the raising. . . . Our famous fanatic of Fort Myers heard the story first and began raising hell, as usual. He wrote the Senators and the Congressmen, but failed to see the prosecuting attorney who lived in his own town."[24]

Glenn was not alone in his dislike for Hanson; even the mild-mannered Mrs. Stranahan became indignant over his actions and statements to the press and wrote to Collier expressing her concern: "Stanley Hanson has always kept the Indians at enmity with any friendly feelings toward the Government (I mean the Indians he holds contact with). I never meet or speak with him but I know how he made Mr. Spencer's life miserable by his false accusations and Mr. Spencer had not yet been buried when he was flying over the state politicking for the position."[25] There is a clear implication of territoriality in this statement. Elsewhere, Mrs. Stranahan testified that she had no contacts with the Seminoles who lived in the wild areas of the Everglades, and apparently Hanson had no influence among the east coast band of Seminoles that had settled into the Dania Reservation. In a 1927 newspaper account Hanson, speaking for the Big Cypress council and medicine men, had stridently denounced Tony Tommie as a "fakir and liar" who pretended to be chief of all the Seminoles.[26] Later, a group of the Mikasuki-Seminoles living on the east end of the Tamiami Trail would employ legal counsel and declare their political independence. So it would seem that discrete spheres of influence were recognized and observed not only by the bands of Seminoles but among their white advocates as well.

Undoubtedly the most widely circulated attack on the Indian Office and Glenn was that published by the *Miami Daily News* in the fall of 1934. A multipart investigative report on the conditions of the Florida Indians written by Cecil R. Warren was compiled under the title "Florida's Seminoles: An Eye-Witness Story of Indian Want and Privation as Published by the *Miami Daily News* with affidavits and accompanying documents."[27] In an editor's foreword it was claimed that the survey was made in response to conflicting reports on conditions in the camps and presented "without bias" to bring relief to Florida's truly "forgotten man." In the first of his fifteen articles, however, the reporter declared that he had found "sound basis" for reports that disease was sweeping the Indians to an early grave and that there was shameful surgical and medical neglect of the Indians. The situation was one in which game was scarce and labor infrequent, Indians were denied access to the relief rolls, and the only government employment available was limited to the Dania Reservation. Thus the stage was set for a major exposé.

Warren spent almost a month visiting the various Seminole communities accompanied by an entourage which always included an Indian interpreter. When he went among the Muskogee-speaking Seminoles living north of Lake Okeechobee, Sam Tommie acted as his interpreter and leading informant. As in any instance when the interrogator and informant are communicating through an intermediary, there is always a possibility for error, and it is exacerbated when the interpreter has his own agenda. The articulate and gregarious Sam Tommie was another son of the old matriarch Annie Tommie, who, like his brother Tony Tommie, aspired to a leadership role among his people; he may have seized upon this opportunity to establish his credentials as an unofficial spokesman with the white community, at least through the press reports. In any case, Sam was a most willing and cooperative auxiliary to the Miami newspaperman. During the questioning about health conditions and food supplies in the various camps, he provided interpretations to questions that confirmed the worst suspicions of neglect and incompetence by the Indian agent. Furthermore, Sam Tommie signed a sworn affidavit attesting to the existence of these conditions, and it was appended to the compilation of articles (37).

The picture that Warren painted of the squalid, poverty-ridden camps occupied by defeated and desperate people was perhaps overdone to achieve journalistic impact. Nonetheless, he did inadvertently draw some interesting ethnological comparisons between the situation north of Lake Okeechobee, where the Indian people were more dependent upon working within the local agricultural system, and the nature of survival in the Everglades camps. He noted that the camps in four locations—Okeechobee, Saw Grass, Hog Island (Fort Drum), and Cow Creek—were generally in poor condition and littered with rubbish, a sign that the Indians were not moving about as much as usual either to hunt or to pursue work. Their chikis were judged to have been built lower to the ground and to have been more poorly constructed than those of the camps in the Everglades. The northern group wore more white clothing, especially the men who had turned almost exclusively to pants and shirts; the women crafted their traditional dress from cheap cloth, and it was far less colorful than the patchwork garments found in the Mikasuki-speaking camps. Many of the Indian families subsisted primarily on garfish, gophers (land turtle), and cabbage palm buds, although a few of them kept hogs as a source of meat. Most did not have

crops planted because they maintained temporary camps along canal
banks or on land they did not own. Some well-known Seminoles of this
region were numbered among the hard-core unemployed. For example,
Dan Parker was now out of work after living for nine years on the
Summerlin farm near West Palm Beach. Jack Tommie had recently
worked for three months in the CWA project at Dania but had no job
at the time of the survey. Sam Tommie, too, had earned some money
at the CWA project but was also unemployed. Naha Tiger and a group
of twenty-three persons from the Cow Creek band were temporarily
camped on the prairie west of Okeechobee; it was huckleberry season,
and they could get sixty cents a gallon from the local storekeepers. On
the other hand, there was relative prosperity in the camps of Morgan
Smith, Johnny Josh, Ely Morgan, and the medicine man Sam Jones; all
had been employed for about six months working railway crossties out
of a nearby stand of timber. The camps of the elderly Billy Bowlegs and
his grandson Billy Stewart were the best of the lot; they were located
on high land in rich hammocks, with wells and pumps and several acres
cultivated in corn and pumpkins. However, Warren hastened to point
out that those camps were above average in situation and convenience.
Most damning of all, though, was the accusation that "most of the Indians said they had not seen the Indian agent for months, in most cases
from three to six months, and that the cessation of aid had worked hardships on them (12). This theme was repeated throughout the articles.

When Warren turned his attention to the Mikasuki-Seminoles living
near the town of Immokalee, the picture brightened but only a little.
He still found them leading a "poor and precarious existence," selling
a few hides and venison in season to pay for their meager supplies.
When visiting the camps of Robert Osceola, John Osceola, and others,
"If at any time you feel pangs of hunger in a Seminole camp you will
find hot coffee, sofskee, comtie, and perhaps dried venison, duck,
chicken, pork, fish, wild turkey, whooping crane or curlew—if the game
is plentiful and the hunting good. However it is not so good now, since
so many white men are taking pleasure in it" (14). Chesnut Billie was
the Mikasuki-speaking interpreter for Warren during this most difficult
phase of his investigatory trip. From Immokalee they planned to journey forty-five miles southward into the Big Cypress to visit the Indians
living in the vicinity of Guava Camp. After going only fifteen miles their
car bogged down, and the party camped overnight on a palmetto "island" under mosquito netting; the next day they returned to Immokalee
with great difficulty. Undaunted, Warren's party swung westward to the
coast and picked up the Tamiami Trail south of Fort Myers, then traveled to a point just east of the Dade-Collier county line known as the

"door to the Big Cypress," a narrow, shallow passage on the north bank
of the Tamiami canal through which the Indians could pole their canoes
into the interior. They were transported by canoe about twenty-five
miles to the "corn dance place" which was a center of Seminole ritual
and tradition, the spot where the Green Corn Dance was held annually
at the time of the little-moon-in-June. There were several well-kept
camps of Mikasuki-Seminoles nearby, so Warren visited with Frank
Tiger and Captain Tony. He learned that they did a lot of trapping and
that raccoon pelts sold for fifty cents while deerskins brought over two
dollars each. When the reporter inquired if the Indian agent got there
on his rounds, the answer was, "No, never been here." Then when asked
what he would do if his family got sick, the resourceful Indian promptly
replied, "Take in canoe to Miami" (18).

At Deep Lake between Immokalee and Everglades City the reporter
visited the secluded camp of old Johnny Buster, who also told him that
the Indian agent had never been there. Yet, within a few months this
camp would be the one selected by Glenn to receive an official party visiting from Washington—and it is unlikely that he would have chosen an
unknown or hostile site for such an event. From there the newspaperman went to virtually every known Mikasuki-Seminole camp, including
that of the medicine man Ingraham Billie at Turner River, Brown Tiger's temporary camp near Everglades, and the home of Charley Billie
where he spent the night in a chiki. In each camp he reported essentially
the same conditions of poverty, but he developed admiration for the
people: "Life in the usual Seminole village seems to be a continual feast.
Unless the entire tribe is asleep, the fires are kept going and the pots
hot" (22). It was here that Warren made the most serious accusation of
neglect, claiming that his host, Charlie Billie, "has not had the care that
he gives his camp. His right arm hangs useless. The forearm is broken
and has remained unset for 10 years. Whether the old fracture will heal
or not is now doubtful. No white man has offered to aid him. He is willing to have a white doctor fix it, if he can, his son Chesnut Billie, interpreter on the *Miami Daily News* survey, said" (23). This account was accompanied by a picture of the pathetic old Indian with his arm dangling
grotesquely from the sleeve of a colorful Seminole shirt.

Having completed his investigation of the outlying Seminole communities that resulted in a long list of indictments against the Indian agent,
Warren paid a visit to the Dania Reservation to confront J. L. Glenn.
The articles covering their meeting began with a factual description of
the Indian quarters, school, and government facilities and a bland account of the various federal employment projects available to Indians

at the reservation. It moved rapidly to Glenn's rebuttal of the points raised against his administration: "The oft-repeated charge of Indians throughout the Big Cypress and Okeechobee areas that the Indian agent has never visited many of the camps was denied by the Rev. Mr. Glenn. He said he had visited all permanent camps with the exception of that of Charley Fewell, 15 miles by canoe from the place of the green corn dance" (24). Glenn went on to explain the charges that he had not visited the camps in several months by saying that his duties were so many, his salary so small, and the Indians so scattered that it was impossible for him to make the rounds more frequently than he did. Nevertheless, he had spent the night in many camps and was able to check on outlying camps through Indians that he met in Immokalee, along the Tamiami Trail, and on the Hendry County Reservation, saving the necessity for frequent hard journeys into the back country.

As for Indians being denied access to relief rolls, he stated that ten or twelve at Immokalee alone were receiving government subsistence; also, he denied having told Sam Tommie that aid could not be extended to Indians living off the reservation—although the agent admittedly preferred offering the Indians employment rather than assistance except when the individuals were too old to work and could not live without financial aid. Glenn's explanations notwithstanding, Warren wrote that "his stand in this matter may be responsible for the frequent complaint of Okeechobee Indians that charitable aid had been cut off upon instructions of the agent about a month and a half ago, and has resulted in actual hunger among them, since they are unable to find work" (25). Glenn said that he knew about Charlie Billie's arm which was fractured a decade earlier during Spencer's administration but claimed that the Indian repeatedly refused to have surgical treatment—which would have no doubt entailed rebreaking the bone in order to set it. After reviewing the educational and public health efforts in behalf of the Seminoles, Warren concluded with a statement that purported to show the objectivity of his reports but had just the opposite effect: "Conditions at the Dania Reservation of the Florida Indians [are] no index to the conditions existing in the camps throughout South Florida, however. . . . In this article we have tried earnestly to present fairly the information available at the reservation, to show the Rev. Mr. Glenn's side of this discussion and revelation of the condition of the Florida Seminoles today. There have been sharp criticisms and reports of misdoings of the Rev. Mr. Glenn in the administration at the reservation, but the truth of these cannot, naturally, be authenticated at the reservation. Unless they are proven authentic, they cannot be set forth in a survey intended to give the people of Florida facts regarding the Indians" (27). This account left Glenn in a position somewhat akin to the man who is asked when he stopped beating his wife. He had been convicted by innuendo.

The final two articles of the series devoted an inordinate amount of space to the commentary of W. Stanley Hanson, hardly an impartial observer of Glenn's performance, concerning immediate needs of the Indians and the direction that federal policies should take in the future. Even though Warren claimed to have had no knowledge of Hanson's statement submitted to the 1930 Senate investigating subcommittee until his own research was completed, it was not unexpected that he would discern that "the findings of Mr. Hanson, . . . revealed by intimate contact with the Indians for several years, are very similar to the discoveries made by the *Miami Daily News* representative" (28).[28] Hanson's suggestions to the subcommittee could be summarized thus: (1) do not pauperize them with pensions but provide reservations where they can live in peace, secure medical aid, and instruction in hygiene; (2) get them started in raising cattle, hogs, and poultry; (3) assist them in finding a market for their wares and see to it that they are treated honestly; (4) establish elementary and industrial schools where they can learn English and how to use modern equipment; (5) stop the commercial Indian villages and induce them to return to their camps; (6) do not attempt to civilize them overnight by providing white men's houses; and (7) appoint an agent in charge who really has their future welfare and interest at heart—one who understands them, their needs, and their language (30–31). The first five suggestions were amazingly consistent with the announced goals of the federal Indian agents and the sixth a gratuitous slap at the Dania Reservation; the last appeared to be a blatant bid for appointment to the post.

To add a note of authenticity to the report, the affidavits of several persons who accompanied Warren into the Seminole camps were included as an appendix. They essentially confirmed the conditions that he reported and verified the comments of the various Indians as translated by the interpreters. A further boost to objectivity was anticipated by including the commentary of a Florida newspaper editor who would address the issue of Indian poverty and governmental neglect. Under the heading "Florida Editor Speaks," the *News* ran a letter from A. H. Andrews, editor of *The American Eagle*, published in the hamlet of Estero near Fort Myers. Far from being a mainstream Florida newspaper, the *Eagle* was an organ of the Koreshan communitarian religious group which practiced celibacy, encouraged racial tolerance, and believed that mankind actually lived inside the earth rather than upon its surface! This long polemic reinforced an impression that the hardships and privation of the Seminoles, although not initiated by agents Spencer and Glenn, were at least prolonged and exacerbated by their actions. Its major complaint was that the Seminole Agency had been moved from Fort Myers to the east coast, a move attributed to the fact that Captain Spencer's family and property interests were located there. The agent had, however, arranged for the Indians to have access to medical aid; but now Glenn refused to honor bills for medical services, funerals, or supplies purchased at local stores, as had been done in the past.

Andrews also lauded Stanley Hanson as "an active member of the Seminole high council . . . known as 'the white medicine man of the Seminoles.' He enjoys their full confidence, converses with them fluently in their own language, and [is] compiling a dictionary of the Miccosukie (Big Cypress) dialect." By contrast, he castigated Mr. Glenn, charging that while an epidemic of measles was sweeping through the camps, the Indians "to date had received no relief from their preacher agent." Andrews concluded that the Seminoles deserved something more than the "absent treatment" from their "arm-chair agents" to lift them from the sickness, starvation, and squalor into which they had fallen through the white man's encroachments and official neglect. He concluded by urging the newspaper, "by all means keep it up until relief is assured" (33).

It would have better served the cause of journalistic objectivity had the *Miami Daily News* informed its readers that Allen H. Andrews was closely involved with W. Stanley Hanson in the Seminole Indian Association and had often written glowingly of his adventures among the Seminoles.[29] Moreover, the editor evidently had not reviewed Glenn's official report on the number of measles cases treated by contract doctors during 1934, or read the distressed agent's comments concerning the failure of the Indians to take advantage of medical assistance even when it was offered. By his own admission Glenn had many shortcomings as an Indian agent, but he could not fairly be called an "arm-chair agent" with the territory that he covered. Nonetheless, nothing short of Hanson's appointment as the Indian agent was going to satisfy the Fort Myers constituency.

In his memoir written some years later, Glenn dismissed these newspaper accounts as the work of Miami "do-gooders," abetted by low-class, backwoods white men with a vested interest in keeping the Indians in their poverty-ridden condition: "There was a two-by-four snipe that ran around over the glades with some bootleggers and a cattle thief and wrote what he thought was a whale of a story in the yellowest sheet in Miami about the Florida Indian work. He had discovered old Johnny Buster, and had a whacking story about the Florida Indian Service's neglect of him, but he got his name mixed up. I absolutely refused to straighten him out and so he skipped it. But what he had planned to say about this case was as far from facts as all the other items he reported."[30] It is conjectural whether the men who accompanied the *Miami Daily News* reporter were actually "bootleggers and cattle thieves" as portrayed or just local white men earning a few extra dollars guiding the reporter. Actually, the affidavits that the men signed did not list their occupations, although in an article Warren referred to one of them as a "Ft. Pierce cattleman and former merchant."

Despite these fulminations by various anti-Glenn and anti–Indian Office elements in Florida, only one complaint from the Indians themselves has been found in the public records. A letter dated April 19, 1934, addressed to Commissioner Collier and apparently signed by Willie Jumper, Sam Tommie, and Jim Gopher, stated: "We the undersigned Seminole Indians living at the agency do hereby petition you to send us a Special Investigator for the Bureau of Indian Affairs [to] whom we can lay the facts of our complaint. Mr. J. L. Glenn the present Superintendent is disagreeable to us in general."[31] The letter is a bit suspect on at least two points: first, at that time only one or two adult Seminoles were capable of writing a letter, but certainly not one which was so well composed, grammatically correct, and free of spelling errors; second, the legalistic tone of this letter leads to the suspicion that even if it were written by an Indian, its inspiration lay elsewhere.

While this storm of controversy swirled unabated about Glenn, the New Deal projects for the Seminoles continued. Throughout the summer and fall of the year an additional $9,000 was released by Collier to continue the work of clearing palmetto undergrowth and seeding the land for forage crops; and since the enrollment was between thirteen and fifteen, Glenn was authorized to hire assistant leaders and leaders at "$36 and $45 respectively, plus quarters and rations."[32] By November, the aggressive Glenn was requesting an additional sum of $6,000 to keep the work going and proposed that the crews also clear two 40-acre tracts west of the town of Davie which belonged to the Seminole Agency. This land, according to the agent, would support at least 100 head of cattle and provide for their economic future "if the Seminoles may have their proportionate share of the cattle mentioned in Circular No. 3033"; Collier thought this an excessive amount to clear eighty acres and offered $2,000 instead.[33] Glenn responded with a long rebuttal citing data gathered from agricultural specialists that up to 320 head of cattle could be grazed on the land available; furthermore, he had just been notified by the Washington office that the Seminole Agency was to receive 105 head of Angus cattle, and "for the present it is essential that this herd be held near Dania. There are so many cattle thieves in the back country where other Indian lands are located the herd would be stolen. When submarginal purchases are made, and the land is sodded, the herd can be broken up and distributed to the several Indian communities. But until that time the two forty acre tracts are going to be needed to provide for the above herd." Because of the difficulty in clearing the outlying forties, he would need at least $3,000; Collier remained unconvinced, telegraphing, "At this time no additional funds are available for allotment, and it will be necessary for you to carry on your ECW program with the $2,000 allotted on November 22. . . . The clearing of land for pasture purposes, appears to us to be a doubtful project."[34]

At this point nature played into Glenn's hands. In December 1934 there was a severe freeze in Florida, and Glenn telegraphed Collier that it seemed inadvisable to send members of the Seminole Emergency Conservation crew from the agency where they had shelter and an abundance of food "to a game depleted woods. During past season federal tick eradication employees carried out systematic destruction of deer as a measure of freeing lands of ticks. Indians now have less food in woods than formerly." This introduced a major issue that the commissioner would have to contend with in the future—the "Seminole Cattle Tick Controversy" which flared in the 1940s—but for the present the Indians were faced with possible starvation if they were not employed. Glenn asked for $5,000 to provide labor relief for his charges; Collier first released $2,000, then changed it to $4,000 for the Seminoles.[35] The Indians were immediately put to work clearing the outlying acreage. This work brought the total amount of New Deal funds encumbered for fiscal 1935 to over $21,000, an impressive amount compared to 1929, the last year of Spencer's administration; then economic conditions among the Florida Indians had begun to disintegrate badly, yet the total Indian Service annual expenditure at the Seminole Agency was $10,780 for all services including the salaries of federal employees.

By March 1935, one of the forty-acre tracts near Davie had been cleared and fenced, and $1,000 still remained of the last emergency allocation. Glenn requested, and was granted, permission to use $500 of this amount to construct a half-mile trail from the Dania Reservation to the "Davie forty" as a driveway for stock to reach this tract.[36] All of this, it should be noted, was predicated upon the assumption that the Angus cattle would be held there as a temporary measure until larger tracts of land could be obtained for the Seminoles. This land acquisition remained at the top of J. L. Glenn's priorities for ensuring the long-range security and economic progress of the Seminoles, and he was soon to pursue the issue with Commissioner Collier and Secretary Ickes when they visited Florida.

The New Deal for the Florida Seminoles had been launched and enjoyed some minor successes during its first two years. However, it was apparent that the programs would have to be broadened and extended to the majority of Seminoles who still lived in the back country. From 1935 onward most Indian Office initiatives were directed to achieving that transition.

4

A Seminole "Red Atlantis"

In March 1935, almost two years after his appointment as commissioner of Indian affairs by President Roosevelt, John Collier paid his first official visit to the Seminole Tribe of Indians in Florida. Although he was recognized as one of the nation's leading Indian rights advocates throughout the 1920s, Collier's efforts had been focused almost exclusively among the larger, better known tribes in the West and Southwest. As executive secretary of the American Indian Defense Association, he frequently appeared before various congressional committees testifying on issues affecting those Indian groups, which were already familiar to the American public. In the national media his name became synonymous with a progressive commitment to the advancement of native peoples, and it was only natural that Roosevelt had accepted the recommendation of Ickes and appointed the dynamic Collier to create a New Deal for the American Indian.

The most significant legislative achievement of Collier's long tenure as Indian commissioner was the enactment of the Wheeler-Howard Act of 1934, better known as the Indian Reorganization Act (IRA), which incorporated the fundamental principles guiding the Indian New Deal. Essentially, it provided for ending the allotment and sale of Indian lands, allowed the organization of tribal corporate structures to achieve economic independence, and guaranteed tribal social and political self-determination through the formation of reservation governments. One stipulation in the legislation required that within twelve months of its passage by the Congress, the Indian tribes were to vote on whether they wished to be covered under the provisions of the act. Although a general consensus existed calling for action to assist American Indians who suffered greatly from the depression, the bill was not without its detractors. Old-line assimilationist groups like the Indian Rights Association, missionary societies, much of the federal Indian Office bureaucracy, and a large number of highly acculturated, Christian, property-owning Indians complained that the IRA placed too much emphasis on collectivism and risked undercutting the "civilizing" gains made by the Indians during the previous half-century. Constitutional democrats and civil libertarians, on the other hand, objected to the curious language of the bill, which required that a majority of adult tribal members must vote to *reject* the IRA or they were automatically bound by its provisions. There were accusations that Collier had engineered the IRA elections in such a manner that much of the opposition—including the tribal tradition-alists who would never take part in such balloting—were effectively disenfranchised.

The anti-Collier forces very nearly won their fight to kill the IRA; when that failed, they had altered it severely. The powerful Senator Elmer Thomas of Oklahoma—a member of the subcommittee that took testimony from the Seminoles in 1930–had the Indian population in his state specifically excluded from coverage by the act, while one of the bill's coauthors, Senator Burton K. Wheeler of Montana, personally re-drafted Collier's version of the legislation eliminating the most objec-tionable provisions.[1] A radically revised but still controversial Wheeler-Howard Act was signed into law on June 18, 1934. Collier spent the ensuing year in a grueling round of meetings with Indian tribal leaders and their constituents on the reservations, and at regional Indian con-gresses, urging their support for the Indian Reorganization Act, which he believed provided the best hope for the tribes to control their own cultural destinies. Contrary to popular opinion, Collier did not advocate that the federal government abandon all influence over Indian affairs; rather, he believed in the concept of "indirect rule" by which the central government would rely upon native institutions as the vehicle for en-couraging local pride and initiative while bringing about progressive so-cial change. Moreover, he had long been convinced that American In-dian tribal structures were uniquely adapted to undertake this type of self-governance.

Like so many disillusioned philosophical progressives caught up in the climate of intellectual cynicism and despair that prevailed after World War I, John Collier sought a new source of societal values and stability. Rather than rejecting American life and fleeing to Europe, the young idealist accepted an invitation from friends and moved to a new artists' colony at Taos, New Mexico. He soon became enamored of the "primi-tive" cultural values evinced in the nearby Taos Pueblo, especially the consensual decision-making process. In 1922 Collier wrote an article for *Survey Graphic* magazine entitled "The Red Atlantis," which suggested that Northern Pueblo patterns of social integration provided a model that should be emulated by the secular, materialistic, and depersonalized Western industrial societies of that day. He held that anyone observing social education among the Pueblos "will find none so young, above the third year, and none so aged, up to a hundred years, that he has not a communal function, status, intensive productive group experience, and an aristocracy of mental attitude which it is impossible either to flatter or demean. . . . The pueblo is not primitive in the same sense of being primordial. Vast spaces of evolution and of the compounding of cultures lie behind it. But it is primitive in that it has conserved the earliest statesmanship, the earliest pedagogy of the human race, carrying them forward under geographical conditions which have helped to a result probably unique for its complex yet childlike beauty, in the whole world's history. From this statesmanship and pedagogy our present world needs to learn, and tomorrow's world will learn if given the chance."[2]

Despite this intoxication with the Pueblo culture that he had encountered a decade earlier, Collier learned that real-life Indian political conflict resolution was not so idyllic. Following months of wrangling with Indian leaders who appeared reluctant to subordinate their own political influence and interests to tribal organization, and listening to the petty, often petulant complaints of tribal councils, he was beginning to despair that Indian politicians, whether Navajo headmen or Pueblo governors, could be as self-serving and self-indulgent as their non-Indian counterparts. Furthermore, he found that the tribal polities were themselves split over numerous matters ranging from grazing rights to the production of handicrafts for the tourist trade. In reality, the commissioner, who was often perceived as "paternalistic and domineering," had encountered much greater and more sophisticated resistance than he anticipated; one outspoken anti-IRA Indian leader from that period has observed, "The IRA did not allow the Indians their independence, which was guaranteed in treaties and agreements and confirmed in court decisions. It did not protect their sovereignty."[3] As a result of this vigorous opposition, only 181 tribes representing 130,000 Indian people voted for the IRA, while 77 tribes with more than 80,000 members rejected it.[4] The forces that had opposed the IRA believed that the version of the bill that ultimately passed was diluted enough to prevent any attempt by Collier to establish Red Atlantis–style communal governments; still, many of the large Indian tribes, including the Navajos, had rejected it outright.

John Collier was greatly distressed that his idealized version of Indian life had been politically tested and found wanting by the very people it was intended to serve. Nevertheless, by utilizing "unique" legal interpretations of the IRA legislation, and employing the bureaucracy of the Indian Office, he was able to impose many of his ideas on the American Indian; this route led inevitably to conflicts with reformers, Congress, and the Indians themselves during twelve stormy years. Throughout his governmental career Collier would have difficulty reconciling the conflicting progressive values of social justice and managerial efficiency in setting Indian policy. In early 1935 he was still smarting from these setbacks, and it is against this background of disappointment in the apathy and occasional outright negativism among the western tribes that his Florida visit must be viewed.

In December 1934, an exchange of IRA-related correspondence was initiated between Collier's office and J. L. Glenn, who by that time was officially chief financial clerk and acting superintendent of the Seminole Agency. The commissioner alerted Glenn to the necessity of adhering to congressional guidelines in conducting the upcoming vote: "You have received information and material regarding the Indian Reorganization Act and are, no doubt, familiar with its scope and purpose. . . . We must, therefore, plan to extend to the Indians of your jurisdiction the privilege of voting on this important question. We want to know what work you have done among your people to discuss this legislation with them, to advise them of its purposes and advantages, etc., and whether you feel that a date should be set to give them the opportunity to express themselves in accordance with the requirements of the act."[5]

The Seminole agent replied to Collier, informing him of the steps taken and adding his own observations about the impact that the IRA might have on the Florida Seminoles. He believed that the provision for the consolidation of Indian lands could easily be accomplished as none of the Seminole reservation had been allotted. Furthermore, he noted that "the Seminoles of Florida do not even receive leasing benefits from their land. To put this land or any other land to work for the support of this racial group is the largest feature of the Florida program. The new Act makes this possible. And it is not a 're-organization' in Florida. It is rather an *organization*. There is nothing to tear down—no established methods of either occupation or ownership. The territory is virgin."[6] Glenn concluded by suggesting that an election should be held in either March or April 1935, and he needed additional time to inform the widely scattered Indians about the nature of the election. He also requested, and was granted, permission to visit Indian Office headquarters in Washington to discuss the "Florida situation." Following that meeting Collier determined to visit the Seminoles prior to the balloting.

Although the primary thrust of the commissioner's visit to Florida was to enlist tribal support for the Indian Reorganization Act referendum, there were other factors that compelled his inspection of the Seminole Agency. Not least of these were the reports that he had received from the anti-Glenn faction, which included some Indians, protesting what they considered to be inadequate service to the tribe. Undoubtedly the *Miami Daily News* series that ran in the fall of 1934, depicting federal efforts as a failure and portraying Glenn quite unfavorably, had been brought to the commissioner's attention. Then, too, there was Mrs. Stranahan's correspondence complaining about Glenn's overzealous enforcement of government guidelines by withholding rent monies from the Indian Emergency Conservation Work wages. Her effort to involve Senator Fletcher in the matter had caused some disturbance in the Washington office. During the preceding year the Seminole agent had been a persistent and forceful—verging on abrasive—advocate of additional IECW funds for his charges, who often successfully challenged budgetary decisions; this move was not calculated to endear Glenn to the Collier administration.

The most direct call for Glenn's removal came from Congressman J. Mark Wilcox of Miami, who had been approached by various citizens, including a delegation from the Federated Women's Clubs of Miami, complaining about neglect of the Seminoles. On January 3, 1934, he wrote Collier, "I am told by responsible business and professional men, as well as county and city officials, that a large part of the trouble is traceable to the neglect of the present agent in charge of them. Mr. J. L. Glenn is the present agent and I have no knowledge of him except such as is given me by disinterested citizens who believe that he should be removed for the good of the Indians . . . I do not wish it to become a political matter, but undoubtedly the present agent should be removed and another substituted in his place."[7] Wilcox's "disinterested" constituents already had a candidate they were promoting as Glenn's replacement. Collier had not met with Glenn, and he responded to Wilcox that he was getting a full report on the Florida agency from A. C. Monahan, his assistant. Monahan went to Florida and interviewed a number of individuals familiar with the Seminole situation. He reported to Collier that the charges of neglect were unjustified; he found that "Mr. Glenn is a man of limited ability but absolutely honest and sincere, and a tireless worker," and he recommended retaining Glenn in his position at least until he could be exchanged with someone serving on another reservation.[8] There the matter rested for the ensuing year.

Glenn was a former minister, and in most respects he typified the old-line assimilationist sentiment that prevailed among the Indian Office field staff—although his writings present an interesting amalgam of federal paternalism combined with an appreciation of Seminoles as a people. He admired their once proud culture which had been debased through poverty and forced contact with a low class of white society; and while the Indian would have to adapt to modern ways to survive, he hoped the nobler elements of their traditional values might be retained in the process. In this respect he differed significantly from most

Christian reformers who found little in the Indian life-style worth re-taining. Unfortunately, Glenn did not have an answer for how this cultural melding could be accomplished. Yet, he was skeptical and openly critical of Collier's self-determination policies, especially those that de-emphasized the importance of compulsory schooling for Indian children. In later years he recalled, "I have often told the men of this tribe that there were many things that the white men had that they did not want their people to have, but education was one thing that they needed most of all. Because we are disgusted with ourselves and with the wars that curse the higher educated communities of the world, we have ele-vated men to high positions who are so misdirected in their convictions that, as John Collier said to me, they are afraid to teach these Indians to read, for they will then read the newspapers and get in the awful world in which we live. In spite of his ecstasy over the glory and good-ness of primitive life, I think I have seen enough of it to be assured that it too has its 'sweat, blood and tears.'"[9]

Apparently there was an open confrontation between Collier and his Seminole agent during their Washington meeting in January 1935. "I made the mistake," Glenn later recounted. "I went to Washington, and he called me in his office. He said 'Glenn, there's been a lot of criticism of you. What have you got to say?' I didn't say anything. I should have defended myself. I think that he had an open mind in the matter, but we had these politicians."[10] Glenn was, after all, in a vulnerable political position. As a holdover appointee of Commissioner Charles J. Rhoads and the Hoover administration he was naturally suspect among the New Dealers, and he did not enjoy the immunity of Civil Service job pro-tection. Collier had a reputation for suppressing dissent over the IRA; even so, he seemed committed to a personal inspection of the situation before making a decision about the agent's future. Therefore, although pressures continued unabated for Glenn's removal, it was a surprise when the *Fort Lauderdale News* of March 1, 1935, announced the arrival of a new Seminole agent, "Miss Agnes Fitzgerald," who reportedly had worked with the Indians of Wisconsin.

As it turned out, Fitzgerald was evidently never "officially" appointed to the post of Seminole agent; her name does not appear on available government or tribal listings of persons who occupied that position. Asked about this seemingly punitive incident, Glenn said, "Well, they planned with me to work under her. The office had planned for me to be subject to her. She lived in Miami, and so I lived at the Agency. I tried to work with her. She was a rather large woman. . . . I know she got into very bad trouble. She took a notion to take the government car and go back into the Everglades to that reservation back there, and the car got stuck on her, and she was stranded there. She finally got some help. I told the office I thought the work was too hard for a woman, and I think that was one reason they dropped her, because she wasn't able to do the work."[11] By April 1936, Fitzgerald had returned to duty in Wisconsin.

Whatever the motives behind sending Fitzgerald to Florida, the Indian Office still considered J. L. Glenn to be in charge at the Seminole Agency. On March 1, he was notified that Commissioner Collier would be traveling to Florida, accompanied by Secretary of the Interior Harold L. Ickes, his wife, Anna, and their son, Raymond.[12] The Indian Office requested that an itinerary be arranged so as to allow Collier and Ickes to meet with as many Seminoles as possible during their two-day visit, preferably in their natural Everglades habitat. Accordingly, Glenn and Fitzgerald met the Collier party which arrived by train in West Palm Beach on the evening of March 18 and took accommodations at the Royal Worth Hotel. The following day the group motored westward through the agricultural area bordering the southern shore of Lake Okeechobee, for Ickes was keen to view the nearly completed earthen dike being constructed as a federal works project. They then headed south to Deep Lake in Collier County, where the agent had arranged a visit to the secluded camp of old Johnny Buster, the same camp that had been singled out by the *Miami Daily News* for its poverty. The day before Glenn had sent a side of beef to the camp so there would be enough food and the Indians would not be embarrassed when guests arrived. It was about a half-mile away from the paved road, and Glenn had promised, "We will have to do a bit of 'log walking,' but I was in there yesterday and there is no water to wade. It can be reached in ten minutes' walk from the automobile, and is yet so completely 'lost' to the white man that few knew its location."[13] This was just the type of setting that Collier and the Ickes family had hoped to find, and it made a lasting impression which would be recounted in subsequent writings by the commissioner. It was late when the party arrived; Glenn was alarmed that most of the beef had already been eaten and the camp was a mess. But a few of the Indians who had remained came forward and shook hands with the commissioner and secretary. Glenn noted appreciatively that Collier, who had visited many Indian homes, was undisturbed by the disarray in the camp.

Following their brief stop at Deep Lake, the party continued on to Everglades City, their overnight stop. There they met with a large number of Mikasuki-Seminoles who were visitng the small mission run by the Deaconess Harriet Bedell. She was a resident Episcopal missionary who had virtually no success in achieving religious conversions but was instrumental in reviving the production of authentic Seminole handicrafts during the depression. Later during this Florida trip Collier was offered a young fresh-water otter as a gift from the Indians; he declined but subsequently wrote several letters to Bedell and others inquiring as to its fate. Although little time was spent with the Seminoles and little opportunity allowed for promoting the IRA, Collier seemed immensely pleased to have met with them at all.

On March 20 the Collier-Ickes party returned over the Tamiami Trail to Miami, but there is no evidence that they visited the commercial "tourist villages" as originally suggested by the Washington office. Following lunch at Pompano Beach, according to teetotaler Glenn, "an ample supply of whiskey was served, and from the revived spirits of the other guests it apparently did something for their exhausted condition."[14] It had indeed been a trying two days for the agent and his staff, arranging logistics for a party numbering about fifty people including reporters, and driving them over dangerous, nearly impassable roads. In the process Glenn had developed a genuine liking for Secretary Ickes and an almost equal distaste for his wife. Anna Wilmarth Ickes was a quintessential liberated woman of the 1920s; a free-thinking liberal and former member of the Illinois legislature, she had strong views about preserving Indian language and culture with which the agent strenuously disagreed. All in all, it could not have been a pleasant journey for anyone concerned.

Glenn was no doubt anxious to get these dignitaries back to West Palm Beach in a timely fashion, as Collier and Ickes were scheduled to meet with a delegation of Seminoles as the high point of an annual tourist-oriented affair known locally as the "Sun Dance." Unfortunately, this event was staged in such a manner—including martial music and the presence of three companies of National Guardsmen—that it gave the impression of being something of a peace conference. Moreover, the *New York Times,* in an announcement of the meeting, had already proclaimed, "Florida's Seminole Indians, after 100 years of technical warfare with the United States, plan to offer the pipe of peace."[15] This was misleading, however, for neither Collier nor Ickes had any intention of engaging in spurious treaty making—a process that, as Collier had earlier pointed out in a memo to Ickes, was discontinued by Congress in 1871.[16] Therefore, the two government leaders had agreed only to hear statements and accept a petition from a delegation of Seminoles who were requesting assistance in securing more land and federal financial assistance. They could not foresee that even this seemingly innocuous action would later bring strong protests from various Indian advocacy interests in Florida.

Approximately 160 Indians were assembled at West Palm Beach, virtually all of them Muskogee-speaking members of the Cow Creek band of Seminoles who lived north of Lake Okeechobee. The spokesman for this group was the ubiquitous Sam Tommie, who interpreted as the elders had their say and was to be the lone signatory of the petition that they presented to Ickes. The document essentially recognized that the Seminole Indians had been at peace with the United States for one hundred years, lived in peace and happiness in the Everglades, and had pleasant relations with the government. However, many white men had come into their land, drained the lakes, cultivated fields, killed the game, and generally made life more difficult. Therefore, they wrote, "we request and petition you to use your influence with the Congress and the President of the great Government of the United States to obtain for us the following lands and benefits": lands in South Florida counties amounting to approximately 3 million acres, an annuity of $15 per capita per month, and full-time nursing service by trained Indian nurses.[17]

The petition revealed the unmistakable influence of Glenn, who had earlier notified A. C. Monahan about plans for the meeting. He advised the West Palm Beach organizers against promoting any treaty negotiations with the federal government, as the Indians were embittered by treaties. Moreover, a 1924 act had made all Indians citizens of the United States. Therefore, he wrote, "I suggested that any move that should come from the Seminoles should be in the form of a petition to the Secretary of the Interior and the Commissioner that they use their influence with Congress to obtain for the Florida Seminoles the same status with the Government that is enjoyed by the Oklahoma Seminoles. The content of such a petition would follow along the line suggested under the three numerals of my letter of the 20th."[18] The final wording of the petition was almost verbatim that proposed by the agent, although he claimed no role in drafting it. Years later Glenn admitted that the Indian Baptist missionary, Willie King, had done most of the work in promoting the petition among the Cow Creek camps and had probably put the final draft together for the meeting. He also contended that Sam Tommie never signed the petition and that Collier was upset at the lack of any legible Indian signatures on the document. It was Glenn's belief that Sam Tommie's life had been threatened by the Miami-area Indians if he signed.

Secretary Ickes accepted the document presented by the Seminoles, saying, "I receive your petition in the spirit in which it is offered. The Seminoles are a brave and independent people and should be able to live their own lives and sustain themselves and their families if given a proper opportunity. Whether or not it is possible for the United States government to give you all the lands you ask for, it is only fair to say that I think that you should have more land for your own. I promise to do what I can in cooperation with the State of Florida to provide you with lands adequate to your needs."[19] This highly cautionary statement of support by the secretary of the interior failed to commit him to any specific purchases of land. Collier also spoke briefly, heaping praise on the Seminoles as a heroic people who had defended their homeland in the past and had never surrendered to superior forces. He rapturously detailed how "yesterday we went to a remote Seminole camp and met and shook hands with the Indians. This camp was a place of beauty, gentleness, hospitality, and true aristocracy. The handclasp of these Indians the handclasp of an aristocratic people. Their demeanor was the demeanor of kings and queens. You have maintained back in the Everglades a life of singular chastity, temperance, and humility. Surely the United States ought to make restitution for what it has taken from your people. I know Secretary Ickes will do that which he promises. His heart is with you and he has great power. I hope you will not consider this a surrender. Rather it is the beginning of your golden age and a new life in the wild country that you love."[20] The commissioner had evidently seen the Indians he wanted to see—noble primitives—and had come closer to making rash promises of restitution than the more dispassionate Ickes. Certainly these statements of support would be encouraging to Glenn in his quest for an Indian homeland. The gathering reportedly concluded in an aura of good feeling; Mrs. Ickes was presented with a gift of two Seminole Indian dolls, and Collier was offered the live otter, while the Indians performed their "peace dance."[21]

Shortly after Collier's entourage returned to the capital, the Department of the Interior issued a press release reiterating the pledges made to the Seminoles. It particularly emphasized that Secretary Ickes, when replying to the petition of the Seminole leaders, had explained the plan for creating a national park in the southern extremity of the Everglades. In doing so he had stated that the Seminoles ought to have the right of subsistence hunting and fishing within its boundaries for a considerable time to come and that they should always have the labor preference. Collier, however, now cautioned that, "three million acres can probably never be bought by the Government for the Seminoles. A part of the land they have petitioned for—land which they regard as morally theirs already—is highly developed truck and citrus fruit land. The Seminoles' request must be weighed with the land requirements of Indians in other parts of the country." More optimistically, though, he noted that the government was already negotiating for the purchase of three tracts for the Seminoles and that cattle would be supplied for them to herd on their reservation established in Hendry County south of Lake Okeechobee. The Indian Office also hoped that the State of Florida would exchange the 100,000 acres of relatively worthless land and water in the proposed park area, which was set aside for Indian use by state legislation in 1917, for another 100,000 acres north of the Tamiami Trail. Altogether, perhaps a quarter of a million acres could be provided as a permanent reservation for the Seminoles. Then, if the federal government and the state would cooperate, wildlife protection and restoration could be set in motion throughout the park area and in at least a million acres of the Everglades region. Thus, Collier concluded, "with land for planting, and land for stock grazing, and with greatly increased game supply, and with a proper development and marketing of their crafts, the Seminoles undoubtedly will be able to develop a successful life of the kind they want, which is the life of wild Indians living in the fastness."[22]

John Collier was fascinated with the Florida Seminoles, who appeared to manifest those qualities of social integration that he had so admired in the Pueblos. Had he found a "New Red Atlantis" in the Everglades? Certainly his ambivalence about introducing New Deal programs to the Florida Indians emerged clearly in an article for *Indians at Work,* a bimonthly periodical of the Indian Office and CCC-ID which publicized federal efforts to rehabilitate American Indian tribes during the depression. Simply titled: "With Secretary Ickes and the Seminoles," it extolled the virtues of the Seminoles' unique life-style in language vaguely reminiscent of his 1922 "Red Atlantis" article and suggested a few programs that should be implemented to assist them. However, in this case the commissioner expressed a reluctance to be aggressive in pursuit of economic and educational development policies that he had consistently advocated for other tribes. In essence, he proposed an agenda to ensure cultural encapsulation. Collier began with the question "Is it our duty to 'civilize' the Seminoles? They have bad teeth (apparently, bad in the measure of their contact with civilized foods). Probably they have too many enteric disorders, and there are sanitary and health habits which perhaps, they well might learn. They are now too poor. Added to more of wild range, and greater security on the widened range, they need cattle; and they need to farm more extensively (subsistence farming). Their religious custom directs that the man shall always cultivate a field. Somewhat their craft output might be improved, and better marketed. But cautiously. Possibly—it might be—a very few of their young people should be chosen to receive an education most carefully planned—in English, in buying and selling, in modern health science, in biology, zoology, ecology and anthropology. These young people might mediate between the tribe and the white world; particularly they might work to lead their people to become wild life conservationists. Personally, I hesitate at one step more than the above. I deeply doubt the wisdom of schooling the Seminoles. Let English come, and the newspaper, and that kingly confidence, that radiant reality, which is their life in the wild, might grow less, might fade away. And what worth would be the exchange?"[23]

Ironically, the fact that the Seminoles lacked any semblance of a consensual tribal government to uphold their interests did not appear to faze Collier at all—this at the very time that the IRA vote was hanging in the balance. His justification was that "possibly the Seminoles' position is unique among that of all Indians. An almost unique history within an environment unexampled in the United States has created an adaptation—a physical and social structure—most delicate, yet ample, and life sustaining. It may be that no other structure would uphold their spiritual life at all. And it is by the spirit that they live. Hence, beyond restoring those equilibriums of the natural environment which the white man has destroyed, and thus making possible a better life within their own social structure and their own unhesitant and powerful and sane instinct— beyond that point, we should go with extreme caution in Seminole matters, and perhaps we had better not go at all."[24] Was John Collier actually advocating that the Seminoles should *not* be allowed to participate in the governmental aspects of the Indian Reorganization Act? Was this intended as a means of preserving the cultural integrity of his "New Red Atlantis"?

Collier's brief visit among the Seminoles appears to have left him in a dilemma: On one hand he believed that acceptance of the Indian Reorganization Act by the tribes provided their only assurance of ever achieving a degree of self-determination in managing their own affairs; on the other, he feared that the political and economic organization fostered by the act might bring to an end what he had perceived—some might argue inaccurately—to be a relatively pristine culture. However, he soon learned that he would not have to concern himself with this issue, as the Seminoles displayed no enthusiasm for the Indian Reorganization Act. On March 30, Glenn telegraphed the following message to Collier: "Balloting at the Florida Seminole jurisdiction on Indian Reorganization Act tabulates twenty one for the act and none against it."[25] The Florida Seminole population was reported to be over 500 in 1935.

Several days later Glenn sent a follow-up letter explaining the difficulties encountered in getting the Indians to participate in the balloting. "I suppose there will be a lot of fuss," he wrote defensively, "about our election in Florida. Our Indians have never used the ballot to determine their affairs. To educate them in a few months to cast an intelligent ballot is not possible. The matter was administered as justly as I was able to administer it under the conditions." The low voter turnout was due primarily to Indian apathy, but some of the problems were also attributed to the newly arrived Fitzgerald. Glenn continued, "When Miss Fitzgerald came down she told me she planned to have the election postponed. I had already posted the notice of the election at the Reservation, and had visited Indian leaders where I thought a poll should be established. For six months or more I had talked with the Indians about the provisions of the Act. But I thought Miss Fitzgerald might gladly have the responsibility. About a week before the election she asked me if I could postpone it. I told her I thought I had no such authority. We then agreed upon the plan of conducting the poles at Dania, and providing means for absentee voters to vote. Miss Fitzgerald gave her time to the Health Clinic, and the election was left to me."[26] Despite his natural disappointment at the low turnout, Collier's reply seemed to express a sympathetic understanding of the situation which his field officer faced in Florida: "I have read carefully your letter of April 4. The very small Seminole vote was to be expected in view of their traditional detachment from the Government. I am sure that you did everything that you could have done."[27]

In the summer of 1935, Congress amended the Indian Reorganization Act requiring a favorable vote by a majority of each tribe for acceptance of the act, with at least 30 percent of the eligible members voting. However, Collier and the Interior Department solicitor, Nathan Margold, had developed procedural means to circumvent this congressional mandate. Therefore when in 1936 a new superintendent of the Seminole Agency requested a clarification of the tribe's status vis-à-vis the Indian Reorganization Act, Assistant Commissioner William Zimmerman sent the following reply: "Our records show that while a majority of the votes cast at the referendum held for the Seminole Indians was favorable to the acceptance of the Indian Reorganization Act, the total number of votes cast was less than 30 percent. The Act of June 15, 1935 amending the Indian Reorganization Act of June 18, 1934, declared, 'That in each instance the total vote cast shall not be less than 30 per centum of those entitled to vote.' The Solicitor for the Department has passed on the question of validity of such elections and has ruled that it is discretionary with the Secretary as to whether another election shall be called. He says, 'In the discretion of the Secretary, therefore, a second election may be called within the time prescribed for holding elections, irrespective of whether the majority of votes cast at the previous election was in favor of or against the act'. Since in the case of the Indians mentioned herein a majority of the votes cast was in favor of the act, the Office shall hold officially that they have not voted to exclude themselves and therefore, another election will not be authorized or called for these Indians. You may furnish this information to the group of Indians concerned."[28]

The decision at the Washington level to declare officially that the Florida Seminoles had voted to accept the provisions of the IRA would have no immediate impact on the Indians. As evinced by the miniscule number who participated in the balloting, there was little or no interest in the measure. By Glenn's account only those Indians living at the Dania Reservation, and perhaps eight or nine in the Okeechobee area, actually cast ballots.[29] There was no involvement at all among the conservative and reclusive Mikasuki-speaking Seminoles who lived in the lower Big Cypress region or in the Everglades near the Tamiami Trail. This large group still followed their traditional leaders, the medicine men and busk councils, who remained unalterably opposed to any dealings with the federal government. Nevertheless, the inclusion of the Florida tribe among those accepting the IRA would have long-range beneficial results. One ironclad provision of the Wheeler-Howard Act stipulated that the tribes had but one opportunity to vote either acceptance or rejection of the bill; they could not revisit the vote at a future time. So it was fortuitous that those twenty-one Seminoles chose to vote and that their affirmative vote was considered binding on the entire tribe. Even though the Seminoles were too fragmented—ethnolinguistically, socially, and politically—in the 1930s either to seek or to accept organization under the IRA, they had retained the eligibility to do so at a later time. Some twenty years later when the reservation populations felt the need to protect themselves by establishing a tribal government and business corporation, they merely exercised their rights under Section 16 of the Indian Reorganization Act.[30]

If Collier mistakenly assumed that a sociopolitical homogeneity existed among the Seminoles, it did not take long for him to become disabused of that notion. Certainly, from the agent's reports and a 1934 survey, he understood that the Seminoles spoke two languages, belonged to several ceremonial busk groups, and lived in widely separated locations; this information should have provided a hint that there was severe fractionalization. Moreover, he soon learned that each of the Seminole factions had its dedicated and vociferous advocates in the non-Indian community, and they were quick to respond to the Collier-Ickes visit. The most caustic criticism came from W. Stanley Hanson in Fort Myers. On March 21, the day following the West Palm Beach affair, Hanson fired off a letter to Collier which opened with an antagonistic statement: "It has come to the attention of the Seminole Indian Association of Florida that irresponsible parties have been recently heralding to the world the signing of a so-called treaty at West Palm Beach, Florida, between the Seminole Indians of this state and the federal government, with whom it is claimed they are still technically at war, owing to the fact that the Florida Seminoles never surrendered." Hanson then launched into a diatribe in which he lectured Collier on the differences between the various Seminole bands. He held that they were not a tribe in the ordinary sense but were composed of two distinct groups that strayed or seceded from other tribes during the preceding century, hence the name Seminole meaning "renegades or wanderers." The two groups lived entirely apart and spoke different dialects, the Muskogee living north and east of Lake Okeechobee, and the Mikasukis mainly in the Big Cypress country to the south and southwest. Collier was reminded that there was no chief of the Seminoles and that their government was vested in a supreme council of elders; thus it was obvious that no individual or group of Seminoles could pledge the Indian population to any treaty or agreement of any kind without the sanction and endorsement of the medicine men. Hanson also bitterly denounced the participation of both Collier and Ickes, saying, "While it is not exactly plain to the white friends of the Florida Seminoles whether the recent ceremonial at West Palm Beach was merely a burlesque or entertainment for the tourists, or whether it was not, the fact remains that the presence of the Secretary of the Interior and the Commissioner of Indian Affairs lends to the ceremonial a touch of serious reality." His letter concluded with a call for an investigation of unidentified "designing individuals" who were exploiting the Florida Indians.[31]

Even before Collier and Ickes departed for Florida, O. B. White, an attorney representing various Mikasuki-speaking Seminoles who resided in the Everglades west of Miami, had written to protest that the secretary and commissioner would be meeting with a hand-picked group of Indians who did not represent the views of the entire tribe. His clients requested a special meeting with the Washington officials during their visit, and White offered, "I feel certain that in this way the Secretary will be better informed as to their necessities. The Big Cypress Indians, as they usually term themselves, do not feel that they will be able to fairly present their plight through the Indian known as Sam Tommy."[32] Actually, Glenn had met with the disgruntled group of Seminoles residing in the Miami area a short time prior to the West Palm Beach affair and learned of their displeasure; apparently threats were made against any Indians who participated in the meeting. Even so, he arranged to have trucks sent to collect the Seminoles residing in the tourist village at Musa Isle to bring them to the meeting with Collier and Ickes, but their head-men and the owner of the village reportedly intervened to prevent their leaving.

The White letter was sent directly to Congressman J. Mark Wilcox of Florida and was forwarded to Ickes's office, where it arrived after the secretary had decamped for West Palm Beach. Upon his return Ickes replied and dismissed White's concerns: "I should have been glad to have had the information prior to my trip, but I believe that my contacts with the Indians were fairly representative, and that I am now in posses-sion of a true picture of the situation. I was able to visit one of the Semi-nole camps in the Immokalee district, and I believe that the Indians who spoke at West Palm Beach voiced the real wishes of most Seminoles."[33]

Commissioner Collier also produced an immediate, pointed, and characteristically acerbic response to the accusations leveled by Hanson: "Secretary Ickes and I will welcome every bit of true information, and every relevant suggestion respecting the Seminoles. However, I am com-pelled to raise the question why you did not ascertain the facts as to what did take place at West Palm Beach, before you released a newspaper crit-icism and wrote your letter. You refer to a so-called treaty adopted at West Palm Beach by 'irresponsible parties.' This matter is pure fiction; no treaty, real or so-called, was or could be adopted at Palm Beach or anywhere. A number of the Seminoles, at Palm Beach, voiced the desire for secure land titles and a reservation of adequate size. I have no knowl-edge as to whether they were the most representative Seminoles, but I have no doubt that all the Seminoles do desire this advantage, and I share with Secretary Ickes the view that it is the government's duty to supply it to them. The incident was so simple and so large a number of people acquainted with what actually transpired, that I must treat as a remark not made in good faith but for political or publicity purposes, the following words: 'The Seminole Indian Association of Florida here-with registers official protest with you against buffoonery of signing treaties with irresponsible Seminoles.'"[34]

Collier had long been aware of Hanson's great influence among the Mikasuki-speaking Seminoles, as well as his obstructionism and deep-seated animosity toward federal agents Spencer and Glenn who, to-gether, had faithfully served the Florida Indians for two decades. Warming to his attack, Collier questioned both the legitimacy and basic integrity of Hanson's organization: "You are not a Seminole Indian. So far as I can make out from your letterhead, there is not a Seminole on your directorate. Your organization is not the Seminole Association of Florida, as its name evidently seeks to convey and as your letter assumes. You have been for years a candidate for a position in the Seminole work of the Indian Office. That is your inalienable right. But it is not your right to conduct a white organization which pretends to be an organization of Seminole Indians, and it is foolish to make your vociferous protest against an alleged incident which as a matter of common knowledge and of fact never took place."[35]

This slashing rebuttal by Collier was accorded hearty support by Mrs. Frank Stranahan, who had also been in attendance at the West Palm Beach meeting and knew what had transpired. As for the critics, she wrote, "I have just picked up the paper and read the 'outburst' of our old enemy, W. Stanley Hanson, Fort Myers—this is the same old tirade he has been carrying on for years & years. Please pay no attention to him. The Indians who met you and Secretary Ickes Wednesday represented a group of Indians who want the things they petitioned for. Those Indians who do not want that recognition will never be compelled to accept it." The commissioner also received a supportive letter from Louis Capron, an ethnologist and long-time friend of the Cow Creek Seminoles.[36]

The Deaconess Bedell wrote to Collier primarily in response to his inquiry about the fate of the otter offered by the Indians, but she, too, took the opportunity to present yet another viewpoint. She reported that the Indians in her region felt the commissioner was their friend, but with the advent of the Everglades National Park and the meeting at West Palm Beach where few of their number were present, they were more suspicious than ever.[37]

Finally, Agnes Fitzgerald contributed her personal assessment of the Florida situation and seemed to side with the Trail Indians; she even went so far as to suggest that there should be no Indian agent, as the term seemed to be repulsive to the Indians.[38] If Collier still was not convinced that a serious division existed among the Florida Seminoles, the *Miami Herald* of April 4, 1935, reported that six of the traditional leaders and medicine men of the Mikasuki-Seminoles had signed an affidavit prepared by their attorneys, White & Colson of Miami, denouncing the West Palm Beach meeting and reaffirming their continuing opposition to the Indian Reorganization Act. It had become obvious that the two Indian groups would have to be treated differentially when developing policies in the future. No doubt by this time Collier and Ickes, having fended off this limited but intense flurry of criticism, were questioning the wisdom of their public meetings with the Seminoles. Nevertheless, they would follow through on their pledges to support efforts to secure additional lands for the tribe and to protect its economic interests within the Everglades National Park, approved by the Congress in 1934.[39]

What, then, were the substantive results of this brief encounter between John Collier and the Florida Seminoles—an interlude so fleeting that it does not even rate a footnote in most accounts of Collier and the Indian New Deal? Surprisingly, there were several substantial outcomes affecting the Seminole people which are directly attributable to this visit. First and most immediate was the acquisition by the Department of Agriculture and the Resettlement Administration of 30,000 acres of land in the "Indian Prairie" region northwest of Lake Okeechobee. These purchases were already being negotiated in 1935, but the process was doubtless expedited when the Collier-Ickes support became widely known in Washington circles. By 1936 this tract would be opened as the Brighton Indian Reservation and would become a home for the Muskogee-speaking Cow Creek band of Seminoles.[40] The government supplied these Indians with a starter herd of beef cattle, and they became excellent cattlemen.

Second, at the urging of Ickes and Collier, during 1935 the State of Florida exchanged the Seminole lands situated in the Everglades National Park reserve for a 104,000-acre reservation in Broward and Palm Beach counties.[41] The restrictions to be placed on Indian hunting and trapping in the park area, limited employment opportunities as guides, and their inevitable transition to a more sedentary agricultural life-style made it a good trade. Today, the drained areas of this reservation are highly cultivated and prime grazing lands for Seminole cattle.

Third, the consolidation of a Seminole land base provided an isolated, secure haven in which the Indian people could determine their own rate and extent of acculturation. It would take the better part of a generation before most of the Florida Indians accepted reservation life; moreover, a significant group of tribal-traditional people living near the Tamiami Trail never did and ultimately formed a new tribal polity. Nevertheless, this period of reservation formation may still be viewed as a peaceful interregnum in that process which William Sturtevant has identified as a "New Ethnogenesis" of the modern Seminoles.[42]

As for Commissioner Collier himself, it was an experience that seems to have heightened his awareness that tribal entities could develop differential rates of acculturation yet retain their essential Indianness. Almost thirty years after his initial visit to the Florida Seminoles—and he came among them only twice in his twelve-year tenure—Collier, in a wonderfully lyrical style, reflected upon the experience in his book *From Every Zenith:* "There are those who have experienced these primitive societies, disciplined yet possessed by joy, and see no hope that their life can be saved. I myself was one of these, my first wild happiness overcome by the desolating sadness, believing these societies had to die. For the center of their life is spirit—they walk with the gods on every road of man—and what place have our times for such a life? Even in the early days of the New Deal when we were moving night and day to open the channels of modern life to the Indian societies, I was often gripped with anxiety that this spiritual center of Indian life might be lost if we carried the Indians too far along with us. This anxiety was sharpest when I first visited the Seminoles. . . . Possibly the Seminoles' situation was unique among that of all Indians. An almost unique history within an environment unique in the United States had created an adaptation—a physical and social structure—most delicate, yet ample, and life sustaining. It might be, we then thought, that no other structure would uphold their spiritual life at all. And it is by the spirit that they lived. Hence, beyond restoring those equilibriums of the natural environment which the white man had destroyed, and thus making possible a better life within their own social structure and their own unhesitant and powerful . . . instinct—beyond that point we knew that we had to go with extreme caution, and it seemed that perhaps beyond that point we should not go at all. . . . As time went on, and they came to want them, we established schools for the Seminoles, and gave aid to their agriculture and stock, and they borrowed from the revolving fund for economic enterprises, and paid back the loans from the returns of the enterprises. And we joined with them in a prolonged struggle . . . to save their deer from slaughter by the State and Federal Bureaus of Animal Industry. Indeed, the way the Seminole future first appeared to us in 1935 was neither necessary in their case nor representative of the Indian outlook in general. Tribes and cultures more ancient and complex than that of the Seminoles were challenged by the Indian Reorganization Act to give themselves with all their powers to the world's main stream. And they did give themselves, deepening their ancient powers while thus giving themselves to the world."[43]

So, it would seem that in retrospect John Collier's encounters with the Florida Seminoles helped clarify his perception that a true "Red Atlantis" lay not in merely preserving traditional cultural forms but through facilitating that dynamic process by which all Indian people shape their own destiny.

5

Cattle, Grass, and Homes

"I am here to see about some land," Jimmie Gopher informed Secretary Ickes through an interpreter. "I have suffered from not having land to live on . . . I am now crowded out to one little tract and don't know who owns it. My livestock has vanished away. I could start up livestock again and be independent if I had some land of my own."[1] While this Seminole speaker did not have the eloquence of Chief Joseph, agent J. L. Glenn must have felt that there could be no more dramatic statement in support of his own position: if the Seminole Indians were ever to achieve a stable, productive community life it would be a result of establishing them on large, fertile expanses of Florida prairie land where they could raise cattle. He was taken with the idea that in their distant history those Lower Creek people who settled in North Florida during the eighteenth century and were called Seminoles by the British—a corruption of the term *cimarrón,* meaning "wild or runaway," applied to them by the Spaniards—had taken to herding wild range cattle from abandoned Spanish *estancias.* In fact, a chief known as the "Cowkeeper" was a main Seminole leader during the British Period in Florida (1763–83).[2]

However, over a century and a half had elapsed since the halcyon days of Indian stock herding on the Alachua prairies of northern Florida. The Seminoles had passed through three disastrous wars, lost the greatest part of their population to a federal removal policy which relocated them in Oklahoma, and the surviving remnant reorganized its socioeconomic patterns while adapting to climatic and ecological conditions at the southern extremity of the peninsula. In the Everglades they had metamorphosed into a hunting, trapping, subsistence-farming society which eventually developed a profitable trading relationship with the outside world. It was true that many of the Florida Indians had turned to some form of agricultural wage labor during the economically depressed times which began early in this century, especially the Muskogee-Seminoles living north of Lake Okeechobee. There was nothing, however, in the life experience of most Mikasuki-Seminoles—the vast majority of the tribe—that pointed to any inherent ability or latent interest in becoming a cattle-based society. Thus, it was a somewhat idyllic quest that Glenn set himself upon; but he was only reflecting a long-standing goal of countless reformers who sought to civilize the Indian by forcing him into agricultural and pastoral pursuits.

In 1933 the accumulated landholdings of the tribe looked impressive for such a small group, still numbering fewer than 600 according to the agent's census. The largest single tract was the 99,000 acres in Monroe County that the Florida Legislature had set aside for Indian use in 1917.[3] There were also several parcels that had been acquired by the federal government beginning in the late 1890s and culminating with the presidential Executive Order of 1911.[4] The Hendry County Reservation was comprised of 23,061 noncontiguous acres in the lower Big Cypress region on the western edge of the Everglades. There was another 2,166 acres in Martin County, centered near Indian Town and directly east of Lake Okeechobee. In Broward County there were 360 acres at Dania Reservation and another 120 acres scattered in adjacent "forties" along the east side of the Everglades. The Indian Office also owned outright 960 acres scattered throughout Collier County—all in all, over 125,000 acres. To the casual observer this would seem to be more than enough land for the Seminoles, and there had been suggestions that perhaps the Indians should not receive more land until they learned to use what they already owned. However, as the agent often pointed out, most of the land allocated to the Seminoles was worthless for farming, livestock grazing, and even most hunting, or else the white man would have never parted with it so easily! What the tribe needed for effective rehabilitation was land that could support all phases of the social and economic life of the group: it should provide good grazing for livestock and high, dry, fertile sites for homes and gardens. Most important, the tribe should not be broken up into small, widely scattered units; it only led to social and economic fragmentation. Glenn correctly discerned that if they were scattered, they were "helpless in their attempt to resist those social forces which compel them to occupy an inferior social status."[5] This understanding, coupled with a desire to consolidate the Indians so that educational and medical services could be delivered more efficiently and effectively, drove the agent to spend countless hours during 1934–35 in the frustrating pursuit of a permanent homeland for the Seminoles.

The issue of land for the Seminoles was directly linked to the establishment of an Everglades National Park in Florida, and many leading figures took an interest in the process. The 1934 congressional act authorizing the park contained a clause protecting Indian rights: "nothing in this Act shall be construed to lessen any existing rights of the Seminole Indians which are not in conflict with the purposes for which the Everglades National Park is created,"[6] but in a national park there would obviously be constraints placed on hunting, trapping, and other traditional Indian pursuits. Ernest F. Coe of Miami, widely acknowledged as the "father of the park," strongly advocated that the State of Florida swap the 99,000-acre state Indian reservation in Monroe County—which was well within the boundaries of the proposed park—for an equal amount of land just to the north but adjoining the park. There, he suggested, the Seminoles from the Everglades and Big Cypress could make their permanent home, hunt freely, and receive employment as park guides. Coe sold this concept to Roy Nash and through him to Commissioner Rhoads, who ordered the Seminole Agency relocated to the Miles City site. D. Graham Copeland also supported the land swap concept, assuring everyone that the Collier Corporation would sell land to the state at a fair price to make sure that it succeeded. It was also Copeland who recommended Miles City as the ideal location for a Seminole Agency headquarters, and the government obtained options on four sections of land. Although the agent objected to such a move, arguing that the Indian Office was committed to retain Dania as an active reservation, he nevertheless began a land-clearing operation at Miles City as part of the Seminole IECW program.

Glenn also recommended that the Indian Office purchase a large tract of land in the Lake Istokpoga–Indian Prairie drainage basin northwest of Lake Okeechobee[7] as a permanent home for Indians living in that region. It was beautiful country and seemed to fit perfectly the paradigm that Glenn had created for an Indian homeland: lush, natural pastureland, dotted with artesian wells and drained by canals leading to Lake Okeechobee. In spring the flat prairies erupted into wildflowers that stretched away to the horizon in a riot of color. There were numerous cabbage and sable palm hammocks which provided ideal campsites and would support limited subsistence agriculture. Some critics believed that this might be a dangerous place to live, because several miles at the point of flowage ingress was not protected by the great earthen dike which enclosed the remainder of Lake Okeechobee. Many Floridians vividly recalled a recent disaster when the great lake was swept from its bed by the 1928 hurricane and nearly 2,000 persons perished in the surrounding farmland. Glenn dismissed these concerns saying that the land to the northwest of the lake was higher than the southern and eastern perimeters; besides, he held, unlike white farmers the Indians were wise enough to build their homes well back from the water's edge on high ground. In January 1934 the assistant to the commissioner, A. C. Monahan, came to Florida to visit the property; he agreed with the field agent's assessment, and secured an option on four sections of Indian Prairie located in Glades County near the small crossroads settlement of Brighton.

The funds to purchase both the Miles City and Indian Prairie tracts would have to come from the Resettlement Administration. This recently formed New Deal agency, headed by former Undersecretary of Agriculture Rexford G. Tugwell, was established by presidential executive order in April 1935 to coordinate land classification, retirement of submarginal acreage, and relocation of its residents, as well as a general rural rehabilitation program.[8] Collier often turned to the Resettlement Administration for assistance in securing land for Indian communities. The regional director of the Resettlement Administration, Dr. W. A. Hartman, was to become a valuable ally of the Indian agent in attempting to secure new properties for the Seminole people. Both the Miles City and Indian Prairie tracts were submitted to his office for examination and approval. The Resettlement Administration was authorized to purchase submarginal lands, and neither selection technically fit the agency's criteria. The Collier County acreage contained over 7 million board feet of lumber which could be sold at a profit, while areas of Indian Prairie were already being used by Florida cattle interests. However, Glenn argued convincingly that these areas were desired by the Indians and that they fit his plans for rehabilitation of the tribe. Dr. Hartman sincerely wanted to accommodate the Seminoles, although he had doubts about the value of the Collier County land for rehabilitation; both parcels were approved for purchase at prices ranging from five to six dollars per acre, and the recommendations were forwarded to Washington. Unfortunately, the Resettlement Administration office rejected both parcels. It was then suggested by the Indian Office that the plans be resubmitted separately. Despite several revisions of the Miles City proposal, that acreage was never acquired. This time Washington approved the purchase of 2,500 acres on Indian Prairie which became the nucleus of the Brighton Reservation.[9]

This was the situation when Collier and Ickes paid their visit to the Seminoles in March of 1935. James Glenn's elation that for the first time in history a commissioner of Indian affairs had visited the Seminole Indians was tempered somewhat by Collier's refusal to take time to visit the Indian Prairie region during his brief sojourn. The agent still hoped to secure at least 17,000 acres of this lush land as a reservation for the Muskogee-Seminoles, and Indian Prairie was included among the lands requested in the petition presented to Secretary Ickes. When the secretary and commissioner gave such positive responses to the Indian entreaties, and Collier's press release mentioned that "perhaps" a quarter of a million acres could be supplied, Glenn evidently took it as a firm commitment to secure at least 200,000 acres. However, several months passed before action on this front was resumed; in the meantime the aggressive Glenn let his displeasure with the delays be known publicly. The West Palm Beach Chamber of Commerce communicated to Secretary Ickes's office that in a speech the agent had accused Washington of foot-dragging on the matter, and the Fort Lauderdale Chamber voiced a similar concern.[10] These complaints must have displeased Collier and further jeopardized Glenn's position.

If New Deal funds became available there was an opportunity to acquire a large amount of land for the Florida Indians, but Collier characteristically insisted on consulting the Seminoles about their preferences before making any selection. Thus, Glenn spent several months traversing the backcountry meeting with as many Indians as he could find. As expected, few Mikasuki-Seminoles were interested in acquiring a government reservation; they were content to remain as squatters in the secluded Everglades camps where they had been relatively insulated from white intrusion. Some of the hard-liners reiterated their claim to all of the peninsula south of Pease Creek, an idea dating from the Second Seminole War. Following the West Palm Beach conference a small faction of Mikasuki-Seminoles living in the vicinity of Miami, headed by Corey Osceola and William McKinley Osceola, retained legal counsel to protect their interests in any negotiations with the federal government. The obstructionism of this group was encouraged by commercial village operators such as Lasher who saw it to their advantage to perpetuate the image of the "unconquered Seminole" that so appealed to tourists. The council of the so-called Trail Indians[11] living on the west side of the Everglades between Turner River and Naples, led by the medicine man Ingraham Billie, also stoutly maintained its political independence. This fragmentation was also catalogued in Gene Stirling's 1933 report for the Applied Anthropology Unit of the Office of Indian Affairs, which found that the Mikasukis had recently organized themselves into Miami and Big Cypress divisions.[12] Nevertheless, there were members of both Mikasuki groups at the meeting with Ickes and Collier, so Glenn felt justified in insisting that a tract of at least 100,000 acres in Collier County should be set aside for the southern branch of the Seminole Tribe.

The Indian agent found the greatest receptivity to the idea for government acquisition of land among the northern group of Muskogee-Seminoles. They had borne the brunt of white contact and appeared to have suffered the most both socially and economically. Most were living a precarious existence on other people's land as described so vividly in the *Miami Daily News* series. However, when Glenn approached their leaders, including the medicine man Sam Jones and Billy Stewart, they could reach no consensus on what steps should be taken. Billy Stewart suggested that the agent should attend the Green Corn Dance and try to get some direction from the council; but when he and his interpreter, the Rev. Willie King, arrived at the dance ground after a hazardous trip, the Indians were inebriated and the climate was clearly too hostile for meaningful discussions. Some of the Indian families wanted to purchase the small plots of land that they currently occupied, although they were often in undesirable locations near white settlements. Others saw the wisdom in securing a large tract of land for a reservation, which was the position promoted by the agent. Interestingly, at this time Sam Tommie stepped in and assumed a leading role in support of Glenn, traveling with him from camp to camp to gain the people's approval for a reservation. Apparently the acrimony surrounding the newspaper articles of the previous year had been put aside, for Glenn praised the Indian's efforts in a 1935 letter to Collier and was to write in his memoir: "Sam married a Ft. Pierce Indian, and her people made him live with them. Sam's brother had a grammar school education, and Sam had learned from him how to read and write. In my trips with him through the Indian country I found him as good company as any white man. . . . This business of buying land for a Seminole home or homes is a most difficult task, and Sam and Mr. King worked on it a great deal." Many years later an elderly Sam Tommie proudly described his work with the agent despite threats to his safety: "That's 'round about 1929 and '30 and '35. This man here, he work about seven years, you see, his name Mr. Glenn. We went round and talked to 'em. And then, they against me all right. But they didn't do anything to my body. They just talked, you see. And anyway, we worked it out. . . . Gradually to one of the family, to one another and all around. Some families listen to me and some not—but the leaders, they didn't want to listen to me, you see. All right, I worked for my people."[13] Ultimately, most Muskogees agreed that they would like to have land at Indian Prairie in Glades County, Blue Field and Cow Creek in St. Lucie County, and Fort Drum Swamp in Okeechobee County. Glenn believed that it would be best to consolidate all of the Muskogees in one location and that naturally it should be Indian Prairie where the Indian Office already had a foothold.

On May 10, 1935 the Indian Office authorized Glenn to begin negotiating the purchase of the several tracts of land requested by the Indians. As before, the program was to be submitted to Dr. W. A. Hartman for his examination. With his approval the Resettlement Administration would purchase the land. When Glenn conferred with Hartman ten days later, he was informed that only Indian Prairie met the rehabilitation specifications and requirements of the Resettlement Administration. The Indian Office made it clear that Dr. Hartman would have the final say on submission, and he was reluctant to devote the inordinate amount of time and effort required to prepare proposals for over 200,000 acres of land that the Indian agent had options on—especially if most of it might be turned down by Washington. As a scientist Dr. Hartman found it difficult to justify many of the Indian selections to his department. For example, it would require more persuasive argument than Hartman was willing to make to convince land utilization scientists that an area such as Fort Drum Swamp was potentially suited for handling all phases of the social and economic life of these Indians. Therefore, Glenn and Hartman agreed that the tracts would be submitted for approval consecutively, beginning with Indian Prairie. Immediate approval of a 45,000-acre tract was given by Dr. Hartman; Glenn prepared to have it appraised, only to be told by Washington that appraisal could not begin until all of the tracts requested by the Indians had been considered. By June options had been secured on 230,000 acres of land, including 100,000 in Collier County just north of the Tamiami Trail, and proposals for purchase submitted to the Resettlement Administration. Immediately there was a negative reaction in the Resettlement Administration toward the Collier County tract because of its price. At this point progress stalled because of reorganization in the agency, and Dr. Hartman, who was caught up in the political shuffle, hesitated to take any action that would cause undue reaction in Washington. A plan to purchase only the 45,000 acres on Indian Prairie was disapproved because of conflicts between the Indian Office and the Resettlement Administration.

It appeared that the work of Glenn and Dr. Hartman was all for nothing, another victim of New Deal bureaucratic infighting. Then in the late summer the Indian Office allocated $25,000 of the Indian Reorganization Act appropriation to purchase lands for the Seminoles. Given the limitations imposed by such a small sum, and knowing there was resistance to the Collier County tract, Glenn and Dr. Hartman concentrated their efforts on a scaled-down plan for Indian Prairie land which seemed to offer the best possibility for a true Indian rehabilitation program. New options were obtained on approximately 8,000 acres at four dollars per acre, and the paperwork was again sent to the Resettlement Administration, which accepted it—but in November 1935 it was once again rejected by the Indian Office. In addition, the Indian Office removed supervision of the land program from the agent and placed it with Riddle

& Yetter, an engineering firm from West Palm Beach, while Dr. Hartman was replaced as regional director of the Resettlement Administration. In his 1935 annual report a dejected Glenn lamented, "During the whole of this work the Officer in Charge has traveled between fifty and sixty thousand miles. He has traversed almost impassable swamps in meeting the Indians and discussing with them their land needs. He has given no end of thought to land conditions in South Florida, and to the requirements of the Seminoles. At times he has worked through the whole of the night in rushing proposals and preparing maps, and other data for these programs. A large program has been set-up and a great deal of information has been gained on it, but only 2,600 acres of land has been purchased."[14]

At that point there was an abrupt change of fortune, for the State of Florida and the federal government entered into agreements for a rapid series of land exchanges and purchases benefiting the Seminoles. On June 14, 1935, Congress approved P.L. 135,[15] which Senator Duncan U. Fletcher had guided through both houses, authorizing the exchange of lands reserved for the Seminole Indians in Florida for other lands. Shortly thereafter the assistant to the commissioner, A. C. Monahan, met Glenn at the state capitol in Tallahassee, and they received a promise from Governor David Sholtz that the legislature would pass the necessary legislation to effect the swap of lands within the Everglades National Park area. Sholtz was as good as his word, and at its next session the Florida legislature passed legislation authorizing the trustees of the Internal Improvement Fund to exchange state lands with private owners and also to exchange state lands thus acquired with the federal government, "to provide more adequately for the needs of the Seminole Indians in Florida."[16] This law paved the way for establishment of one state and three federal reservations which remained intact for the next three decades.

Prior to 1900 the federal government had purchased 23,061 acres in Hendry County. By Executive Order 1379 of June 28, 1911, another 3,640 acres in Martin, Collier, and Broward counties were set aside for the Seminoles. The exchange took place in the following manner: In Broward County 360 acres were retained as the nucleus of the Dania Reservation, while the 120 outlying acres were traded to the state to gain 115 acres adjacent to the reservation, the net loss of five acres being more than offset by the added value of the land thus acquired. The lands in Martin and Collier counties, about 3,170 acres, was exchanged for 1,280 acres in Hendry County to be added to the existing reservation there and 1,920 acres in Glades County that would become part of the Brighton Reservation.[17]

Although the Brighton Reservation began with the original 2,500 acres acquired at Glenn's urging in 1935, with additional exchanges and purchases it had grown to over 35,000 acres by 1938. Of this total 27,086.10 acres were purchased with Resettlement Administration funds, 6,789.93 acres were secured with Indian Reorganization Act funds, and 1,920 acres by exchange with the State of Florida.[18] The Resettlement Administration acreage was later assumed by the Department of Agriculture and officially transferred to the Department of the Interior by Executive Order 7868 of April 15, 1938,[19] although title to the land remained with agriculture until Brighton was declared to be a reservation for the Seminole Indians pursuant to the Act of July 20, 1956.[20]

The Hendry County holdings were renamed Big Cypress Reservation and formally dedicated with the addition of the 1,280 acres of land in 1936. Over the next decade an additional 18,356 acres were purchased with IRA funds, bringing it to 42,697 acres.[21] The basic configuration of this reservation remained unaltered until the 1980s.

Governor Sholtz and the cabinet of the State of Florida, sitting in their capacity as trustees of the Internal Improvement Trust Fund, approved all of the above exchanges of land with the United States on December 23, 1936.[22] At the same session they took up the matter of changing the location of the State Seminole Reservation as authorized by the legislature in the enabling act of 1935, which held that when, as a result of exchanges of land with the state, the United States had established reservations for the Seminoles in Florida, "the state Seminole Indian reservation in Monroe County, created by Chapter 7310, acts of 1917, shall be withdrawn and returned to said board of trustees; and thereupon the board of trustees of the internal improvement trust fund shall set aside a tract of land of approximately equal size and suitable character, adjacently located, as nearly as may be, to the reservation being established by the United States; and said lands, when so set aside, shall constitute the state Indian reservation and shall be held in trust by the department of general services for the perpetual benefit of the Indians and as a reservation for them."[23] Accordingly, the trustees ordered the return of the 99,200 acres in Monroe County, for which they substituted 104,800 acres in the western reaches of Broward and Palm Beach counties. This tract abuts the eastern boundary of the Big Cypress Reservation and lies almost entirely within a water conservation area of the South Florida Water Management District. In 1965 the Florida legislature authorized the transfer of this tract to the United States to be held in trust for the Seminole and Miccosukee tribes, the former to have full benefit of the top quarter (approximately forty-five sections in Broward and Palm

Beach counties) and the newly formed Miccosukee Tribe (granted federal recognition in 1962) to have control of the lower three-quarters in southern Broward County.[24] Still, the question of federal trust status for both tracts remained in doubt until the 1980s. The Miccosukee Tribe's portion of this land was taken into federal trust by the Florida Indian Land Claims Settlement Act of 1982, while federalization of the Seminole acreage is authorized in the Seminole Indian Land Claims Settlement Act of 1987.[25]

The three relatively small Seminole Indian reservations thus pieced together during the Great Depression of the 1930s were a far cry from what Glenn and others had envisioned for the rehabilitation of the tribe, but economic constraints as well as inter- and intra-agency politics thwarted their attempts to obtain significantly larger tracts. A more farsighted and open-handed Indian Office bureaucracy would have instituted a policy of securing as much land as possible—especially at the low prices prevailing at the time. Rather than 230,000 acres the Seminoles wound up with 180,000 acres, and most of that remained in the capricious hands of state government. And there was always a nagging question: If the state had exchanged Indian lands once, what was to prevent its happening again? Therefore, changing their state reservation land to federal trust status as quickly as possible became imperative for future Indian leaders. But at least these rural enclaves had been set aside as secure havens where the process of bringing a scattered and fragmented Indian people together could begin to regenerate tribal unity. In the beginning, though, the reservations developed as more or less separate communities, each with its own character. As the northern and southern Seminoles were joined by common racial and cultural bonds, so were they also separated by language (Big Cypress people spoke Mikasuki while those at Brighton used Muskogee), internal social and political structure (each constituted a busk group with its own medicine men and council prior to a widespread conversion to Christianity), economic patterns (Brighton people took to cattle herding and sustained off-reservation employment sooner than those at Big Cypress), and a varying capacity for acceptance or involvement in government-sponsored programs such as the CCC-ID, day schools, and livestock associations.

From the outset Brighton Reservation had the potential to become the most successful of the new rural reservations. The Muskogee-Seminoles living in widely scattered camps north of Lake Okeechobee had frequented the Indian Prairie for many years. They added a touch of local color at the Mediterranean-style hotel which was built in this isolated setting during the 1920s by James H. Bright, a partner with aircraft pioneer

Glenn Curtiss in developing Hialeah and Miami Springs.[26] The new community of Brighton, which Curtiss named after his partner, lay equidistant from two major railways that provided easy access for sportsmen drawn by the hunting and fishing on Indian Prairie. The hotel was envisioned to be the centerpiece of a huge Florida real estate enterprise encompassing an entire township in Glades County plus more than 7,000 acres in Highlands County, and the company spent a great deal of money installing gravity canals to drain the area before the land boom collapsed. The great hotel closed and fell into decay, but as many as ten Seminole families were living on Indian Prairie permanently in the mid-1930s.[27] They made their camps among the numerous palm hammocks, some as large as twenty acres, that dotted the landscape. The fertile hammock soil supported crops of corn, pumpkins, and potatoes, while dense undergrowth in the uncleared areas provided perfect forage for wild hogs. The Indians supplemented these food sources by fishing, gathering huckleberries in season, or hunting the turkey, quail, and deer that were still available throughout the region bordering Lake Okeechobee.

Francis J. Scott was named superintendent of the Seminole Agency in January 1936, replacing Glenn who remained three months more as disbursing agent before reentering the ministry.[28] The new field officer continued the effort to relocate Muskogee families to the Brighton Reservation, which had an abundance of high hammock land where Indian families could establish widely separated campsites according to their custom. However, it soon became apparent that there were certain negative features that had to be corrected before the reservation was fully habitable and rehabilitation programs could be instituted. The most objectionable of these was the heavy flooding that occurred during the rainy season, despite the fact that the terrain was drained by the large Indian Prairie Canal to the north and the Harney Pond Canal to the south, both emptying directly into Lake Okeechobee. The new flooding, though, was caused by the dikes, ditches, and canals constructed on the white-owned farms and ranches that surrounded the Indian lands. Much water management would have to be undertaken over the ensuing years with funds initially provided by the IECW and its successor, CCC-ID. Any program for flood control was complicated by the fact that part of the acreage was still being purchased as late as 1938. Even then the Brighton Reservation was not a unitary block of land; during the land boom at least forty persons had acquired title to over 11,000 acres all lying within the reservation boundaries, while the Lykes Brothers cattle ranch owned 480 acres.[29]

Over time the Muskogee-Seminoles of the Brighton Reservation more than fulfilled Glenn's predictions that they would excel as cattlemen. He based that prediction in part on the successful experience of the Seminoles at Dania Reservation who, in 1933, had purchased twelve head of wild range cattle which they tended and sold for a profit.[30] As a result of this venture, the Indian Office later supplied them with seventy-two purebred Angus cattle, which were also successfully grazed on the improved pasturage provided through the IECW program at Dania.[31] It was assumed that the Muskogees would do even better if they had more land and cattle to work with, but the Brighton cattle program got off to an inauspicious start and narrowly averted disaster.

One of Glenn's final duties as agent had been to submit a rehabilitation plan for the Seminole tribe to Dr. Philip Weltner, the new regional director of the Resettlement Administration. Although the agency approved a plan in 1935 that called for an expenditure of $40,000 and the resettlement of forty Seminole families on Indian Prairie, it ruled that the money could only be committed as a loan. Glenn refused to accept the loan and the plan was dropped. Like his predecessor, Dr. Weltner took a benign interest in the Seminoles. He had access to 2,000 head of cattle from drought-stricken western states which he offered to the Indians as a starter herd; "five hundred and forty-seven head were transferred immediately, and arrangements were completed for the shipment of another five hundred head."[32] In the meanwhile the Indian Office had turned down Glenn and Hartman's proposal for purchasing better grasslands. The first shipment of Herefords arrived by railroad and were driven through the town of Brighton, then turned out on the original four sections of unimproved pasture. Many of them were soon dying from malnutrition. Old-timers recalled that part of the prairie was known as "Sick Island" because cattle wandering into its fastness rarely returned, and those managing to escape were covered with a thick mud and so emaciated that they quickly died.[33] The second shipment of 500 head was abandoned. By the time Florida and federal government had completed their land negotiations, only a fraction of the original herd remained.

Superintendent Scott took the initiative in getting Brighton and the cattle program on a sound footing. Beginning in 1936 the focus of the Seminole Agency IECW/CCC-ID budget was shifted to outlying reservations to provide fencing, to sink wells for a water supply, and to improve pastures by planting Bermuda and other grasses—even though title to some of the land still had not been secured. These moves proved a double benefit to the Seminoles by providing immediate employment income for families as well as improving tribal lands. However, the person usually credited with organizing the cattle program at the Brighton Reservation and setting the Muskogee-Seminoles on the road to self-sufficiency was Fred Montsdeoca, who came to his position as the agricultural extension agent for Okeechobee County in January 1937. A graduate of the University of Florida and a ranch-owner, Montsdeoca had had a long-standing interest in the Indians since his college days and would be associated with the tribe until his retirement. He recalled that the Brighton Reservation was less than an ideal place to raise beef cattle in the late 1930s: "There were a few people who could work as cattle hands. My job was to locate cattle on ranges, get minerals and ample pasturage and train workers. I had to teach the practice of weaning yearlings, rotating pastures, increasing the calf crop by using good bulls. The native range and climatic conditions were very bad—no drainage, much high water, and drought in winter. Everything was very difficult."[34] For over three decades Montsdeoca encouraged the Indians to take an interest in the proper care, management, and treatment of their cattle and hogs, as well as assisting them with range control and improvement. In recognition of these efforts Montsdeoca was accorded the honorary title "assistant county agent for Indian affairs" in 1955. More important, as Garbarino's study from a later period revealed, the Seminoles listened, learned, and followed his advice. One of the Indian cattlemen readily admitted, "I do what Fred says to do. Even if I don't know for myself, he knows because it is his work."[35] By 1938 the Indian stockmen had progressed to a point where *Indians at Work* reported that the Seminoles took a creditable part in the Florida State Fair by exhibiting their Herefords. The story was accompanied by a picture of Charlie Osceola and the stockman each leading a pair of Hereford calves.[36] When Fred Montsdeoca passed away in 1974, he left as a legacy a firmly established Seminole Indian cattle industry functioning on both the Brighton and Big Cypress reservations.

From the outset all costs associated with the cattle program at the Brighton Reservation had been met by the federal government. Because the Indians did not have sufficient range or experience in the cattle industry to enter the business individually, the cattle were held as a tribal herd until such time as the whole tribe was interested and had the experience necessary to be successful cattlemen. The cattle had been held in possession of the government and none of the calf crop was disposed of; in June 1939 there were 1,103 head of cattle in the herd. At this point it was determined that the Muskogee-Seminoles had attained the requisite experience to assume control of the herd. A "Trust Agreement to

Reimburse for Cattle" was approved by Collier and duly executed on August 10, 1939.[37]

The trust agreement was made between the commissioner of Indian affairs and three trustees acting in behalf of all members of the Seminole Tribe of Indians of the State of Florida. Although Montsdeoca and the Rev. Willie King organized an "election," the Indian people were not accustomed to selecting their leaders in this manner, and the result was less than satisfactory. Apparently the women voted for everyone nominated, and as a result one of the men elected to the board was not even a cattle owner.[38] The first men chosen as Seminole cattle trustees were Charles Micco, John Josh, and Willy Gopher. The Seminole cattle enterprise was featured in the March 1940 issue of *Indians at Work*. Although John Collier was the foremost exponent of Indian self-determination, this agreement was not intended as an exercise in democratic leadership selection. The document required that cattle trustees be appointed by the commissioner, and he could "remove any or all of the said Trustees at any time, for reasons deemed by him satisfactory or necessary so to do. Any vacancies otherwise occurring among the Trustees shall be filled by the Commissioner." Moreover, every aspect of the cattle program was strictly regulated by the Indian Office. Severe limitations were placed on the ability of the trustees to operate the tribal herd without permission of the local superintendent; while they were admonished to "determine and decide all business affairs concerning the sale herd in accordance with good management practices now established and followed in the cattle industry in the area . . . the Superintendent may require the discontinuance or any operation or management plan or practices which are not in accordance with such plan or practice advocated by the State Agricultural College."[39] A strict repayment-in-kind schedule required that the Indians return to the government one yearling heifer or one purebred bull for each animal originally placed in the common herd. Repayment would be at the rate of 25 percent of the herd each year, starting in 1942 and ending in 1945. Theoretically, the trustees represented the interest of all Seminole people, but practically speaking the cattle program remained almost exclusively a Brighton Reservation affair until the mid-1940s.

There were economic activities other than the cattle enterprise at the Brighton Reservation.[40] Each family was assigned a five-acre fenced plot where corn, sugarcane, pumpkins, and potatoes could be grown, and there were also orange and grapefruit trees and banana plants growing in the eighty acres of cleared hammock. Practically all Indian families claimed to own some of the wild hogs that foraged on wild nuts and cabbage palm berries. When the Indians requested it, the Glades County agricultural agent would come to the reservation and, for a small fee, innoculate the hogs against cholera. This sideline of raising hogs became profitable, and it was reported that $1,000 worth of hogs was sold in a two-month period to a Tampa packinghouse. Close cooperation was maintained with the Everglades Experiment Station at Belle Glade and the Florida State Extension Service, both of which supplied specimen plants and technical information to the Indians.

The CCC-ID program, which had done so much to improve the cattle program by fencing, draining, and revegetating 1,699 acres of range, also contributed to the general quality of life on the reservation. Among other things, a four-mile telephone line was completed to link Brighton with the outside world. Thirty-three wells were dug to provide fresh water to many Indian camps. An all-weather road and truck trails were built. Most of this work was supervised by the mechanic Byron L. Yates, who had been with the program from the start and drew an $80 monthly salary, raised to $135 in 1937. By 1939, IECW/CCC-ID funds in excess of $99,000 had been expended on the Seminoles, most on projects at the Brighton Reservation.[41] Only minor maintenance and renovation jobs were continued at the Dania Reservation, so a number of the residents moved to the rural reservations seeking employment—a dramatic reversal of the process that took place when IECW began in 1934.

The work relief budget for the Seminole Agency was limited, and Superintendent Scott was constantly pleading with the Washington office for additional funds. The Indian workers in the CCC-ID earned about $2 a day with per diem but did not work every week, so it was estimated that the average wage earned was under $500 a year. This money was virtually the only source of cash income for most of the 160 Seminole males eligible for enrollment in the CCC-ID, but only a small percentage could be employed year-round; in 1937, Scott complained that "we cannot carry our present crew of more than thirty men, throughout the fiscal year, without additional funds, and owing to our limited funds we cannot give employment to many deserving Indians who are in need of work and would like to join our CCC group."[42] As a result of this plea the Seminole allocation of CCC-ID monies was increased substantially over the next two years—in part because the program was also extended to the Big Cypress Reservation. With a source of assured income, the Brighton people continued to make slow but steady progress in building their community.

There were several encouraging signs that those Indians who had resettled on the Brighton Reservation were making a rapid adaptation. In 1938, the Muskogees requested a day school for their reservation.[43] At a conference held between the Indian leaders and Assistant Commissioner W. A. Zimmerman, Richard Osceola, one of two spokesmen for the Muskogee people, stressed their need for a school, a hospital, a community center, and better livestock. The Indian Office agreed with most of these requests and sent Mr. and Mrs. William Boehmer to initiate the educational and community development work. They had come from an assignment among the Sioux of South Dakota and knew how to develop rapport with an Indian community. At first they lived in a trailer and worked side-by-side with the Seminoles in erecting the school building and teachers' quarters, both of which were built using $7,000 of CCC-ID funds. The school was dedicated on November 16, 1938, with the missionary Rev. Willie King conducting the ceremony and Richard Osceola translating Scott's speech into Muskogee for the assembled residents. Even the reclusive old patriarch Billy Buster, estimated to be over one hundred years of age, attended these exercises.[44] The Boehmers remained for thirty years and in the process became not only teachers but also friends and advisers to the Seminole people.

The Boehmers were also the prime movers in organizing the Seminole handicrafts industry as an additional source of income. When they arrived the Seminole women were making articles of inferior quality, and there was little attempt to sell their items to the public. Contact was made with the Indian Arts and Crafts Board in Washington, a division of the Office of Indian Affairs, and Alice Mariott was assigned to work with the Muskogee group in writing a constitution and bylaws for a proposed organization. The Seminole Crafts Guild of Glades County was approved on August 11, 1940, and its membership was open to all persons on the reservation, Indians and employees, who were interested in the development and sale of Seminole arts and crafts. There were to be five officers, "two men and three women, who shall be Indians," and a secretary-treasurer, "who shall be an Indian Service employee."[45] William Boehmer filled the latter post on a part-time basis for many years. The women and young girls were soon producing dolls, patchwork clothing, basketry, beadwork, and small canoes according to standards set by the guild. Each article was inspected, given a tag issued by the Seminole Agency, and sold to tourists who visited the Brighton Day School. Those articles that did not meet standards were exchanged for groceries and gasoline at nearby stores and service stations. After a time the high quality items were also sold to outlets at commercial Indian villages and gift shops throughout Florida. In 1939 the income from sale of handicrafts was estimated to be $7,000, and by 1941 it had risen substantially. Through a small markup on sales the guild accumulated a revolving fund from which it was able to pay cash for finished products rather than taking them on consignment, and this method brought a degree of financial independence to many single women. Although the development of a handicrafts industry was a positive step in the early years, it would later become controversial. Following World War II there was a need to develop more viable employment opportunities for Indian people, but a paternalistic Indian Office continued to encourage the traditional handicrafts even though there was a limited market and low prices for such goods. When the Seminole Crafts Guild finally ceased operation, it had an estimated two-year inventory of unsold goods in storage.

The school building, which housed a classroom, a community workroom for crafts, a shop, men's and women's showers, a laundry, and quarters for the teacher's family, became the hub of community life at the Brighton Reservation before the wholesale conversions to Christianity brought Baptist churches. In 1939, to celebrate the sixth anniversary of the CCC-ID which had been so important in their lives, the people at Brighton Reservation held their first field day—a round of festivities including games, athletic contests, rodeo events, and feasting on traditional Indian foods—which was attended by Indians from other reservations, citizens from nearby towns, and national CCC director Robert Fechner who was visiting Florida programs. The event received several pages of photo coverage in *Indians at Work* and became an annual Brighton affair.[46]

Around 1938 the Baptist missionary Willie King had turned his efforts to the area around Brighton and Okeechobee City and was beginning to have some limited success in making conversions. In addition to pastoral duties, he intended to translate the Bible into Muskogee but needed assistance if the work was to continue. Having reached sixty-seven years of age, the exhausted missionary wrote to his Oklahoma Association pleading for them to send a younger man to take up the work, saying, "I have done all that can be done for them towards their welfare. Some have to be taught in life-living and then in religion."[47] Although King was perceived as a threat by some Indian religious traditionalists, Christian influence as measured by numbers of converts was minimal throughout the early 1940s.

Perhaps the only outside appraisal of conditions at Brighton Reservation was that provided by the anthropologist Alexander Spoehr, who wrote to John Collier in 1939 at the conclusion of his extended fieldwork among the Muskogees.[48] In this letter, written at the request of his colleague Donald Collier, the commissioner's son, Spoehr briefly touched on virtually every aspect of the government program and personnel. He evaluated Superintendent Scott as having, "done a very successful job so far in getting the Seminole reservations started and on their feet, and I see no reason why the success should not continue. So far as I know he is well regarded by the Indians." With regard to the cattle program, Spoehr agreed with the plan of the government holding the herd to be turned over to the Indians at a later time, for, "if the cattle are apportioned out to the Seminole as individuals, it is probable that the herd will not last long, for only a minority of the men know enough about cattle to take care of them. The preferable plan is undoubtedly some form of communal ownership and management, even though the Seminole are in some ways rugged individualists."

However, the ethnologist cautioned that while it was fine for the government to promote future economic self-sufficiency through cattle ownership, there were dangers inherent in the policy of offering the Seminoles jobs on the reservation: "The older men are very strong characters, are used to hoeing their own rows, and are independent in spirit; many of the younger men are on the whole less responsible, are becoming accustomed to working for the government when and if they wish, and do not seem to realize that their jobs are not going to last forever. There is a danger here in too paternalistic and helping an attitude on the part of the government leading to a loss of initiative and responsibility on the part of the young Indians, of which I believe Mr. Scott is cognizant. I might add that the Seminole are embarking on a period of social change undoubtedly greater than any they have known before, with the possible exception of the Seminole wars; the coming years are bound to impose the severest strain on the adaptability of their little society." He held that the best way of easing this strain was by nurturing those traits of independence and self-sufficiency for which the Seminoles were known, and he implied that it could probably be achieved best in economic activities other than those that the CCC-ID promoted.

Spoehr also suggested that a policy should be formulated governing missionary work on the reservations, because, "with the Indians now on reservations, pressures from missionaries will probably increase and I should not be surprised if proposals were made to build missions on the reservations themselves. Inasmuch as the Indians have evinced little desire in the last fifty years to adopt the various forms of white religion offered them, I should hate to see it forced on them, if only because of the social disruption so often entailed." These comments from an eminent scholar were gratefully accepted by Collier, and he wrote Spoehr that "All the items are helpful and all of them seem right."[49] The letter was duplicated and distributed among the Indian Service staff.

John Collier was so pleased with the progress at Brighton and Big Cypress that he devoted a section of his 1939 annual report to discussing the economic and educational advancements among the Seminole Indians. "In no section of the country has the attitude of Indian wards become more responsive than among the Seminoles. . . . These measures are at last meeting with the most enthusiastic cooperation from those Seminoles, about one-half of the tribe, who have established themselves on the two new reservations."[50]

By 1940 the Brighton Reservation had begun to take on the dimensions of a model Indian community along the lines envisioned by John Collier. It was on the road to building a prosperous cattle industry, the general living conditions had been dramatically improved, a day school had been established at the request of the Indians, and a viable arts and crafts program was under way. It appeared that only one link was missing from this chain of development: the Brighton people should organize themselves politically under provisions of the Indian Reorganization Act. The groundwork for such a move was established by those twenty-one Seminoles who voted in favor of the IRA in the 1935 election, thereby entitling the tribe to participate. Furthermore, a provision of the IRA held that the right to organize was not restricted to a collective group or tribe. Again the solicitor, Nathan Margold, had ruled that an individual group or distinct tribe of Indians occupying a definite geographical area of a reservation could seek their own recognition.[51] This move is apparently what Collier was advocating for the Muskogee-Seminoles at Brighton. It was recalled that these were the people who had petitioned for a reservation at the West Palm Beach conference; also, by allowing only a portion of the Seminoles to organize formally, any opposition from the Mikasuki-Seminoles should be negated.

A departmental memorandum of March 4, 1941, initialed by DMcN (probably D'Arcy McNickle, assistant to Collier) left no doubt as to the direction Collier favored: "The Seminole Indians residing in Glades County, sometimes referred to as the Cow Creek Indians, are interested in taking over the cattle enterprise recently started for the benefit of the Seminole Tribe, and are considering organizing under the Indian Reorganization Act. Mr. Zimmerman and Mr. Collier indicate a desire to see the Cow Creek Indians organized separately. . . . The questionnaire on Tribal Organization submitted in 1934, showed that the Seminole Indians are made up of three groups, each group having a separate council, and occupying different geographical areas. At present there is little inter-council organization. . . . One of the three groups is the Cow Creeks, composed of eighteen or twenty families or approximately 100 individuals. They live near Lake Okeechobee, 100 miles north of the other groups and speak a different language, the Muskogee dialect. They have their own tribal council of four members headed by a medicine man. The tribal council meets annually on a date arranged by the medicine man; it has complete jurisdiction over the Indians, and its execution of Indian law is thorough and exacting."⁵²

This memorandum gave a succinct and accurate description of the Muskogee-Seminole situation, and it had hit upon the major source of their reluctance to organize: the continuing influence of the medicine man and busk council. In the early 1940s many of these Indians still followed the traditional leaders who had not moved onto government land, and they participated in the Green Corn Dance which was always conducted in a remote location away from the reservation. Although they had made great strides in adopting the white man's material culture, they were still affectively Indian. There was little desire or willingness to embark on a formal organizational scheme except among a few of the highly acculturated Indians who were involved in the cattle enterprise. This reluctance was dramatically pointed out when a $20,000 rehabilitation grant was awarded to the Seminoles later in 1941 and trustees were appointed to sign the necessary documents. After initially signing to accept the money, two of the trustees, John Josh and Jimmie Gopher, refused to sign any more papers on orders from the council of elders. The field officer and an interpreter went into the backcountry in an attempt to meet with the leaders but to no avail; an exasperated agent telegraphed Collier, "Big Cypress delegation and Cow Creek head men living Ft. Drum area now at corn dance have directed trustees not to sign voucher rehabilitation and refuse grant. Our repeated meetings and efforts explanation unavailing. Head men insisting money being paid tribes in return for young men who will then be placed in army. Trustees fully understand grant but are overruled by head men."⁵³ Although this issue was later resolved in favor of accepting the grant through an elaborate voting process conducted among only those Indians living on the Brighton Reservation, it nevertheless points up the strength that the traditional Seminole leaders still had at that time. Also, there was a lingering suspicion of the government's motives in dealing with the Seminoles; because of it the Seminole Agency had received permission to omit the fingerprinting of Indians applying for CCC-ID identification cards, as "some misunderstanding and trouble would probably result if thumb prints are required to employ them."⁵⁴

Experiences such as these caused Assistant Commissioner Zimmerman to rethink the Indian Office position on the matter of promoting a separate tribal organization for the Muskogees. In a letter to the superintendent of the Seminole Agency, he reviewed all the reasons why the Muskogees could legally be considered a separate band eligible for tribal organization, but he concluded by reiterating the fundamental policy of

the Indian New Deal: "It is understood that the Indians will decide
whether or not, and when, tribal organization should be attempted."[55]
This review apparently signaled the end of an active effort to organize
the Brighton Reservation people apart from the other Seminoles. Although the singling out of this model Indian community would have no
doubt pleased Collier—who acknowledged that the Mikasukis and the
Muskogees should be treated differentially—the long-run effect on the
Florida Indians could have been disastrous. Had they pursued the option of seeking a political and economic identity apart from the other
Indians, the resulting fragmentation of loyalties and dissipation of limited economic resources would have made it exceedingly difficult to organize a unified Seminole tribal government in 1957. Initially, as a result
of the experiences gained from interacting with non-Indians throughout the New Deal era, the small Brighton Reservation population would
provide much of the economic stability and political leadership for the
nascent Seminole Tribe of Florida.

While the Brighton Reservation was well established in the years just
prior to World War II, the same could not be said for the wild and remote Big Cypress Reservation, even though from 1937 on it shared
equally in the attention of federal authorities. Moreover, even after a
number of Mikasuki-Seminoles accepted reservation life and converted
to Christianity, they remained seemingly impervious to those economic
and social motivations that operated so effectively among their Muskogee kin to the north. For years, long after the federal government formally chartered the Seminole Tribe of Florida, there would be less than
full integration of this reservation population into the social and political
affairs of the tribe.

6

Just Leave Us Alone!

The morning of February 22, 1936, dawned clear and cool; it would be a fine day for a conference with the Seminoles in the Everglades, just what Florida Governor David Sholtz had in mind. The eloquent and publicity-minded New Deal governor intended to make political capital of the recent state efforts to exchange Indian lands in the Everglades National Park for an even greater holding to the north, which would become the new State Indian Reservation. Thus, a meeting with the Seminoles to explain what the state had done and to show that it was solicitous of their needs seemed to be in order. Political and business figures in Lee and Collier counties were eager to arrange any "media event" that might boost Florida's slumping tourist economy. And the leaders of the Mikasuki-Seminoles and their white advocates were anxious to gain some official recognition of their existence to counterbalance the impact of the West Palm Beach meeting the previous year. Although many federal policymakers continued to view the Seminoles as a monolithic tribe, the Mikasuki element was determined to maintain its separate identity.

Governor Sholtz and his party of state officials, including the chief justice of the Florida Supreme Court and several members of the cabinet, traveled in a police-escorted motorcade from Fort Myers to a point near Monroe Station on the Tamiami Trail. They were greeted there by a group of 270 of the "Trail Indians" who accompanied the official party to a parley ground prepared in a nearby pine hammock. Sholtz, much to his delight, was borne there in a ceremonial litter carried by the tribesmen. After the usual round of picture taking, all cameras and newsmen were hustled away, leaving the state officials to confer with the Mikasukis led by Doctor Tiger with Corey Osceola as spokesman. The Indians allowed the attorney O. B. White and their trusted friend Stanley Hanson to remain as witnesses to the meeting. During the brief interchange that followed, the governor solemnly inquired what the State of Florida could do for the tribe, and was told, "*Pohaan checkish* (just let us alone)!"[1]

The governor emerged from the meeting and recounted for the press what the Seminoles had said, explaining they were afraid of being moved from their villages. "They fear the white man will keep on moving them until they are in the water. That was the expression they used. I told them they could depend on the State Administration to defend their rights and do what we can for them. They are a sturdy self-reliant people. They did not ask for relief or aid of any kind, just to be left alone."[2] Even so, the Sholtz administration initiated the practice of providing free automobile tags for the Florida Indians. Seminole resistance to being involved in any state programs—and by inference federal Indian programs as well—was conveyed in a letter from Sholtz to Secretary Ickes summarizing the outcome of the conference. First, Sholtz interpreted being "left alone" to mean that the Indians did not want to be limited to a reservation. Neither did they want the Everglades National Park set up to interfere with their present territorial run. They did not want schools, believing in their own system of education. Finally, they wanted an Indian agent who understood their problems and whom they trusted. Sholtz wrote that the Indians had reiterated their complaints about the previous agent and that the West Palm Beach meeting had been a "staged affair" in which the true desires of all Seminoles had never been put forth through their real leaders. The governor assured Ickes that all members of the cabinet joined him in putting forth the name of Stanley Hanson for appointment to the position of Indian agent. He attempted to defuse any concerns arising from Roy Nash's report: "I have personally had Mr. Hanson thoroughly checked and we are all convinced that an Agent should be appointed and to get the best results, Mr. Hanson should be at least given temporary appointment as Indian Agent, although I am personally convinced his appointment should be made permanent."[3] Evidently Hanson's presence at the conference, his language fluency and reputation as a "white medicine man," as well as the support of a Fort Myers constituency, had impressed Governor Sholtz.

A reply from Ickes addressed these points. While he agreed that it would be unwise to force schooling on any Seminole group, he had concerns about the other three points. He thought it wiser to set aside a large protected area for hunting, trapping, or farming, as the case called for, rather than let the Seminoles roam all over the already heavily drained Everglades. He said that he still hoped to arrange for Seminole "privileges" within the Everglades National Park but clearly implied that it was a dim prospect. He bristled a bit when responding to the suggestion that the meeting with the Seminoles in West Palm Beach should not be considered legitimate: "I do not doubt that the meeting held at West Palm Beach was a 'staged affair.' It is equally true, however, that large numbers of Seminoles were present and the petition which they delivered to me impressed me as being a dignified and well thought-out plea for those things which the Seminoles desire. I regretted the effort that was made, after that meeting, to discredit the Indians' petition. I do not know whether my information is correct, to the effect that Mr. Hanson, whom you mention, was a leading factor in that effort." In any case, federal law required that Indian Office superintendencies be filled from the Civil Service register. Having thus dismissed out-of-hand any possibility of a Hanson candidacy, he assured the governor that it was the government's intention to provide a competent superintendent for the Seminoles. He affirmed his support for the incumbent superintendent, Francis J. Scott, who had a fairly wide and successful experience with Indians; but if he proved inadequate to the needs of the Seminoles, he would be replaced. Secretary Ickes concluded by lauding Governor Sholtz for recognizing that the Seminoles were a valuable element in the life of Florida and the Southeast and predicted that "with cooperation between you and the Federal agencies, a better situation should become possible."[4]

Despite these rosy predictions, the Seminoles' conditions did not improve. In fact, in April 1936, Scott wrote to Collier contending that the establishment of the Everglades National Park would be a decided disadvantage to the Indians: A large portion of their hunting grounds would be materially reduced if not eliminated altogether, and many of the Indians living along that portion of the Tamiami Trail to be included in the park would have to abandon their camps and garden patches and move into inhospitable country. Furthermore, he labeled as a "pipe dream" the theoretical supposition that in some mystical way the game would flow from the protected park area into the Indian lands, there to be slaughtered by the Indians; usually the opposite happened, because the game learned to stay inside protected areas. If the game should migrate, it remained questionable whether Indian hunting lands could be protected for their exclusive use. Finally, Scott debunked the notion that the Seminoles would prosper as tourist guides in a park that would be visited heavily for only a few months each year, in which no hunting was allowed, and where the Indians were not easily accessible to those who might hire them. For all these reasons he cautioned Collier, "as you know the Seminole of Florida has been pushed about from place to place for the past century and if he is to be pushed again into a forbidding wilderness with his hunting grounds greatly reduced, I have only to say that their predicament is going to be most serious."[5]

Naturally, advocates of the park such as Ernest Coe and Sholtz maintained that the Seminoles would indeed benefit from its existence.[6] Sholtz wrote to Collier a short time later that he had met with Scott and understood his concerns, and there was no mention of appointing another Seminole agent. Sholtz then contacted Coe, calling on the Everglades Park Commission to work with Scott and make every concession possible to the Seminoles, because "in my judgment, it would add great color if they remained in the confines of the park area and, of course, were permitted also to do the hunting necessary for existence in the territory. I believe they would be willing to limit this north of the trail as to hunting and living, but I am sure that a common sense arrangement can be worked out which will satisfy the Indian Department and at the same time show a cooperative spirit on the part of the State and your Commission." These negotiations became deadlocked, and Florida newspapers were soon reporting that the traditional Mikasukis headed by Corey Osceola and Josie Billie were preparing to resist their eviction from the park area, with force if necessary. As late as 1938, a plan to use Seminoles in some capacity as boat guides in the park was still under consideration by Collier, but it became a moot point when in 1937 there was a significant schism among the Mikasuki-Seminoles. It occurred when the leading medicine man, as a result of decadent and antisocial behavior, lost his moral and political authority and was driven out by the archconservatives; two groups emerged to try to fill the resulting organizational and leadership void. An extreme nativistic faction kept their camps on the western side of the Everglades in the vicinity of the Tamiami Trail and thus retained the identifier "Trail Indians." A second group, called for convenience "Reservation Mikasukis," split with the busk council and moved to the newly opened Big Cypress Reservation.

Scott had foreseen that there would probably be an influx of Mikasukis to the Big Cypress Reservation once the new Everglades National Park boundaries were set and economic conditions worsened. The park project was suspended until after World War II, but the tribal schism and the need for employment accelerated the movement of families to the reservation. In March 1937 both state and federal reservations were still virtually unpopulated, and Scott reported that "during part of the year only three families live on the Hendry County Government Reservation. . . . Of the three Indian families living on the reservation, the family of Wilson Cypress is well taken care of by one of the leading merchants of the city of Miami. Wilson Cypress is employed by the merchant as a guide and his needs are taken care of throughout the year whether he is acting as a guide or not. Whitney Cypress . . . lives in the same camp with Wilson Cypress. Cuffney Tiger lives in the southeastern part of the reservation during part of the year but during the tourist season the family spends most of the season along the Tamiami Trail running west of the city of Miami."[7] But by November he was appealing to the head of CCC-ID, D. E. Murphy, for additional funds to extend the work projects to the Big Cypress community where there were many indigent families. He suggested that considerable improvement and development work could be undertaken which would not only provide work opportunities for the needy Indians among the southern group but would also make the reservation habitable. One such project called for extensive repairs to the range fencing that had first been put up in 1926 during Spencer's administration. Since the Indians got their water supply from standing ponds or canals, wells should be put down at each camp. A public campground should be developed at the old headquarters site, which would then become the center of CCC-ID activities. Finally, the entire reservation should be posted against hunting. These projects would give ample protection to an unprotected area where game hunters took the game that should be protected for the Indians and where hunters stole or shot hogs owned by the Indians.[8]

A major problem in organizing any CCC-ID program, obviously, would be to find a supervisor who could work with the Mikasukis, most of whom had limited knowledge of English. Therefore, he informed Murphy, "If you enable me to start some projects on the Hendry County Reservation, it will be necessary for you to authorize me to employ a local man, who has the confidence of the Indians and who can speak their language, as mechanic, who will also act as foreman. There are no local Indians capable of filling such a position."[9] Only one person fit this description, and W. Stanley Hanson was hired as the mechanic at a salary of $135 per month. He soon moved into the small frame caretaker's cottage on the reservation, and through his personal appeals at least seven to nine Indian families moved their camps there. The employment of Hanson, whom he had reproached so vigorously two years earlier, must have seemed ironic to Collier, but there is no record that he ever discussed the subject. Of course, Hanson was mentioned in numerous reports from the Seminole Agency, as well as several articles in *Indians at Work;* also, it is probable that the commissioner had contact with him during a visit to the Big Cypress Reservation in 1940. Political agendas aside, it was obvious that Hanson certainly had the best interests of the Indians at heart, while they in turn trusted and respected him. Once

he had obtained a long-sought staff position, Hanson seems to have become a model Indian Office employee, and Collier accorded him treatment appropriate to his position.

It was Stanley Hanson who escorted the ethnologist Ethel Cutler Freeman to the Big Cypress Reservation when she undertook five weeks of
fieldwork there during the winter of 1939. He introduced her among
the camps and helped her to understand the ways of the Mikasukis as
well as a bit of their language. There was no modern housing or other
facilities on the federal reservations for many years, so it was still possible to observe an Indian life-style that had been modified only a little.
This experience was so successful that Freeman, who was sponsored by
the American Museum of Natural History in New York, returned with
her young son and daughter to spend several months the following winter. She was overwhelmed by the isolation of the Big Cypress setting and
the insularity of the people who failed to recognize any bond with the
Seminoles living north of Lake Okeechobee. When asked about the Cow
Creeks, Hanson had been somewhat misleading in answering, "Oh,
they're Creeks and speak Muskogee. The two branches of the Seminole
don't mix and don't like each other."[10] Her writings based on these visits
were to yield a narrowly focused but sensitive portrayal of the Mikasuki-
Seminoles at the very time when they were undergoing a period of fundamental cultural transition, the stresses of which were exacerbated by
internal frictions.

Despite the economic uncertainties of the late 1930s, at least three
other significant studies of Seminole life were taking place. In addition
to Freeman's work in the Big Cypress, folklorist Robert Greenlee also
gathered information in the Mikasuki camps on their social organization
and medical practices. Fifty miles to the north, Alexander Spoehr from
the University of Chicago and the Field Museum was studying the camp,
clan, and kinship system of the Muskogees of the Brighton Reservation
and environs. He, too, had captured an Indian society on the brink of
major adaptations in material culture but maintaining a traditional pattern of social organization and religious beliefs. In addition to Spoehr's
highly analytical works, Louis Capron produced useful descriptive studies of two Muskogee ceremonials, the Green Corn Dance in the spring
and the fall Hunting Dance.[11] Capron was not a professional ethnologist,
but he had access to reliable informants with whom he built close friendships over long years of interaction with the Muskogee-speaking Seminoles. From these works it is possible to piece together a rough mosaic
of Seminole life as it had evolved by the concluding years of the Great
Depression—at least in rural settings. In actuality what emerges is a tri-

partite comparison between the acculturated Muskogees who had settled into a relatively prosperous existence on the Brighton Reservation and the bifurcated Mikasukis who maintained separate sociopolitical identities while struggling for economic survival.

Anthropological studies generally strive to identify dynamic elements that contribute to continuity and change in a culture. Interestingly, among the Florida Indians the most enduring aspect of cultural continuity was provided by their languages, which historically had also divided them! In the Creek Confederacy of the eighteenth century the dominant Upper Creeks spoke Muskogee, while a number of smaller dependent tribal entities, collectively known as Lower Creeks, spoke a variety of Hitchiti tongues, one of them Mikasuki. Although these two tongues derived from the same language stock, they were mutually unintelligible; however, Muskogee became a lingua franca for political, trade, and religious purposes throughout the confederacy, and many of its elements were incorporated into the languages of the Lower Creeks. Therefore, the Mikasukis laid claim to a separate ethnolinguistic origin from the Muskogees, and both groups objected to being identified as Seminoles—the term was not employed as an ethnonym in either language. There were, of course, specific labels for the two languages spoken by the Florida Indians. The Mikasukis call their own language *i-laponki* and the Muskogee language *ci-saponki,* while to the Muskogees their own language was *oci-soponaka* and that of the Mikasukis *cilo-kkita.*[12] White observers who came among the Florida Seminoles during the intensive trading-contact period in the late nineteenth century heard primarily Muskogee terminology from their Mikasuki linguistic and ethnographic informants. It was, therefore, well into this century before outsiders fully understood that the northern and southern divisions of the Florida Seminoles did in fact speak different languages and concluded that this barrier accounted for much of their social and political fragmentation.

The basic social unit for all three Seminole bands was the extended family camp. The term camp had two meanings: the actual physical setting in which a family lived and the people who lived there. For example, "Guava Camp" identified a specific site as well as the related group of individuals residing together. Physically, the camps of both Mikasukis and Muskogees were similar in pattern and appearance, consisting of a number of palm-thatched, open-sided chikis, the Mikasuki name for house, which were erected around the perimeter of a clearing. At the center of the clearing stood a cook house, a thatched roof supported by four posts, which served as a weather shelter for the communal cooking fire laid out on the bare ground underneath. The other chikis were larger and more substantially built, with platform floors underneath raised two to three feet off the ground. Each family unit maintained its own house, which was a multipurpose area for eating, socializing, and sleeping. They stored supplies, clothing, bedding, and mosquito-bars in the eaves during the day, and the women and girls sewed on the platforms using hand-cranked Singer machines or made baskets and dolls for sale to tourists. There was also a smaller version of the chiki known as a "baby house," where a mother and her newborn lived apart for the first four months following birth. Indian babies were always delivered in places some distance from the camp proper, with only the assistance of a midwife and other women.

The material culture of a Seminole camp revealed an extraordinary eclecticism. A traditional wooden mortar and pestle used for grinding corn or coontie root stood side by side with a steel coffee mill, phonograph, and sewing machine. Modern rifles and ammunition had all but displaced traditional bow and arrows for taking deer, bear, and other large game, while the fish gig and a steel-shanked "gopher puller" used to extract the land tortoise from its burrow were part of each Indian's arsenal. Scattered around the camp was an assortment of tubs, basins, knives, axes, cooking utensils, and farming implements, and the day's activities ranged from cooking, sewing, gardening, or butchering hogs to hunting, trapping, and fishing. The camps were lively, bustling places by day where chickens, dogs, and pigs wandered freely among the activities of adults and children, while other Indians were coming and going in a constant round of visiting back and forth among relatives.

All Seminoles followed the practice of matrilocal marriage, in which a married woman and her family took up residence in the camp of her mother. Thus each camp had a matrilineal core of women all belonging to the same clan. Unattached males of the family also resided in the camp of their mother. This system offered a built-in support group to assist in raising children in case a father died; more important, though, only the members of the child's clan could pass on knowledge of their appropriate social, political, and ceremonial roles in the life of the people. The biological fathers of Indian children could not participate in passing along this nonmaterial aspect of culture, but these males were expected to participate in the instruction of the children of their own clans.

The matrilineal exogamous clan formed the basic kinship group for both the Mikasuki and Muskogee Seminoles. This pattern was typical of southeastern Indian cultures in which descent was counted through the female line and members were required to take marriage partners outside their own clan. The clan was a group of families which claimed a common lineage, generally connected with a totemic animal, and provided the individual with a social and political support group that cut across camps and regions. An elaborate system of kinship terminology articulated an individual's relationship to every other member of his clan and the clans into which they were married. Traditionally, the clans came together, and each played a specific role in the annual busk ritual or the Green Corn Dance, which was held each spring and served to unify the widely scattered camps. In the 1930s several of the clans were reportedly represented in both the northern and southern Seminole bands. Among the Cow Creek Seminoles there were five matrilineal exogamous clans, Panther, Bird, Talahasee (Old Town), Deer, and Snake, four of which were totemic. Among the Mikasukis there were nine exogamous clans, Panther, Wildcat, Tiger, Bird, Otter, Wind, Wolf, Snake, and Big Town, seven of them totemic.[13] There were several Mikasuki clans represented on the Brighton Reservation in the persons of single old men who had come there when they married Muskogee women and remained in the region. By the 1960s at least two of the Mikasuki clans had reportedly died out, and two others were in danger of extinction.[14]

Within Seminole society there were sex-differentiated roles that created no conflict between the men and women carrying them out. Historically, males had been responsible for providing the subsistence and maintenance for the camps. Seminole men always played the leading role as keepers of the "fire" and were in control of tribal political and religious affairs. This unquestioned status-role relationship began to break down as environmental and social conditions changed. When the hunting and trapping economy began to play out after the Everglades were drained, a period of uncertainty and insecurity for Indian men followed, especially for the Mikasukis who had less contact with a wage labor economy than did the Muskogees. With typical resilience, many Indian families initially confronted this problem by spending part of their year in the commercial camps of Miami; then after the Tamiami Trail was completed in 1928, temporary villages were set up along that highway to attract tourists. Among those families who moved their camps to the federal reservations during the 1930s, the men found working in the CCC-ID programs a viable economic substitute for hunting and trapping that allowed them to resume their position as providers. But the Trail Indian men had been reduced to a marginal economic role with a concomitant loss of self-esteem; unable to occupy themselves with hunting and trading, they tended to spend more of their time just lounging about the camp, and there was a greater incidence of drinking and antisocial behavior. The confidence of the traditionalists

would be further eroded when a large segment of the Mikasukis abandoned their old ways and moved to the Big Cypress Reservation, where
many took up cattle raising and ultimately converted to Christianity. One
might be tempted to argue that those Mikasukis who took up residence
on federal land were merely exhibiting that trait of flexibility that had
enabled them to adapt and survive over the centuries. However, there
were more complex motives underlying that schism.

The status of Seminole women underwent a significant strengthening
during the difficult period of adjustment early in this century, even
prior to the Great Depression. Actually, they were always secure in the
knowledge of their position within the tribe, which was neither inferior
nor superior to that of men, and there was no overt competition between
the sexes. Their roles did not conflict but rather complemented each
other. Men had the subsistence responsibility, women the social. Therefore Indian women became the conservators of the cultural tradition.
During the era of intensive trading in plumes and hides around the turn
of the century, the women always remained in the background and took
little part in the commercial transactions at the trading posts. They neither learned nor spoke much English, thereby becoming the conservative guardians of the Seminole languages and oral traditions. Occasionally, they also had to exert social control in the physical sense over Indian
men who too readily accommodated themselves to the whites' ways, especially to the use of spirituous liquors which could be purchased at most
trading posts. When the men became uncontrollable after a drinking
bout, the women often took away their weapons and tied them up until
they returned to their senses.

Among the Mikasukis, the women were also the perpetuators of what
might be called their ideology of independence. It was manifested in
their deep-seated desire to remain free of contamination by the white
man's culture and values. For this reason the traditional Mikasukis were
reluctant to move to federal lands and tended to keep their camps deep
in the interior of the Everglades and Big Cypress. Even when they temporarily occupied tourist villages along the Tamiami Trail, the living
quarters were generally well hidden from the prying eyes of visitors by
palisade walls covered with a thick palmetto thatch. A corollary to this
was the Mikasuki determination not to be lumped in with the Muskogees
in a tribal amalgam known as "Seminole" and thereby lose their separate
identity. The women were in a perfect position to transmit this value
core to the next generation. Through the matrilineal function they were
primarily responsible for child rearing with the support of clan kinfolk.
The women's essential function was molding each new generation,
teaching the youth to conform to accepted values while adapting to new

conditions. This outlook led to ambivalence in the trading relationship. Indian men interacted with the white traders, but antagonism had developed into a cultural pattern in which Mikasuki women were not allowed to speak or look at whites while youngsters were conditioned to dislike and distrust them. No similar pattern of antagonism toward whites was manifested by the Muskogees, one of the major points that differentiated them from the Mikasukis.

The Seminole women displayed a remarkable ability to adjust to changing social conditions and economic pressures. They would alter a foreign concept or material trait so that it could be absorbed into their life without impinging on old cultural patterns. For example, the women were historically acknowledged as the owners of the family camp and goods; they determined where the camp should be located and when it should be moved. They were responsible for household chores such as food preparation, washing the clothing, tending the garden; not infrequently they also kept a herd of hogs. Over time, though, women mastered the sewing machine and began to produce patchwork clothing and dolls, and then basketry, for sale as a means of supporting their families. The women were first to accept the necessity of picking crops for wages when such work was available, especially when they were heads of single-parent family units. In the process of accepting wage labor they also modified their clothing and hair styles, adopting the practice of combing the hair over a piece of cardboard to produce both a practical eye shade and an attractive arrangement that became a colorful part of their costume in the 1940s. The important point that should be made here, though, is that the male-female relationship was not radically altered. Women did not attempt to usurp male leadership roles but were content to remain in the background as powerful figures who were always consulted by the men of their clans before any major decisions were made. Unquestionably, the women remained a bulwark of stability in a transitional society.

The unifying religious ritual for both the Muskogees and the Mikasukis was the annual busk ceremony, commonly called the Green Corn Dance—although it was but one of many dances performed. This annual ritual of renewal was usually held in early summer at the time of "the little moon in June," when the new corn crop ripened. It was conducted by two medicine men who had spent years in training for the role. The position was achieved rather than ascribed, although the medicine men had to come from traditionally designated clans—Panther and Wind for the Mikasukis, Panther and Bird for the Muskogees. The medicine men were trained to handle the medicine bundle, a collection of sacred artifacts which originally had a medicinal function but in this century came to signify the spiritual unity of the people. The bundle was displayed only once during the several days of the ceremony. The busk ritual was intended to preserve the life in the medicine and to insure the health of the individuals in the coming year. It also provided a sense of common identity and belonging for the people through participation in stickball games and communal dancing. During the four days the medicine men and council performed various annual rites which provided another dimension of continuity, such as court day, when transgressors against tribal laws were judged and punished, and the granting of adult names to young men who had come of age. After fasting and then purging their bodies with an herbal emetic called the Black Drink, the men were spiritually and physically renewed. A feast at which the new corn was eaten was the concluding symbolic act of the ceremony.

During the 1930s there were three independently functioning busk groups among the Florida Seminoles.[15] The medicine man Sam Jones conducted the busk for the Muskogees, but he and the councilmen who lived away from the reservation exerted only limited moral and political authority over the increasingly acculturated Brighton Reservation people. The medicine bundle passed to Frank Shore in the early 1940s, but few Muskogees attempted to preserve the traditional ways. Within the decade there would be a significant Christian missionizing effort among the Brighton people. The medicine men remained far more influential among the Mikasuki groups. Cuffney Tiger held the medicine bundle and conducted the busk for those traditional "Reservation Mikasukis" who lived on the Hendry County Reservation. It was not uncommon for the medicine men to attend each other's dances although they technically could not participate, a sign that there were no significant differences in the religious beliefs of the three groups. In fact, Cuffney Tiger died while attending the Green Corn Dance of the Muskogees in 1947, and his medicine bundle became inactive for several years; by the time it was restored, Christianity had made significant inroads among the reservation population.

The third medicine bundle, that of the ultraconservative Trail Indians, had long been kept by one of the most famous Seminole medicine men, Josie Billie. He was widely renowned as both a spiritual leader and practitioner of herbal medicine. Unfortunately, for all his charisma, Josie Billie was often drunk and violent, and he committed crimes—he was accused of killing at least two Indians. For a time he was reportedly under a death sentence from the council and hunted by the clan of one of the victims. As a result of these incidents the Mikasuki council of elders ostracized him in 1937, and he went to live on the Big Cypress Reservation. Naturally, this action was extremely disconcerting to the Mikasuki traditionalists who believed that the medicine man interceded with the Great Spirit on their behalf. At about this time a group of Mikasukis who disagreed with the council on various issues, possibly including the removal of a medicine man, also moved to the reservation.

In 1945, Josie Billie converted to Christianity, and twenty-two of his followers and their families followed his lead. A cynical appraisal of this event might hold that it returned Josie to a position of spiritual and political authority as leader of the Reservation Mikasukis. Freeman contends that these Indians had come to the reservation and converted "because they did not belong to clans which would inherit official positions or status. Status could no longer be gained by war and hunting prowess. The acceptance of Christianity gave these Seminoles prestige. Church positions became goals for the ambitious."[16] Soon Baptist church members were forbidden to attend the Green Corn Dance, and the ceremony could no longer be held on the reservation. This move exacerbated the social disruption that not only split reservation dwellers from their relatives on the trail but ultimately led to a division among the reservation people as well. In any case, Josie Billie passed his medicine bundle to his brother, Ingraham Billie, who then became the chief medicine man of the traditional Mikasukis. He, too, was a strong and purposeful character who was committed to preserving the old religion and customs, and he conducted the annual busk until his death in the 1980s.

Actually, the acceptance of Christianity by a large number of the Reservation Mikasukis in 1945 was the culmination of a missionizing process that had been taking place for several years.[17] During the early 1940s, as the number of converts among the Cow Creeks stabilized, the missionary Willie King turned his attention increasingly to the Big Cypress people. He had learned the Mikasuki language, and in 1943 he began meeting Seminoles from the reservation when they came to the town of Immokalee to trade at the store of W. Dius Roberts, a leading figure in the community and an ardent Baptist layman. At Roberts's suggestion King was invited to preach on a periodic basis at the local Baptist church, and Seminoles were invited to attend. The Indians accepted this arrangement and continued to attend the Immokalee church when the missionary was there, but they also began to invite King to their camps where he preached and made a small number of converts. This basis of trust and receptiveness was firmly in place when the charismatic Rev. Stanley Smith came in 1943 to assist the old missionary. Smith was a spellbinding speaker with a dynamic personality who aggressively challenged the Indians to accept Christ. Even though he did not speak Mikasuki and used an interpreter, Smith, like his elder colleague, had relatively greater success among the Big Cypress people than with the

Cow Creeks. Gradually he won over the old medicine man Josie Billie, and that would be a turning point in bringing virtually the entire community into the fold. On the day when Josie and his fellow Mikasukis joined the church, Smith made sure that several officers of the Florida Baptist Home Mission Board were present to take part in the ceremony, for which he received most of the credit. From this point on, the Baptist Indians would be the major political faction in the life of the Big Cypress Reservation, and they remained a force for social conservatism.

It was this group of Reservation Mikasukis who were undergoing a fundamental shift in their life-style and religious orientation, that Scott had to deal with in developing the Big Cypress Reservation. As it turned out, he had taken an appropriate step in hiring Stanley Hanson to work with them during this difficult period, for he understood their motivations and fears and could literally and figuratively translate their concerns to the government field officer. And there would soon be a chance for the Indians to present their views first-hand to a ranking official of the Indian Office from Washington.

In April 1938, Commissioner Collier wrote an open letter to the Seminole Indians of Florida complimenting them on the reports of their progress which he had received from an Ataloa, a western Indian woman who had spent two months among them. He promised to send Assistant Commissioner Zimmerman "to visit you within the next month or two, and we hope you will tell him your needs. When he returns we shall do everything in our power to see that these needs are met."[18] Zimmerman visited Florida the following month and met with both the Brighton Indians and the Mikasukis living on the reservation in Hendry County. He heard the latter group ask for purchase of at least forty sections to the west of the swampy and poorly drained reservation so that they could have better farming and gardening plots. The nearest town where supplies could be purchased was Immokalee, thirty miles away, so they requested a heavy-duty truck with four-wheel drive and a front-mounted power winch for hauling out of mud bogs, so they could make the trip during the rainy season. During this visit the spokesman for the Brighton residents presented Zimmerman with a list of requests which included a hospital and school building—a rough indication of the difference in developmental levels between the two reservation populations.

By July, Scott's plans to continue the work of fencing, pasture development, and improving the water supply at both Big Cypress and Brighton were placed in jeopardy when he was notified that the Seminole allocation of CCC-ID funds was to be reduced from $25,000 to $18,000 because of the worsening national economic emergency.[19] It would be impossible to continue employing an average of thirty-five workmen, and none of the badly needed equipment could be purchased. The superintendent immediately began a protracted correspondence with Zimmerman and D. E. Murphy, head of CCC-ID, in which he eloquently stated the Seminoles' needs. He continually reminded them of Collier's letter to the Seminoles and his promise to "do everything in our power to see that these needs are met." The budget cuts were restored and the allocation was actually increased to $38,000 by October 1938.[20] It was not the last time that CCC-ID funding for the Seminoles would be decreased: in its budget proposal for fiscal year 1940 the Seminole Agency requested $40,000 but got only $30,000, a net reduction of $8,000, and the 1941 allocation was only $30,500 to cover all of the work relief and rehabilitation projects.[21]

Superintendent Scott was incensed at the apparent inability, or unwillingness, of the Office of Indian Affairs to acknowledge the importance of the Seminole work. In frustration he wrote a long letter to Collier, Zimmerman, Murphy, and the Indian Office department heads summarizing the dilemma facing the Seminole CCC-ID program: "Under our present policy we try to make our reservation programs attractive enough to draw the Indians away from the commercial camps and other cesspools of iniquity and provide employment for the men at subsistence wages to enable the families to become established on the reservations. Must we now change our policy and throw out discouragement rather than encouragement in order that we may keep the number of employables low enough so that we can operate within the quite limited funds provided for our activities?"[22] In a second letter to the Indian Office department heads a month later, he noted that the appeal for increased funds "springs from the thought that, by implied or expressed promises or encouraging action, we have placed ourselves under a very definite moral obligation to a large group of the Florida Seminoles and we must discharge this obligation by enlarging, rather than reducing our program if we are to keep faith with these Indians. My last desparate appeal is being made with the hope that we may prevent a nullification of the good work already accomplished, which is almost certain to take place if we do not carry on in a manner that will provide a living wage for the many Indians who have settled on our reservation areas and for the limited number who will settle here from time to time in the future."[23] As was the case with his predecessor Glenn, Scott had become outspoken and was willing to circumvent traditional protocol to get his message across.

Although his appeals for additional funds went basically unheeded,

Scott moved ahead to employing Seminoles with the money that was made available. His FY-1940 plan called for building truck trails and vehicle bridges, erecting 256 miles of range fence, revegetating 500 acres, stringing seven miles of telephone line, sinking fifteen new wells, and placing fifty signs, markers, and historical monuments on the reservations.[24] His highest priority, though, was construction of an all-weather road from the Big Cypress Reservation to connect with a state road leading to Immokalee. Permission was given to use CCC-ID workers to improve the roadway even though the right-of-way did not run entirely over federal land and Scott was constantly besieging the Washington office to provide a dragline and other road-building equipment; however, the grading was barely begun during his administration. It would fall to his successor, Dwight Gardin, to complete the project.

The establishment of a cattle enterprise on the Hendry County lands, later known as the Big Cypress Reservation, had been a goal of Seminole agents since L. A. Spencer first advocated it in 1918.[25] The possibility for such a program had been discussed periodically but was initially discouraged by the Indian Office. However, when in 1941 the Seminoles received a $20,000 grant from the Rehabilitation Division to restock and upgrade their range, a delegation of Big Cypress residents led by Josie Billie attended a meeting at Brighton and expressed approval of the arrangements. To verify this, three men from Big Cypress—Billie Osceola, John Cypress, and Harjo Osceola—signed one of the agreement papers, although only signatures of the tribal trustees from Brighton appeared on the grant itself.[26] In theory, the funds were granted to the entire Seminole tribe, and the cattle were to be held at Brighton until such time as a similar program opened at Big Cypress. Before there could be any thought of placing cattle on Big Cypress, though, the Indian Office authorities would have to resolve the controversy over efforts to eradicate the cattle tick in Florida. The preeminent biographer of John Collier, historian Kenneth Philp, has provided a penetrating analysis of this significant struggle which both saved the Seminole deer and paved the way for a Big Cypress cattle program.[27] To understand this event that was so central to Seminole development during the late 1930s and early 1940s, a brief synopsis of the Philp study is included here.

Beginning with an act of Congress in 1906, there had been a joint federal-state effort to rid the cattle in the warm-weather states of the tropical tick *Boophilus annulatus,* variety *australis,* which penetrated the hide, ruining its commercial value, and caused a fever of the spleen. Many cattle died; those that survived were of poor quality. The U.S. Bureau of Animal Industry cooperated with various state agencies in setting up quarantine areas and helping cattlemen dip their stock. So successful was this program that virtually all of the South and Southwest became free of the tick except Florida and a small section of Texas along the Mexican border. Florida was the last state to participate in the joint eradication project, but in 1923 the legislature authorized the Florida Livestock and Sanitary Board to cooperate with the federal authorities. When ticks continued to appear on cattle that had been dipped but grazed near swampy areas and game preserves in central Florida, it was determined that tick-infested deer were the carriers and had to be destroyed. In 1937 legislation was passed authorizing payment of bounties to hunt the animals in four counties, and during the next two years over 700 deer were slaughtered. This seemingly wanton killing of animals that were not proven carriers brought an outcry from conservationists, sportsmen, women's groups, and schoolchildren of the state; the matter came before the Florida Supreme Court, which issued an injunction halting the eradication program. Neighboring states retaliated by placing all of Florida under quarantine, thereby effectively crippling the cattle industry of the state. The Florida Supreme Court later reversed itself on the constitutionality of the law, and the killing of the deer resumed. By 1939 the state legislature had passed a second law authorizing the destruction of additional deer that inhabited the Everglades and Big Cypress Swamp in the southern part of the peninsula.

The Big Cypress Seminole Reservation was near the center of this infested area and blocked the state's effort to conclude a successful eradication program; since it was federal property the Indian Office would have to give permission for entry to the reservation. On December 19, 1939, state officials met with Scott and requested the right to destroy all the deer on Seminole land. Scott argued that the Indians needed the deer for food to supplement their meager CCC-ID incomes and questioned whether the deer were actually infested. The Florida officials then contacted their counterparts at the Bureau of Animal Industry, who in turn explained the deer removal to John Collier. The commissioner promised to investigate the situation before making a final decision. True to his word, Collier traveled by air to Florida during the first week of January 1940 to gather firsthand information. He was accompanied by the CCC-ID director Daniel E. Murphy. After meeting with state officials and representatives of the Department of Agriculture at Miami, he concluded that the deer had to be destroyed—but he needed Indian approval, and that meant a trip to the nearly inaccessible Big Cypress Reservation. In his report to Secretary Ickes the commissioner recounted his seventy-mile journey that required ten and one-half hours of "very hard, continuous going, our light car being helped along by a six-tired truck, a huge jack, planking and logs, ten men to push and haul; this, though winter is the dry season."[28] At the Seminole encampment he tried to explain why the government wanted to shoot the deer, but "the Seminoles were unanimous that under no condition and for no price would they consent to the extermination of their deer. And it is my recommendation that you should withhold consent."[29]

The adamant opposition of the Seminoles, according to Philp, led Collier to have second thoughts about the wisdom of coercing the tribe to accept destruction of the deer. Similar attempts to force western tribes such as the Navajo to accept stock reductions had led to open resistance and violence, and Collier did not want a repetition of that experience. He discussed the situation with Ickes, and they agreed to take the position that the Agriculture Department's arguments were not compelling enough to order destruction of the deer. Collier explained their stand in a press release on January 22, 1940,[30] in which he made three basic points: (1) The southern Seminoles depended for their livelihood, in part, on the deer and would never agree to their destruction because without the deer they would require additional relief expenditures and could be driven back to the unsavory show camps at Miami; (2) the extermination would violate the pledges that Ickes and Collier had made in 1935 to leave the Seminoles undisturbed and would be an unwarranted invasion of their rights under the Indian Reorganization Act; (3) the government had not proven that destruction of the deer would eliminate the cattle tick infestation—in other states where deer had not been destroyed eradication programs had still succeeded. The commissioner ventured the opinion that the Everglades was "a region of the country ideally suited to deer, and poorly suited to cattle,"[31] and in a sincere but seemingly naive attempt to resolve the impasse he recommended that the state erect a high single fence or six-foot double fence around the reservation and let the deer roam free within!

As he had following the previous visit, Collier eloquently and romantically described his latest contact with the Seminoles: "The power of the Indian! I witnessed it anew in the deep Everglades of Florida a few days ago. These Seminoles . . . they are a people both gentle and wild. A life of extreme simplicity on the material side is lived within a complex of effectual, group-supported disciplines on the social side. The blood is still pure. In their own way, and not much helped by modern medicine, the Seminoles are healthier than their white neighbors, and their rate of increase is considerably greater than that of the general population. Their arts and crafts, which strike their own peculiar, unique and exquisite chord among the many musics of Indian art, have important possibilities of enrichment and expansion. . . . Their country is a place of glory. And its elixir is in their blood." Still, he acknowledged a fundamental division of the tribe, noting that the northern band had an all-Seminole cattle trusteeship on a reservation where cattle raising and farming were possible. Thus, "the Seminoles illustrate how it is that there is no one goal or one way for Indians. Within this group of fewer than 600 Indians, life moves in the one direction toward wilderness, in the other toward plowed acres, fenced fields and a tidy livestock industry. Indian CCC has been an epoch-making help to the Indians."[32] In this interesting commentary Collier affirmed that he had already accepted the reality of multiple patterns of tribal development.

Meanwhile, in Washington the cattle tick issue was still far from resolved. Florida's Senator Claude Pepper was angered by Collier's suggestion for fencing the reservation, and he called a half-day conference in Washington on March 28, 1940, to bring together all parties to hammer out an agreement. Representatives of the Florida Livestock and Sanitary Board and the Florida Cattlemen's Association met with Collier, Undersecretary A. J. Wirtz, and others from the Department of the Interior, but no agreement could be reached. The Indian Office added to the tension several days later when Superintendent Dwight Gardin posted no-trespassing signs on the Big Cypress Reservation after unknown hunters had shot some deer. Gardin would pursue an aggressive policy of patrolling the posted land, and Collier lauded his efforts.

Throughout the summer of 1940 the issue remained deadlocked as three strong-willed personalities—Collier, Ickes, and Secretary of Agriculture Henry A. Wallace—engaged in political skirmishing but failed to reach a solution. A major casualty of their struggle was interagency cooperation, for the relationship between Interior and Agriculture would never be the same again. In May 1941, Senator Pepper introduced a bill that would have prevented Ickes and Collier from interfering with the tick eradication project and provided for replacement of any infected Indian deer lost in the process. After hearing much heated testimony, the Senate Indian Affairs Committee voted to recommend passage of S. 1476 with two changes: Collier and Ickes were not prevented from interfering with the program but rather it became their duty to cooperate with it, and Florida had to replace all deer killed, not just those found to have been infected with the cattle tick. The Senate concurred, passed the bill, and sent it on to the House, where it ran into immediate trouble. The bill was still being debated when in January 1942, at the instigation of a Florida congressman, the House Appropriations Subcommittee inserted an amendment in the 1943 Agriculture Department appropriation bill giving the secretary authority to conduct tick eradication on the Big Cypress Reservation and creating a fund of $5,000 to buy meat for the Seminoles until state officials restocked their deer herd. Ickes immediately informed President Roosevelt that the legislation must be defeated; a new secretary of agriculture, Claude Wickard, supported the proposal. The president, preoccupied with the war, pointedly suggested that the cabinet members solve the matter themselves or "put the whole thing off until we find out whether we are going to win the World War or not. If we don't win it, ticks on animals and humans will doubtless take over the nation. If we do win the war, we can start a great national tick campaign for the unemployed." After reflection, he sided with Ickes and wrote to the secretary of agriculture warning that he did not want any deer killed on the Seminole reservations until after the war, saying, "No one knows whether these unfortunate animals are host to the cattle tick or not," and threatening to impound the $5,000 if the measure was passed by Congress.[33] The bill passed, and Roosevelt impounded the funds. Still, the Bureau of Animal Industry did not lift its quarantine of Collier and Hendry counties. Ickes and Wickard soon reached a compromise permitting the slaughter of sixty-seven deer which, if found free of ticks, would result in the quarantine being lifted. Even this fragile peace almost collapsed when Collier, still mindful of his promise to protect Indian wildlife, allowed them to kill only forty-three deer. Finally, weary of the controversy, Wickard capitulated to Ickes in a letter of March 2, 1943. He criticized the Indian Office for arbitrarily terminating the hunting but admitted that no fever ticks had been found on the Seminole animals or others taken in areas adjacent to the reservation. Therefore, his department would not request removal of any more deer, and he released the Big Cypress Reservation from federal quarantine restrictions.

It is easy to accept Philp's assessment that the cattle tick controversy revealed deep divisions among New Deal reformers. While all were devoted to conservation of natural resources, the agencies could not agree on how this goal was to be achieved. The Department of Agriculture was run by scientific experts who believed in the rational and efficient use of natural resources; they sided with the Florida cattle industry, finding its economic well-being more significant than preserving the deer. The Office of Indian Affairs, on the other hand, viewed the social and economic benefits that the Seminoles derived from the Everglades deer herd to be of overriding value—besides which they were morally and legally committed to protecting Indian interests. Philp therefore concluded that "in the end Collier and Ickes's position was vindicated, and they preserved the last seedstock for wild deer in Florida." He is less convincing when arguing that "in many ways they won a Pyrrhic victory.

Their introduction of cattle on the Big Cypress reservation and the killing of many of the Indians' deer in order to block successfully the plan of the Bureau of Animal Industry was a violation of earlier promises to keep the Indians' land free of outside disturbances."[34] Certainly Collier and Ickes did not initiate the eradication program or extend it to Seminole lands; they were only resisting a policy perceived as detrimental to Indian interests. As for the compromise allowing destruction of some Indian deer, it seemed an acceptable price to save the total population from extinction—and then Collier intervened to hold losses to a minimum. Most important, though, the introduction of cattle to the Big Cypress Reservation was not imposed by administrative fiat but came at the request of the Reservation Mikasukis themselves.

On September 10, 1941, a group of ten men from the Big Cypress Reservation signed a letter to the commissioner requesting that cattle be made available to them. In 1942 it was found possible to place 398 head of cattle on the limited pasturage available there, and two years later Collier asserted, "These cattle were put on the Big Cypress for the dual purpose of establishing something definite with regard to the alleged tick infestation and to actually start the Big Cypress Indians in the cattle business." In January 1944—only nine months following the "capitulation" letter from Secretary Wickard—Collier began to explore the possibility of setting up a cattle trusteeship for Big Cypress, where $25,000 of rehabilitation funds had already been spent to develop a herd. He wrote to the incumbent superintendent of the Seminole Agency informing him that "the fact of the matter is . . . we now have a cattle operation at Big Cypress which in effect still being managed by the Government," and asked him to begin discussions with the Indians to ascertain whether they preferred one unified Seminole cattle enterprise or two separate units.[35] Apparently this request generated a heated debate in Washington, for the following day the Seminole agent received a telegram ordering him to hold no discussions with the Indians until he heard from the commissioner. Collier's next letter informed the agent, "We feel that you should lend your influence toward the establishment of an over-all Seminole tribal organization rather than two separate and distinct tribal organizations,"[36] yet he clearly left open the possibility that the Indian Office would accept whatever the Seminoles preferred. By November 1944, following many tribal meetings, the Seminoles had decided on a structure providing for separate Brighton and Big Cypress cattle enterprises, each with its own elected trustees, and a Central Tribal Cattle Organization to exercise general supervision over policy, budget, and marketing operations; this central organization would have three members, one appointed by each of the cattle enterprises, and a third person appointed by the superintendent.[37] Again, there were delays in getting things organized, and it was not until 1946 that the first cattle trustees were selected from the Big Cypress Reservation.[38]

The Reservation Mikasukis seem to have adapted readily to life on the federal trust lands of South Florida and were making rapid acculturational strides, but they remained socially and economically conservative and had a long way to go to approximate the gains manifested by the Brighton people. The total development at Big Cypress Reservation lagged behind the other Seminole reservations well into the 1960s.

7

Reading, Writing, and Being Red

Under John Collier's deft direction, the Indian New Deal dramatically and systematically reversed half a century of federal assimilationist policy. The cornerstones of this policy, aimed at the destruction of tribalism, were the dissolution of the Indian land base, which was set in motion by the Dawes Act of 1887; the destruction of traditional Indian leadership and its replacement with government-endorsed courts and councils; the stifling of Indian religious practices while encouraging Christian missionizing; and the compulsory education of Indian youth in white schools.

The Florida Seminoles escaped the worst of these changes. Their reservation lands, because they still had not been fully acculturated and remained mostly unoccupied well into the 1930s, were never subjected to individual allotment. There was no centralized political authority to be replaced, as the medicine men and busk councils generally maintained camps far away from reservation lands. Serious missionary work among the Seminoles was just beginning during the depression and would not become a serious factor until the late 1940s. Likewise, federal schooling for Indian children did not take hold except in isolated instances—Dania in 1927–36 and Brighton after 1938—while there was no question of admitting Seminoles to public schools until well after World War II.

In many respects the schooling provided for Seminole pupils showed in microcosm the major trends afoot in American Indian education during the 1920s and 1930s, primarily in reaction to the overweening assimilationism that had prevailed in government schools since the 1880s. When Captain Richard H. Pratt opened the Carlisle Indian School in 1879—following a brief stint in Florida, where he supervised Plains Indian prisoners at Fort Marion in St. Augustine and made a comprehensive report on the Seminoles—it became a rallying point for the reformers who thought that off-reservation boarding schools, especially those offering industrial training to their charges, were the answer to assimilating the Indian into American life. There also remained some old mission schools, operated primarily by the Catholic Church, and on heavily allotted reservations Indian children usually attended public schools and in the process became highly acculturated. Boarding schools either on or off a reservation required removing Indian youth from familiar surroundings and from the psychological support of the family and reservation, changing their manner of dress, speech, and grooming and providing training that would help them to work in the white world. However, these schools were expensive to maintain, and critics questioned whether the curriculum prepared Indians to return and become productive and accepted members of their reservation communities. Many of the skills learned were useless on underdeveloped lands, and returning graduates were often ostracized by their peers. In essence they were forced to make a choice: either to acculturate fully and lose their Indian identity and heritage, or to "return to the blanket," which meant throwing off what they had learned and resuming the traditional lifestyle of their people. Despite these problems, the Indian Office was still operating many boarding schools in the third decade of this century.

The next step was to build reservation day schools. These were less expensive and more acceptable to Indian parents who did not want to send their children away even to boarding schools at the other end of their reservation, which could be far away on a vast preserve like those of the Navajo or Zuñi. But the federal schools closer to home on the reservations remained formidable institutions featuring harsh discipline, a rigid curriculum, and inflexible methods of instruction. It was inevitable that when the Indian Office came under attack from the "New Reformers" during the 1920s, education was one area singled out as most in need of change. The ensuing public clamor for reform in Indian policy led the government to appoint a committee of one hundred to suggest changes, but it was the publication of the blockbuster Meriam Report of 1928 that brought immediate response in the highest levels of government. In 1929, President Herbert Hoover appointed Charles J. Rhoads as commissioner of Indian affairs with a mandate to clean up the Indian Office. Rhoads tried to implement the reforms outlined in the Meriam Report but had made little progress after almost a year, and reformers again began to clamor for action.

The task of revamping Indian education then fell to Dr. W. Carson Ryan, professor of education at Swarthmore College, leader of the Progressive Education movement, and a fellow Quaker appointed by Rhoads in 1930 to be educational director of the Indian Office. Ryan was a nationally recognized authority on educational survey techniques who had directed the preparation of the education component of the Meriam Report and wrote its main recommendations. Thus he came to the job with impeccable credentials and support from the critics of Indian education who expected immediate change. The Meriam Report strongly suggested that the primary task of the Indian Office was education. It should provide Indian youths and their parents with the tools to adapt to both worlds, white and Indian. This approach was a far cry from schooling with the goal of assimilation, and Ryan called for a total reshaping of Indian education through a threefold program: development of a community school system oriented to the needs of existing population centers on the reservations; federal-state contracts that would rapidly accelerate the number of children attending public school; and the gradual phasing out of boarding schools. Ryan would find it difficult to implement this plan during his five years in the post because of increasingly stringent budgetary restrictions and entrenched interests in the Indian Office bureaucracy, particularly among teachers and administrators who clung to their assimilationist philosophy and practices. But he did make a beginning at decentralizing the system; moreover, the fact that he retained a free hand in the first three years of Collier's administration attests that the commissioner, also a devotee of the community-centered educational tenets of Deweyan progressivism, concurred in the direction that reform was taking. But lest the point be missed, Margaret Szasz emphasized, "The fact that he remained in office during the early years of Collier's administration indicates that Indian education reform began not with Collier but during Rhoads' commissionership."[1]

The influence of Deweyan thought is clearly evident in Ryan's strong emphasis on the necessity for community schools adapted to the needs of specific Indian populations. The fact that most Indian communities were in rural areas would necessitate a curriculum geared to raising crops and animals, conservation, and improving living conditions. Such schools should not be expected to conform to either the infamous Uniform Course of Study for Indian Schools or state curriculum standards. Neither was capable of helping Indian children develop a sense of their role in the social and economic life of their people; but the school would use all the resources of family and community to produce the integrated personality which Collier had admired earlier among the Northern Pueblos. Szasz provides another intriguing notion: that "Ryan was using the Indian Service as an experiment to test his interpretation of Progressive Education, and the Indian Service for the first time in its history was serving as the avant-garde in school change."[2] But Ryan, aware that if Indians opted to enter the white world they must be prepared to survive there economically, was a strong advocate of vocational training. Rather than seeing it as limiting their prospects to blue-collar occupations, he perceived it as broadening Indians' opportunities to enter the economic mainstream if they wished. So the groundwork was laid for vocational guidance and instruction, primarily in the remaining Indian boarding schools, and for liaison with employers in the world outside.

The day school that agent Lucien A. Spencer opened at the Dania Reservation in 1927 might be labeled the right kind of school established for the wrong reasons. Spencer was unabashedly assimilationist in his strong desire to bring the benefits of schooling to his Seminole wards, even if it created conflict, like that between the Cow Creek headmen and the women who had their camps near Indian Town. Spencer thought it appropriate to force the issue by cutting off rations to the dependent women, knowing that when things became desperate enough they would defy the headmen, move their families to Dania, and enter the children in school. To Spencer this move simply meant placing them in a classroom that was organized and equipped in the same manner as any white elementary school and run by a competent teacher. It never occurred to him that the curriculum should be community based, yet from the beginning the school offered more than the basics. Spencer readily admitted that "so far as actual 'book learning' is concerned, we have made little progress. The Florida Seminoles are a primitive people and mental concentration, to them, is very tiresome." As for the teacher, "while Mrs. [Lena] King probably could not pass the required examinations for a teacher she is thoroughly competent to give them a start and the only way we can ever get hold of them is through one of their own people. She is a trained welfare worker and in addition to her school work maintained classes in needle-work, etc., as well as maintaining night classes for the men who were at work during the day."[3] So was the seed of a day school planted.

The little school at Dania operated for just four months in 1927 but maintained a six-month term throughout the remainder of Spencer's administration. A November-through-April calendar was based on the observation that attendance was negligible during the hot months in Florida. In 1928 the agent reported that the school was still an experiment; it had not attempted any academic work beyond the first grade level as the children were still learning English, and the only industrial training was instruction in planting and caring for crops. He was not prepared to recommend schooling for the tribe in general until he saw how things went at Dania.

Indian Day School, Dania, ca. 1933 (courtesy National Archives)

The report of a local citizens' committee that visited the school in 1929 provided the first suggestion that the Dania day school was developing along the community school model later promoted by W. Carson Ryan and others. There was an integration of academic and practical in the program that appeared to be almost purely Deweyan. The children prepared their noon lunch and took care of the dining room and kitchen, and supposedly these experiences with nutrition and sanitation would transfer to their camp life over time. There was also time in the afternoon for gardening; the vegetables raised were not only an exercise but were used to supplement family diet. There was also time for aesthetic development; the committee noted that the "examples of drawing and clay moulding are indeed interesting and satisfactory."[4] Such activities were certainly consistent with the goals of meeting community needs.

After two years Spencer had begun to believe there was hope that his experimental school could succeed. In 1929 he wrote, "I now feel that if it can be continued under the present regime for a year or two longer that its success is assured. The tribal objection is giving way and with the teacher having full confidence of the Indians, the school will soon be a fixed institution among these Indians."[5] The agent was preparing to spend funds on repairs and on building new playground equipment, and he looked forward to planning the school program for the next two years. Much of Spencer's confidence in the success of the project was due to the fact that the teacher, Mrs. John Marshall, was his daughter; she had grown up around the Florida Indians and knew how to deal with them on a personal basis. Although some persons saw the employment of Spencer's daughter as nepotism, it was quite legal as Mrs. Marshall was a certified teacher. She had not sought the position, and only filled in when the teacher originally employed had to back out at the last moment. Also, because there were no teacher's quarters at Dania, it was convenient that the wife of an employee already residing there was qualified to serve in that capacity (her husband served as farmer on the reservation). During Mrs. Marshall's three-year stint (1928–30), attendance was erratic, and the only real achievements seemed to be building goodwill and preparing a few Indian children to advance to second grade. Although Spencer did not live to see Roy Nash's caustic appraisal of the education program, he could not have disputed the assessment that little had been accomplished.

When James L. Glenn was appointed to take Spencer's place in 1931, he brought a special interest in Seminole education. He and his wife were both teachers before coming to Florida, and they had operated an open-air school for Indian children at the camp near Everglades City. Following the lead of his predecessor, Glenn was determined to move the day school from the realm of an experiment to an accepted institution both at the Dania Reservation and for the entire tribe. The school term was increased from six to nine months, the position of the teacher was raised to Civil Service status, and the facilities were greatly expanded with the addition of a kitchen and bathrooms. Nevertheless, there was a constant struggle to persuade parents that their children should attend school. In 1932, Glenn noted that of the 185 school-age youngsters in the tribe, only fifteen, or 8 percent, were receiving any instruction.[6] The enrollment figures for the decade during which the school operated are deceiving, for they often included adults; even so, it seems to never have been greater than twenty in any year.[7]

Attendance was another matter altogether, and discipline was practically nonexistent. Glenn found that even those who did attend were so far removed from the unknown system of education that they observed neither adequate order nor regular schedule: "It is not surprising that pupils at Dania were satisfied if they remained in the classroom for one, two, or three hours each day, and were present for two or three days each week. Nor is it surprising that the student should walk out of the room at any and every impulse, or should torment the teacher by jumping out of windows or throwing dirt through the screens. The Seminole genuinely loves to play pranks on his associates, and this form of play was legitimate fun to him." Moreover, he added, the teacher could not hope to resort to traditional disciplinary measures as "the local Indian temperament presented a new problem in school discipline. Punishment in its various forms may be justified as a last resort among white pupils, but it is the first occasion for revolt among the Seminoles. Kindness and patience are major equipments for maintaining order within the class room."[8]

Seminole indifference to schooling and the lack of parental concern is verified by a Seminole informant who attended the day school and would later become one of the first high school graduates from the tribe. In the 1930s "some of them [parents] sent their children to school. We weren't forced to go. We could go if we want to, but we didn't have to go. But once in a while the curiosity got us so that we would get there. I think we were pretty loud or mean or something that they didn't know what school life was and we just won't cooperate, that's all. . . . I remember that they tried to get us to sit down and teach the books and all that. Of course, our grandmother told us that we were not supposed to go to school. . . . we come and spend a few hours, and we would just walk out when we feel like it. I went to school all right, but it is just that I didn't stay long enough to know what it was all about. That's why I didn't know nothing until I went to [boarding] school on my own."[9]

Despite these drawbacks the teachers apparently did a good deal more than teach cognitive skills at the day school. Agent Glenn wrote of the first teacher he hired, Helena Higgins: "She is engaged in teaching the Indian children not merely reading and writing, but how to LIVE. She required them to bathe from twice to three times per week, to brush their teeth, comb their hair, wash their hands and faces, clean their finger nails, wear clean clothes, and show proper regard for others through the social conventions, to eat a suitable diet, and she binds up their hurts, and administers proper medicine when ill. She does for them the things a mother in a white home does for her children."[10] For performing this surrogate role she received an annual salary of $1,356.

A problem of a different sort was presented by the heterogeneous nature of the student body at the day school. In 1934 the ages of the pupils ranged from five to sixty years, all grouped together in a single room and all endeavoring to learn the same simple things. Approximately fifty individuals had some part in the school program, but many of them were from the rolls of the Emergency Conservation Work crew and received only five hours of classroom instruction a week. "But" the agent contended, "at least these boys have learned to write a card or send a telegram to the Officer in Charge of the Seminole Agency to ask for additional employment. Some of the more regular students of the school can write as legible a hand as the usual college president, and carry on correspondence with both white and Indian friends, and can read with ease the usual material of school books."[11] No doubt there was a bit of exaggeration, but if even a part of his assessment was true there had been great improvement in the school since Roy Nash's visit in 1930.

Some idea of the day school curriculum may be gleaned by examining student report cards from the period. Beginning in 1933 more time was devoted to the work of a regular elementary program; the Seminole children reportedly developed an appreciation for stories and were making satisfactory progress in learning to read and write. Still there were certain aspects of the curriculum that did not fit with the Indian worldview; for example, "the white man's story of a round world is still not convincing, and affords the parents many a chuckle over the foolishness of the things taught in the school."[12] In addition to the usual elementary subjects such as reading, arithmetic, English, and spelling, the students also received marks in agriculture, drawing, physiology, and hygiene, as well as home economics in which cooking and general home training were emphasized. As Glenn described that aspect of the program, "To adapt at my school to the immediate, primary, and basic needs of children . . . I required the teacher to set up a class in cooking. The Indian Service provides the noon lunches for all Indian school children. I therefore asked them to cook that food, and in cooking it to learn not only cooking but sanitation."[13] There were also evaluations of their efforts and deportment. What the teachers wrote on the cards was generally an appeal for more regular attendance. It was evidently an accepted idea to "fail" children even in the lower grades, as "not promoted" also appears on the cards. Viewed from this perspective it is possible to conclude that virtually every aspect of the school was unconsciously tailored to enforcing conformity to non-Indian norms of behavior and achievement.

In a theoretical sense it could be argued that the Dania day school was not a true community school. Even though it provided Indian children with a number of academic and practical skills, the curriculum was externally imposed. There was little evidence of any attempt to draw upon the resources of the Indian community to meet its needs. In addition, the degree of adult involvement and use of the school facility was not

Indian children at Dania Day School, ca. 1933 (courtesy National Archives)

as great as that envisioned by Ryan and Collier when the concept was adopted. Ideally, the school would, in Collier's words, "serve as pioneering agents, going far beyond the public schools in the flexibility of their curricula and in the many sidedness of their uses."[14] In a true community school the people themselves play a central role in determining the content and method of instruction—as well as the values and behaviors to be reinforced. That was not the case at the Dania day school in the early 1930s; it was clear that the agent and the teacher were firmly in control. Nevertheless, Glenn believed that he was operating a community day school and advocated that "the Indian community school should be introduced among the Seminoles, and a more diligent effort made to reach a larger number of these school children."[15]

If this system appears to have been overly paternalistic by contemporary standards, it was certainly acceptable in the social context of half a century ago. Both Spencer and Glenn were representative of the benign assimilationist sentiment pervading the Indian Office staff when the Indian New Deal began. They sincerely felt that the schooling they fostered would benefit the Seminole people in the long run. Furthermore, they were not oblivious to the fact that these Indians had effectively managed the informal education of children, transmitting a cultural heritage from generation to generation. To them the problem was simply that young Indians would be confronted with a rapidly changing world demanding skills and knowledge that the traditional enculturation process could not provide. Glenn vigorously disagreed with Collier's position that every Indian community should make its own decisions concerning the type and amount of education appropriate for its children. Yet he perceptively and sympathetically summarized the difficulties that Indians faced in making the transition from traditional patterns of education to formal schooling: "The Seminole Indians of Florida are not opposed to education. In common with other races they have developed a given system through which they train their youths for the role of adult life. For study about the camp fire of the home they are more proficient and industrious than the members of the white race. . . . Every Indian household has its program of teaching its children certain fundamental things. Since the vocation of the race is different to that of more advanced social groups the aims and the methods of Indian education do not conform to those of the more mature races. But the Indian believes in training his children. He objects rather to the strange and complicated system together with the unfamiliar objectives of the public school system. For example he questions the wisdom of employing a system of marks through which sounds, words, and thoughts were represented on paper. The white man, through inducing him to sign legal documents, has utilized the system to rob him. He fears that it is an instrument of evil. These are his problems of education, and he will think them through with time."[16]

Despite this general support for the concept of a community day school, Glenn had misgivings about the idea of opening a second Indian school to serve the Seminole children in Dade County. It would be a poor substitute, he thought, for the Dania school, where the reservation children profited from constant association with federal employees, an influence that would be lacking at an off-reservation contract school. He also believed that this scheme was fostered by certain white elements in Miami opposed to his administration. The federal government decided, nevertheless, to proceed with negotiations for another school. In 1934, Glenn reported that "during the early spring of the present fiscal year Dr. J. [sic] Carson Ryan, Jr., . . . visited the Agency, and in connection with the Officer in Charge made arrangements with the Dade County School Board looking toward the establishment of another school in the

Miami area."[17] A few weeks later a teacher was assigned to the work, but she became ill and remained so throughout the year. For that reason the schooling that had been planned was never initiated. Following this visit, Ryan became a bit skeptical about the possibility of immediately beginning a school program for the Mikasukis living in villages along the Tamiami Trail. Reflecting on the success of social workers among the western tribes, he suggested that "if these villages are to continue, it seems possible, some provision will have to be made for social, health, and educational service beyond what is now made. The desirability of school in the ordinary sense would seem to be highly questionable unless the groups become larger and more permanent. An itinerant worker, preferably of Indian blood, would be useful."[18]

Although convinced that it would be a waste of time to attempt schooling among the "Trail Mikasukis" who were still resistant to any government intrusion, Glenn was more enthusiastic about sending teachers to settlements perceived to be receptive to education, such as those north of Lake Okeechobee. "In so far as possible" he wrote, "the school should be taken to Indian camps . . . by setting up Indian rural schools. Whenever the children of three or four Indian camps can be grouped into a small school a teacher should be provided. . . . the future of the Seminoles, whatever it may be, is lodged in the plastic nature of these Indian children."[19] His own limited experience in teaching Indian youngsters in their wilderness camps had been a rewarding one for Glenn and his wife, and it may have colored his views on how effective such a program could be over time. It was at best a high-minded but hopelessly impractical and expensive plan, given the economic situation at that time.

James L. Glenn would not have to preside over the demise of the day school, for at the end of 1935 he was relieved of duty as special commissioner to the Seminoles. The months that followed were a period of retrenchment in Indian Office programs, and one of the casualties was the Dania day school. In May 1937 the new Seminole agent, F. J. Scott, prepared an article for *Indians at Work* in which he announced that "efforts to interest the Florida Seminoles in large numbers in conventional school have come to little. . . . [The Dania school] was operated for a period of nine years with mediocre success. Because of a lack of sufficient interest and attendance the school was abandoned at the close of the school year in 1936. Present Government policy has been to abandon large scale attempts at education but to encourage the few who are interested. So far none of the Southern Seminole group has shown any interest in following the ways of whites, nor is the Indian Office attempting to force changes in their point of view."[20]

It is ironic that at the time the Dania school was about to be phased out, it appeared to be emerging as a true community day school fulfilling the role that Collier and his directors of Indian education had envisioned for such institutions—at least it was providing the prescribed activities. In 1936, Willard Walcott Beatty became Collier's second director of Indian education. Over the next decade Beatty, who had served as president of the Progressive Education Association, was equally committed to the philosophy underlying the community day school and perhaps articulated its goals more broadly than his predecessor. Like Collier, he believed that the Indian community could provide the dominant culture with a new and more meaningful model of social interaction. His initial message carried in *Indians at Work* acknowledged that "the vision of the new Government community day school as an educational center for the entire community was that of Carson Ryan before me. It is a picture envisioned by my leader, John Collier. . . . it is an experiment in the betterment of rural life which, if successful, may point the way to an enrichment of life for millions of white Americans, also."[21] Both the commissioner and his education director thought it possible for the Indian to have the best of both worlds, holding that "adults of the community are using the school to promote their own better living, and through this experience are learning to cooperate with and trust the school in the leadership which it is offering them and their children in learning to respect and dignify that which is fine in Indian tradition and adapt to their own needs that which is worthy in the culture of the white man."[22] This noble sentiment ignored the fact that the very experience of participation in the day school was itself a transforming act for the Indians: the language of instruction was English, which could not carry the cultural nuances of tribal tongues; few bilingual materials were available, and most teachers were ill equipped to serve as cross-cultural mediators. Thus, the possibility existed that what might look like a community day school, when judged solely by its curriculum and activities, could in reality be something different.

In the same year that Beatty assumed his new post, the Seminole day school at Dania was featured several times in *Indians at Work,* the implication being that it was an appropriate exemplar of the new community day school that the Indian Office was promoting. One piece, written by Elsie H. Devol who was the teacher from 1934 until the school closed, gave a litany of activities designed to upgrade Indian life, many of the type frequently mentioned by Beatty. The pupils had been pursuing a week-long unit on "camp improvement" which was based on serving the noon meal. The children served lunch in the camps each day, and their mothers were "invited" to come and help prepare the meal in the school kitchen; they used the Camp Fire Outdoor Book which contained recipes for many dishes combining vegetables and meat in "a wholesome meal." A program was held at the end of the week in which six campfires were lighted in the road fronting the school—"these fires were laid in the typical Seminole style with logs pointing outward in the four directions"—and the children gave oral compositions and readings about good diet. "Then songs were sung to emphasize healthful food and camp sanitation. An original song, composed by Seminole School students, set to the tune of 'Billy Boy' was sung by Howard Tiger and Moses Jumper. Mary Tommie, one of the Seminole Camp Fire Girls, was presented with a Wood Gatherer's Ring by the Guardian, which marked that Mary made another step in Camp Fire work. . . . the last number of the program was given by Mary Tommie, who explained and demonstrated how to toast a bacon and cheese sandwich on a pointed palmetto stick." As the teacher described the scene, "The gay dress of the Seminole school children, singing and speaking on the school porch, while their parents who were sitting in the grass watch[ed] the performance, was picturesque in the fire light." The white teacher concluded that the entire affair gave the Seminoles an opportunity to mingle with the federal employees and their families and that this activity cultivated that spirit of trust and confidence so essential in the success of any project looking forward to the "betterment of the Seminole people."[23]

Where was the cultural interchange? Where was the integration of Indian values and ways? What was the assurance that there would be any carryover into the life of the Indian camp if the people themselves had not generated an interest in better diet and sanitation? Except for the reservation setting there was little to set this exercise apart from similar Camp Fire Girl ceremonies at a white middle-class school. It was devoid of anything uniquely Seminole—save perhaps the traditional log fire. There is something disquieting about inducting a Seminole child into an organization ostensibly based on traditional Indian values, much less as a "wood gatherer" (actually, the ring was awarded for gathering and marketing huckleberries and cleaning up around her camp) when that function was no longer culturally viable for her people in their setting. The entire unit had the appearance of a teacher-contrived and -orchestrated acculturational activity in the guise of meeting Indian needs, and it points up one seeming ambiguity in the way the community day school concept functioned in Florida.

The decision to close the Dania day school was ostensibly taken in a general effort by the Indian Office to economize. It was argued that those Seminole youngsters who wanted to continue their education could do so in the nearby town of Dania. Moreover, officials held that attendance in public schools would accelerate the acculturational process for Indian pupils. So confused was Indian education policy early in the New Deal that officials who urged this course of action seemed at odds with Collier's policy of Indian self-determination but also consistent with that section of the reformist Meriam Report that held that "the present policy of placing Indian children in public schools near their homes instead of in boarding schools or even in Indian Service day schools is, on the whole, to be commended. It is a movement in the direction of normal transition, it results as a rule in good race contacts and the Indians like it."[24] Unfortunately, in the case of the Seminoles the Indian Office had conveniently discounted the lack of parental support for schooling, the children's low state of readiness for entering a public classroom, and the refusal of the public school at Dania to accept Indian children because of racial segregation policies. Even their friend Mrs. Frank Stranahan, appearing before the U.S. Senate Subcommittee which came to Dania in 1930, had declared that Seminole youngsters were not ready to enter public schools because they had poor hygiene and little academic preparation.[25] Despite these obvious impediments to continuing the education of most Seminole Indian children, the Dania day school was closed permanently.

Within two years, the Indian Office reversed itself to support day schools for the outlying Seminole reservations—although a few children from these remote locations would also be sent to the Cherokee School each year. The people of the Brighton Reservation built their day school in 1938, and it functioned for sixteen years. The teacher, William Boehmer, gave a succinct account of the situation: "We opened the school with eight children. . . . We helped with the building and also became acquainted with the people. . . . a few could speak some English and understand some, but neither my wife nor I could speak the Creek language which the Indians at Brighton use. . . . They ranged in age from six years to about sixteen, and only one of these had ever been in school. There really was not much support for the school at the beginning. The people on the Brighton reservation are good workers; they are hard working people. If there was not work on the reservation they would go out to the ranches and farms, sometimes thirty or forty miles away, to work; and when the winter's truck farming season opened they often would take the whole family and go to these farms until the crop was harvested, and take the children along. In fact, the children worked too. Our attendance for the first two or three years probably ranged in seventy-two to seventy-five percent attendance. But as time went on the parents learned that the children did not learn unless they were in school; they had to attend regularly in order to continue to progress. The parents saw this, and later on they would go to the farms to work, but they would leave the children at home with an aunt or grandmother or somebody to take care of them. . . . 1954 was the last year that we had school."[26]

A day school opened at Big Cypress in 1940, but it had a spotty existence. Commenting on this school, which initially operated in a converted chiki, Freeman found in 1945 that "the school which our Government has tried to establish on their Reservation has been abandoned at least temporarily . . . it is only within the last two years that the Big Cypress [people] have made an exception and allowed their children to go to the boarding school in Cherokee, Carolina, where teachers and pupils are Indian."[27] In the 1950s the Big Cypress day school was reactivated, and it continues to function as a modern elementary school but now under tribal direction.

Superintendent Scott's article announcing the Dania school closing featured a picture of three Seminole youngsters—Agnes Parker, Betty Mae Tiger, and her younger brother, Howard Tiger—who were the first to be sent away to an Indian boarding school. During the 1936–37 school year they had been attending the Cherokee Indian School in Cherokee, North Carolina. The basic educational costs for these pupils and those who would follow were borne by the Indian Office, but they also received assistance from the Friends of the Seminoles, which Mrs. Stranahan had organized in 1934. Later, the Daughters of the American Revolution in Fort Lauderdale also joined in the local effort, which sponsored Seminole children at the boarding facility from 1937 through 1954.[28]

It is difficult to imagine the trepidation of those youngsters facing that trip into the unknown, far away from family and friends, in search of an education. A montage of their experiences and motivation has been pieced together from two sources, the letters they wrote back to their sponsors in Florida and the oral accounts of Indian adults who attended the Cherokee school. They were confronted immediately with the shock of a new living situation, a strange geographical setting and climatic conditions, and being thrown together with other Indians in a highly structured institutional environment. They were homesick, and this situation worsened when some of them came down with measles during the first year. One of the girls recalled, "I didn't like it at first, I was homesick. I didn't like the snow. They'd build us a snowball, and they'd hit us. It was the first time we ever see snow. First I was homesick, then I got used to it and I kind of like it up there." Another stated simply, "I liked it, that's beautiful country. When I first went away . . . I was homesick but I determined I was going to finish . . . and I did." It was soon apparent that they lacked adequate clothing for the winter temperatures in North

Carolina. Their letters evinced great anxiety over not having appropriate clothing to wear to class and school functions; the older children expressed a touching concern for the younger ones, especially in having their outgrown clothes replaced. There was a constant appeal for funds to buy clothing, shoes, books, and other school materials not provided by the government. One Seminole recalled her experience as an impoverished young girl: "I have nothing like a lot of people, a lot of the kids take their extras, you know, a lot of socks and all this. I got one pair of socks I wear there. . . . I thought I had a hard time but I make it. I never been that way up north before. . . . I didn't know nothing about it. . . . it's cold. . . . my aunt, she couldn't write . . . and they don't know what we need from there to here."[29] The club women in Florida tried to meet these needs as best they could with shipments of donated clothing and occasional gifts of cash, although times were hard. Even so, at least one student wrote to complain that, as a disciplinary measure, she was being denied money sent for her use by the Friends of the Seminoles.

The Cherokee School was established in the 1880s by Quakers, and long before it was taken over by the government it had a well-established tradition of combining practical vocational pursuits with standard academic subjects.[30] When not in classes each student was assigned additional duties, the girls having domestic chores and the boys working in plant maintenance and keeping the grounds. The children lived in dormitories, two and sometimes four to a room. The day usually began at six o'clock when students dressed and undertook early assignments, including helping the younger children. One of the young Seminoles reported, "I stayed in the girls building most of the time because I helped little girls get ready for school. You know, in the morning we'd get them up and dress them for breakfast. We eat at seven o'clock . . . and some of us stayed in the dining room to help clean the dining room and everything. And at eight I come back and help little girls fix their beds and everything. Get them ready for school by eight twenty, we had to be at school at eight twenty. It was all day."[31] Academically, the school was oriented to traditional subjects found in the public schools—English, literature, mathematics, history, etc. One of the girls wrote about her typing course which took two periods a day along with three academic periods and three "detail" periods—a euphemism for the domestic arts program. During the 1930s both Ryan and Beatty had begun a reorientation of the curriculum in Indian boarding schools to reflect the realities of the times. As Szasz pointed out, "While the self supporting system was in part a matter of necessity, some kinds of school labor also served as training for students who were to return to their reservations."[32]

Because the Seminole children, particularly in the first few years, were older and had a checkered pattern of previous schooling, they were often assigned to a special class at Cherokee until they could accurately be placed in a grade. This placement was difficult at best. One of the girls who went in 1937 was fourteen and would take eight years to finish. As one of her companions recalls, "We were kind of bigger than those school kids . . . we were about eight or nine and they put us in third grade." Another woman who attended in the 1940s said, "I'd never gone to school before and I went at sixteen in the first grade." Most of the Indian children would attend only a few years, and for this reason there was a heavy emphasis on the basic subjects and the domestic arts program. In that sense the work that they did around the school contributed to their acculturation, despite the insistence of Ryan, Beatty, and Collier that they did not have to accept white ways. One Seminole who attended for only a year and a half still thought it was a valuable experience despite limited academic attainment: "They helped. We don't know how [to] fix a bed, for one thing. That's what we learned. We learned how to fix a bed, and we learned how to set the table, learned ironing clothes and folded sheets, and all this kind. They'd teach us to after school, they'd call it work, and they had some lunch and everything." Somewhat ruefully she also added, "That's all I learned."[33] However, during the years that they attended, a number of Seminoles did well academically, at least enough to graduate. In 1945, Agnes Parker and Betty Mae Tiger became the first of their people to graduate from high school. Agnes never returned to Florida permanently, but Betty Mae took nurses' training at the Kiowa hospital and returned to serve her people; she later married classmate Moses Jumper and raised a family with all of the children completing public school—a privilege not afforded their mother. In the 1960s she was the first woman to be elected to head the Seminole Tribe of Florida.

Except for the great amount of out-of-class work expected of them, most of the Seminole adults recalled that they had been treated kindly by the staff and had found their quarters and food generally acceptable. Yet, one remembered a bit of difficulty in adjusting to the new diet: "Oh, we didn't like it at first. We missed our sofkee. That's our main food among our tribe. They had hash and beans, mostly potatoes and beans."[34]

In addition to their obligations at the school, some industrious Seminoles still found time to undertake a variety of activities in the community such as babysitting and housecleaning to earn additional money. The wage for such work was only fifteen cents an hour, yet they could make as much as $18 to $20 each month to use for socks, shoes, and personal items. They often worked as late as eight o'clock in the evening, then went back to the dormitories to study until bedtime.

Such a schedule did not leave much time for social activities, and indeed there was little for the young Indians to do away from the campus. Occasionally those who had the money would attend a movie in the town on a Saturday afternoon or go shopping. There were student activities such as clubs, student council, and athletic teams at the school. They served as class officers, played on the athletic teams, and took a leading role in the Cherokee Festival held each fall. On Sunday morning they were transported to a nearby Baptist church and attended midweek prayer meetings as well. No one seems to have questioned whether there was any aspect of compulsion involved in this religious observance; it was just accepted as part of the scheme of things at Cherokee. Moreover, by 1940 there was a strong Baptist missionary effort among the Florida Seminoles, and the youngsters attending boarding school came from that segment of the tribe most receptive to Christianity.[35]

There can be little doubt that these were atypical Seminole youngsters. Years later Glenn offered a candid appraisal of their relationship to the tribe: "The Florida school was an expensive affair, and in some ways these children learned faster after they were separated from their people. But it made more difficult the gap between the educated Seminoles and their own people, and there were a smaller number of children who would go to school under these conditions." This problem of social distance also troubled anthropologist Alexander Spoehr, and he had mentioned to John Collier: "With respect to education, I am very skeptical about the advisability of sending Seminole children to the Cherokee boarding school in North Carolina, for I am afraid they will merely become alienated from their own society, while fitting into no other; there is one girl now at Dania who is not very well adjusted to her own group, largely, I think for this reason." When this information was passed along to W. W. Beatty he confided to the superintendent at the Cherokee Agency that he thought Spoehr's point "well taken and one which should be given consideration in the future,"[36] but there was no interruption in sending Seminoles to Cherokee until the 1950s.

In reflecting on their experiences at the Cherokee School after forty years, the Seminole adults interviewed were almost unanimous in their acceptance of the education they received and were grateful for the opportunity. Asked if it was worth the hardships, one of the group replied, "It's up to you, you want to make up your mind what you want to be. . . . I know we need our education. There was only a few of us that speak

English at that time. . . . I thought to myself if I could go home and speak three or four words in English I could help my people." The combination of desire for both personal advancement and to be of service to their people suffused virtually all of the accounts. Perhaps the one Seminole who has spoken and written most extensively of her frustrations and fulfillments in seeking an education is Betty Mae Jumper (née Tiger). She was a trailblazer who set a pattern for others to follow. When asked why she chose the boarding school route, she answered, "well there was no school here and we wasn't allowed to go to public school. I wanted to go to school . . . my father says he got me in either Oklahoma or North Carolina. And so I told him North Carolina because in Oklahoma if I go there it would be a language to all of us, they talk in Creek and I do too, so I can't learn fast. But if I went to Cherokee I can't understand them so I figured that I would learn faster there. They have to talk to me in English. So yeah, I learned." Betty readily acknowledged that Superintendent F. J. Scott was helpful in arranging for her to go to Cherokee, but her comments also confirmed the gap which resulted between the children and the tribal elders as a result of this decision. "My people didn't believe in boarding school" she said, "they fought me going because my grandmother was really against it, because they didn't believe in school."[37] Nevertheless, she persisted, and wrote to Mrs. Stranahan shortly before her graduation, "I hope that it will be possible for more to follow and as I saw children following in my footsteps toward an education I knew then I would never quit school which my grandmother wished me very much to do, because it means everything to me to see my tribe take an interest toward the school which we need so badly. All the years I have been in school I pray that someday all my people may realize the needs of an education and that my influence may mean something to them."[38]

A teacher who worked at the Cherokee School for over twenty-five years recalled the Seminole children, especially those who attended during the war years of the 1940s.[39] Betty Mae Tiger and her future husband, Moses Jumper, were among her favorites, as was Betty's brother, Howard. During these years, life at the school was spartan. Many of the Indian boys left school to join the military services. There were no field trips because of gas rationing, and sports activities were similarly curtailed. Classes spent much of their time combing the area for scrap metal and writing to the boys in the service. Mostly, the old teacher remembered how well the Seminole youngsters fit into the school's life. They were neat and well mannered, they looked out for one another and responded to the academic-vocational program. Once she accompanied the children on their return trip to Florida and was shocked at their meager existence on the reservations there. This trip confirmed her belief that the boarding school with its orderly routine, healthful food, and sanitary living conditions was a positive experience for these children who came from a background of poverty. Nonetheless, the residential facility was closed in 1954 as a result of improved roads, busing, and increased public school attendance throughout the Cherokee communities in North Carolina. The Seminoles and children from other tribes who had attended the school would have to transfer elsewhere in the federal boarding school system or enter the public schools of their home states. Fortunately, following World War II much of the resistance to accepting Indian children into public schools had disappeared in Florida, and they enrolled in increasing numbers. The day school at Brighton Reservation was closed at the request of the residents, and their children were bused to public schools in Okeechobee County. In 1957 the first Seminole graduated from a public high school in Florida: Joe Dan Osceola, son of Richard Osceola, who had been a moving force in organizing the Brighton school in 1938.[40] Thus, education for the Florida Seminoles had come full circle.

The Seminole youngsters who journeyed to the Cherokee school were archetypical of those from their generation who accepted the notion that white ways could be adopted, and adapted, for survival. Figuratively, they were the first passengers on a twenty-year bus ride in search of the assumed advantages of acculturation. For decades the Office of Indian Affairs, aided and abetted by private societies and missionary groups, had as a goal the Christianization and assimilation of the Indian. In the 1930s and 1940s, despite the reforms of the Collier administration, these were still viable goals for many, both in and out of government. Indeed, the commissioner himself wanted it both ways; as has been pointed out, "although Collier walked the thin line between proponents of assimilation and proponents of reservation heritage, he too believed that the Indian could achieve a balance between these seemingly contradictory ways of life. . . . Both Beatty and Collier recognized that their aims conflicted with almost all of the earlier goals of the Indian Service. However, at least in the 1930s, they did not seem to regard their goal— that the Indian choose the best of both worlds—as unattainable."[41]

It was in such an educational-ideological milieu that the Seminole students were fostered, in the full expectation that they could return to their reservations unchanged as Indians and as individuals except for the employment of newly acquired skills and knowledge. According to anthropologists such as George and Louise Spindler, this position was psychologically untenable, for at its root acculturation is a process of personality reorganization for adaptation to changed cultural conditions.[42] Having once undergone this process, the individual is never the same and often encounters a conflict between old and new value systems that can be devastating. Moreover, it was an ingrained tenet of Indian Office policy, especially at the field staff level, that schooling should be accepted by the tribes; to the extent that those Seminoles who attended boarding school were promoted as role models among their people, the assimilation process was enhanced. They were singled out for special recognition and support by both government functionaries and Indian aid societies in Florida, and they played an important role in the tribal political renascence during the 1950s. Attendance at school thereby became synonymous with high status and economic gain for successive generations of Seminoles—though only a small number of youngsters fulfilled this expectation until recent years. Therefore, one of the most significant residuals of the New Deal era for the Florida Seminoles— although not immediately apparent among the conservative elements— was the initial acceptance of white schooling with all that it implied for the undermining of their own culture.

8

Demise of the Seminole
New Deal

When Dwight R. Gardin stepped into the position of superintendent at the Seminole Agency in April 1940, replacing F. J. Scott, he was no stranger among the Florida Indian camps. For several years he had served as the "itinerant shopman" attached to the CCC-ID program, and he knew Indians on all the reservations, thus providing greatly needed continuity to the projects already begun among the Seminole people. He confronted an immediate crisis when it was found that the annual CCC-ID allocation had already been expended by Scott, and additional funds had to be secured from the Rehabilitation Division of the Indian Office to continue the work and provide relief for the Indians until the end of the year. Gardin notified D. E. Murphy that in order to avoid a repetition of this problem the Seminole budget request for the following year was higher than the funds allowed for 1940; furthermore, he explained that "this shortage of funds was probably due to the fact that more and more Indians are coming into the reservation all the time to live and work, in preference to staying in the commercial camps. This to my mind, is a healthy and laudable condition and means that the reservation areas are becoming more attractive to them, from an economic standpoint, than the commercial camps and I think we should encourage this attitude as much as possible." He then reminded Murphy, "as you perhaps realize from your visit," little improvement had been made to the Seminole reservation in Hendry County compared to other areas where the CCC-ID work had begun earlier: "As I expect a gradual but constant influx of new Indians toward the reservation areas I think it wise that we should make provisions in our estimate for accommodating them."[1] Gardin's pleas were to no avail, and on June 12, Murphy notified him that the Seminole CCC program for fiscal year 1941 was approved in the amount of $30,500—an increase of only $500.[2] Like his predecessor, Gardin would have to make do with shrinking funds as the president's New Deal policies ran into increasing opposition in Congress.

Nationally, the political climate had turned dramatically more conservative during Franklin Roosevelt's second term in office. Throughout the so-called Second New Deal, a conservative coalition of Republicans and southern Democrats had stiffened in their opposition to the president's policies and spending requests. Their stance became particularly bitter following the 1937 fight over Roosevelt's "court-packing" plan, which drew national criticism and failed to get through Congress. Because it was one federal agency with high visibility and political vulnerability, the Indian Office was singled out for extreme criticism from unreconstructed assimilationists and their supporters in Congress. Commissioner John Collier, who increasingly became the object of personal attacks, was constantly called before congressional committees to defend his policies, personnel, and budget requests. Collier had openly supported the president's plan for restructuring the federal judiciary, believing that a court system more receptive to the New Deal in general would be a protection for the hard-won gains of the Indian. Ironically, Senator Burton K. Wheeler—who had never totally abandoned the goal of Indian assimilation even though he coauthored the Wheeler-Howard Act—became one of the leading voices opposed to Collier and the Indian New Deal.

Working within the budgetary constraints imposed upon the CCC-ID program, Gardin proved to be an energetic and aggressive administrator. One of his major accomplishments was seeing through to completion the construction of an all-weather road connecting the Big Cypress Reservation with the town of Immokalee in 1941. This project provided greatly needed employment for the Indians; one of the Seminole elders, Willie Frank, recalled how "Gardin help[ed] with CCC program. He did help with finding work and helping with assistance for food if needed. . . . We built roads, this main work through Big Cypress, 833 road."[3] Unfortunately, early in his term Gardin committed the political and fiscal indiscretion of grossly overspending his FY-1940 budget—by $1,344.99 —and that placed him at a continuing disadvantage with the Washington bureaucracy. On July 23, 1940, D. E. Murphy received a scathing memorandum from the Indian Office auditor detailing the extent of Gardin's transgression, concluding, "If the situation is truly as it looks, I should not know how to phrase a letter about it. It would be the worst I ever heard of."[4] On August 7, Murphy, stung by the criticism, demanded an explanation from Gardin as to why he had overspent his budget by more than 15 percent without authorization; the superintendent did not reply to that inquiry until January 23, 1941.[5] Even then, no justification was given other than there had been a changeover of both superintendents and clerks near the end of the fiscal year, and in the rush of work they had simply neglected to secure approval for the amounts expended in excess of that budgeted. Murphy was assured that there was no intent to disregard his instructions and that in the future proper procedures would be followed. Nevertheless, there would be a change in superintendents within six months. Commissioner Collier would report that Gardin had been replaced because he was unable to get along with Florida officials and for "other indiscretions."[6]

The superintendent was enthusiastic about getting a cattle program under way at the Big Cypress Reservation, although during that period the Ickes-Collier position in the cattle tick controversy still had not been affirmed by presidential intervention. It was Gardin who accompanied Collier and Murphy when they visited the "Reservation Mikasukis" in 1940 and took the photographs that ultimately illustrated Collier's article concerning Everglades deer for *Indians at Work*. On April 1, 1940, the Big Cypress Reservation was posted with no-trespassing signs after unknown hunters had killed some of the Seminole deer, and this action placed Gardin in the middle of the controversy. He corresponded directly with Collier concerning efforts to deter deer hunters from entering the posted areas of the reservation and was urged to enforce vigorously the no-hunting regulations. As part of this enforcement effort the superintendent requested permission to purchase two horses for use in patrolling the Hendry County Reservation. The *Miami Herald* also vindicated his actions when it ran a series of articles in opposition to killing the Seminole deer.[7]

Meanwhile, in a letter dated August 2, 1940, Gardin expressed the view that "the Big Cypress Indians are very anxious to start raising cattle and I am heartily in favor of stocking that range as soon as it is deemed advisable"—this even though the region was still under quarantine. Nevertheless, it was anticipated that a survey would show that the cattle there were tick-free, and while he realized that no cattle could be sold or removed from the area until the quarantine was lifted unless they were dipped for twenty-one days under supervision of the State Livestock Sanitary Board, Gardin insisted that "we can legally stock the range at any time and the cattle will be increasing all the time even though the quarantine is still in effect." The superintendent was admittedly concerned that if they waited until the quarantine was lifted, the Indians would have lost several years' time and the natural increase of the stock; he noted that cattlemen adjacent to the reservation were stocking their range in anticipation that the quarantine would ultimately be lifted. More important, though, he suggested that "in view of the present situation abroad and in the United States, I believe we should do all we can to hasten the day when they will be more or less economically independent. The southern group is now almost wholly dependent on CCC-ID work and I am afraid that the next Congress will dramatically reduce the appropriation or kill it altogether."[8] He continued to hammer at this theme in subsequent correspondence until, in the summer of 1941, Assistant Commissioner Zimmerman answered, "The office is of the opinion that it may be unwise at the present time to organize a cattle industry for the Big Cypress group. We agree with you that some type of economic development must be worked out for these people, but until the tick situation is clarified it may be risky to attempt such a move."[9] So, through the remaining months of his superintendency Gardin backed away from the Big Cypress cattle issue. He was, however, responsible for getting the Muskogees at Brighton to select three trustees and acceptthe $20,000 rehabilitation grant in 1941; in the long run, tribal acceptance of that grant insured that the cattle program would ultimately be extended to Big Cypress.

Gardin also found himself embroiled in the controversy surrounding Seminole opposition to registering under the Selective Service Act. Covington has provided a useful overview of this episode.[10] By 1940, events in Europe had left the Roosevelt administration with no doubts that the United States would be drawn into that conflict, and there was a rush to build up the nation's military strength. In August, Congress passed the first peacetime Selective Service Act: it provided for the registration of all eligible males between the ages of twenty-one and thirty-six on October 16, 1940. As required by the act 16.4 million men registered and, after their numbers were drawn in an October 29 lottery, 1.2 million of the registrants were summoned for one year of military training. While there was a mixed reaction to this process, which was obviously gearing America for war, the vast majority of citizens accepted it as a necessary step to insure national preparedness. This ambivalence was also reflected throughout the American Indian tribes, and several questioned whether the Selective Service Act applied to them. There was outright opposition among a few tribes. The young men of the Papagos were advised to resist the law, and when policemen entered the reservation they were disarmed. The Zuñis of western New Mexico resisted by declaring that all of their young men were priests and should receive religious deferments; consequently only 213 of the populous Zuñi were taken into military service. The president of the Seneca Nation decided on a court test to see if Indians were subject to the law. However, there were also Indian voices in support of the Selective Service Act. Another leader of the Senecas ruled that all men of ages eighteen to thirty-five must register, while the leader of the Yaquis living near Tucson, Arizona, announced that his tribe was grateful to the United States and offered full cooperation with the registration law.

Commissioner Collier addressed candidly the question of the Indian attitude toward the war in his 1942 annual report to the secretary of the interior: "One would expect the Indians of the United States to be confused and complexed by the war situation. Essentially they are a rural people. Many of them live in remote areas, speak only their native languages, and have little access to newspapers, radio, or other forms of communication. How could they be expected to understand the clash of ideologies which has precipitated the world crisis?" Moreover, he continued, there had been little in their treatment at the hands of the federal government over the last century and a half that would engender sympathy and loyalty to the nation or leave them willing to defend it against its enemies. But surprisingly some Indians had responded earnestly and enthusiastically. For example, the Zia Pueblo "engaged in prayer before the second selective service registration," while among the Navajo Tribe, "Even the old people were insistent that they be allowed to enlist and the actions of the Selective Service officials in turning down so many young Navajos because of their inability to read and write or speak the English language has been felt very keenly by the entire tribe."[11] By 1942 the Cheyenne Tribe of Oklahoma had formally declared war on the Axis powers.

The Florida Seminoles had a well-deserved reputation for opposing the government in Washington, so there was no reason to expect that they would respond to its dictates in the matter of registration. However, the initial indication was that they might actually go along with the draft. The *New York Times* published the erroneous information that a ceremonial council of elders had agreed that the young men should register for the draft. Plans were made to visit each of the isolated villages so that men might enroll. At the Brighton Reservation, the teacher, William Boehmer, and stockman Fred Montsdeoca waited at the school building to register Seminoles; their wait was in vain. Only two Indian women showed up during the day to blow ceremonial tobacco smoke on the building to protect anyone who might register. After darkness had fallen two men who had a knowledge of English came in and filled out the eight-page registration document. At the Big Cypress Reservation the registration process went a bit better. The influential medicine man Josie Billie came in to assist his friend Stanley Hanson, who was assigned to enroll the Mikasukis, and together they were able to register twenty-nine of the sixty-four eligible men.

The Baptist missionary Willie King had barely begun his work among the Mikasukis when World War II broke out, and he found them anxious to learn about the meaning of the war. On those occasions when they came to him for information he used the opportunity to witness to them about Christianity. The military also impinged upon his work in other ways; he reported that on one occasion, while preaching to the small congregation back at Dania, "We enjoyed singing our old Creek songs. But those war planes [from a nearby base] made an awful noise above us that it drowned our voices."[12] Throughout the war years King became increasingly influential; he continued to keep his flock informed about international events and encouraged them to support the war effort in various ways, but there is no evidence that he ever urged them to register or volunteer for service.

At first superintendent Gardin was unconcerned over the situation, pointing out that no Seminoles had been drafted in World War I and it was unlikely that any would be called this time. He said that he would keep after the Indians during the rest of the week, urging them to register, but most of the sixty-four eligible Seminoles had taken the advice of their leaders and gone into hiding. The extent of this Seminole aversion to military service has been alluded to elsewhere, but a conversation with the Big Cypress medicine woman Susie Billie pointed up just how pervasive was their distrust of government programs which they linked with the registration. "Oh yes, people didn't have social security cards then. People heard you have to have it to seek employment. At that time people were working digging ditches. When they heard, they quit work thinking they were going to get sent off for military reasons. Thinking if signing anything they were being prepared for draft. They quit work and went into woods and started farming their own food, but shortly after someone explained the purpose of Social Security, and that no harm has come to the people. So people signed the papers and returned to work."[13]

Against such ingrained opposition Gardin was predictably unsuccessful at registering Seminoles in his second attempt, and on October 29 he was forced to report this fact to Commissioner Collier. In response, Collier requested that he report the names of those "recalcitrant" Indian leaders who had advised their people against registration. This list was to be made available to the state Selective Service director, who would take appropriate action. The superintendent forwarded the names of William McKinley Osceola, Cory Osceola, John Osceola, and Josie Billie. Gardin expressed the opinion that if all four were taken into custody they would soon advise their followers to register. But no federal action was taken against the Seminole draft evaders in 1940, thus encouraging other potential registrants to follow the lead of the recalcitrants; eventually, a few individuals did trickle in and sign the papers.

The inclusion of Josie Billie among the strident resisters represented an apparent lack of communication between Hanson and Gardin, since the Indian had been very helpful to Hanson in the initial registration. However, he had come under such heavy pressure from his peers for taking part in the first registration that he refused to have anything to do with subsequent attempts. Stanley Hanson, who spoke the Mikasuki language fluently, visited the villages to make a thorough investigation of the Indians' attitude toward Selective Service; he found no desire on their part to register for the draft. Hanson believed some whites had misinformed the Seminoles that they did not have to register for the draft because they were not citizens of the United States—which they were, as stipulated in the citizenship act of 1924. When officials in Washington and Florida wanted to adopt a tough stand and force the Seminoles to register, it was Hanson who pointed out that this move would destroy cordial relations with the Indians (to say nothing of causing a public relations problem), so they backed away. In June 1941, Gardin encountered strong resistance from the Cow Creek and Big Cypress medicine men over the rehabilitation grant, and he wrote to Collier complaining that "the Selective Service Act has had a far reaching effect on these people and has hindered us in a program that had seemed to be well on the road toward helping these people toward economic security."[14] In July 1941, Dwight Gardin was removed as superintendent of the Seminole Agency, to be replaced by William B. Hill.

The issue remained dormant until the commissioner of Indian affairs issued directions for a third registration for men who had reached their twentieth birthday by December 31, 1941, and had not passed their forty-fifth birthday by February 16, 1942. The registration was scheduled to take place on the latter date, and the state director of Selective Service was to have full responsibility for the registration of the Seminoles. Although it would have been preferable to have a non–Indian Office employee conduct the registration, it required someone with a knowledge of the people and language; Stanley Hanson was again given the task. He claimed to have traveled 2,136 miles in attempting to locate and register Indians from Silver Springs near Ocala to Miami. By June 1, 1942, of the 108 eligible Indians, 67, or 62 percent, had registered. This relatively low figure did not disturb Hanson for he believed that since a draft card was needed to secure employment, the holdouts would gradually register as they had done in 1940. Opposition to registration remained strongest among those Seminoles not living on the reservations and therefore least likely to seek government or private-sector employment.

By the final week of February 1942, the Selective Service officials had investigated the Seminole Indian registration problem and concluded that the matter could not be corrected. Captain Ralph W. Cooper was assigned to make a thorough investigation of the matter and report to the state director of Selective Service for Florida. In the two-day period of February 25–26 he visited the Seminoles residing at Dania, Brighton, Everglades, Fort Myers, and in camps along the Tamiami Trail. From this rather hurried trip he concluded that the Seminoles possessed little knowledge of English and were somewhat unsanitary, and it would not be worthwhile to use force against them; it would produce only limited results and arouse greater distrust toward the government. A few months later, by April 1942, federal officials in Washington had reached a decision on the Seminole registration problem. The issue had been brought to the attorney general for an opinion, and he decided that it was a State Selective service matter, not a federal one. The Florida selective service officials, in turn, decided to accept Captain Cooper's assessment that even if all the Seminoles were forced to register, the number actually accepted into military service would not justify the effort and the resulting distrust.

While this decision ended any active effort to register Seminoles for military service, both Hanson and Captain Cooper insisted—though in retrospect their claims appear somewhat naive—that the Indians could be of value if they were willing to assist the government in the war effort. Since Florida was dotted with army and navy aviation training schools, the Seminoles could assist in any rescue work at crashes that might take place in the Everglades. Also, they contended that if enemy troops should land by boat or parachute in or near the Everglades, the Indians would serve as guides to locate them. In June 1941, Hanson reported that some Seminoles were willing to serve on patrol and guide duty; this information was passed along to Secretary Ickes and Secretary of War Henry Stimson, and they referred it to the State Defense Council of Florida. As Covington summarized the situation, "So far as can be determined no use was made of the Seminoles in that capacity and they were not required to register if they did not desire to do so."[15] In this instance the U.S. government had acted with great restraint and unusual patience in handling a delicate situation.

Although World War II did not have a direct impact on the Florida Seminoles as a whole, individual Indians and their families played a role in the war effort as they saw fit. Since most of the Seminoles lived in rural settings, they continued to find work on nearby truck farms and filled the place of laborers who had been drafted. By 1943 thirty to forty men worked in defense-related jobs as truck drivers, carpenters, laborers, and mechanics. An illustration found in the *Miami Herald* reported that "four families of Seminole Indians have encamped on Federal highway to take war jobs. Richard Osceola, spokesman for the group, said he and his brother, Billie, and a nephew, Bell, are driving trucks on a night shift at an airport, while his sister, Lena Tiger, is working with a crew of women at the field. John Tiger and his brother, Frank, also are employed on the project."[16] One tribal elder, Willie Frank, who had lived in the Everglades west of Miami, recalled, "Mostly working farm labor, but around that time, along 1941, during war with Japan we helped build boats and things for the war." His may have been the earliest direct involvement in wartime production, but there were evidently other Mikasukis—their camps were the closest to an urban center—who were also employed in work relating to the military. Buffalo Tiger once recounted that he and two men from his village were employed in building light aircraft around 1942. The plant foreman, believing that Tiger should use an anglicized name, began calling him "William," and the name stuck. The 1942 census roll of the Seminole Agency also bestowed an anglicized name but erroneously listed him as "Frank (Buffalo) Tiger." During the years when Tiger served as chairman of the new Miccosukee Tribe, he always signed correspondence and official documents as William Buffalo Tiger.[17]

The 1942 wartime census roll compiled by the Seminole Agency listed a population of 619 Indians, virtually all of them residing in Collier, Broward, and Glades counties.[18] This enumeration, authorized by superintendent W. B. Hill and conducted by Stanley Hanson, was extensively annotated to show contemporary and historical family relationships, as well as their place of residence. Because of Hanson's extensive knowledge of their culture and language, as well as family genealogies among both the Mikasukis and the Cow Creeks, this remains a valuable ethnohistorical document.

Their resistance to the draft aside, Seminoles took a number of actions that became symbolically important as demonstrations of Indian support for the nation's struggle. Some Indians who had extra cash purchased war bonds and savings stamps, nineteen-year-old Betty Mae Tiger buying the first bond before returning to the federal boarding school at Cherokee. The Seminoles stood in line to accept their ration cards for sugar and gasoline. The demand for beef during the war also stimulated the development of the herds at Brighton and Big Cypress, just as it rejuvenated the entire Florida cattle industry. In all of these experiences there was an increased Seminole bonding with the society outside their immediate camps or reservation communities, which could not help but accelerate the pace of acculturation for the individuals involved.

In 1943, three Seminole males—Moses Jumper, Howard Tiger, and Jack Osceola—volunteered and were accepted for military service. The first to enlist was Howard Tiger from the Dania Reservation, who became a member of the U.S. Marine Corps at age seventeen. Like his older sister, Betty Mae Tiger, he had been attending the Cherokee Indian School in North Carolina. There he was a star athlete, excelling in basketball and track, but he also displayed a fine aptitude for mechanics and would have graduated in two years were it not for the war. When many of his Cherokee friends began enlisting and were taking part in the fighting, young Howard determined that he, too, would go to fight the Japanese. His mother, Ada Tiger, was just as adamant that her son should remain in school; she was the same strong-willed matriarch who had defied the Cow Creek headmen in 1926 and moved her family to Dania where the children could attend Spencer's school. Howard had previously promised his mother that he would not join the military prior to his eighteenth birthday without her approval. When the school term ended in June, he returned to Florida and obtained employment at the Opa Locka Naval Air Station in Miami, but he still wanted to be in uniform. Finally, on August 17—two days before his birthday—his mother gave her consent and her blessing, and Howard Tiger joined the Marines. A newspaper reporter came to his home at Dania when the family gathered to celebrate his eighteenth birthday, the women resplendent in their patchwork skirts and Howard in his Marine dress uniform, and questioned the young man about his motivation for joining the service of a nation with which his people were technically at war. "Guess it was the Japs. Let me shoot Japs and I'll be happy," he reportedly declared. It was just the thing to make the front page of the *Fort Lauderdale News,* and the story was reprinted in *Indians at Work*.[19] Howard Tiger got his wish to fight the Japanese, serving with distinction in the Pacific theater during the battles for Guam and Iwo Jima. He returned to Florida following the war, married a Cherokee girl from the Snowbird Community whom he had met at school, and became a prominent member of the Seminole tribal government. His was a special kind of acculturational experience denied to all but a few young Seminole men but shared by over 24,000 other American Indians. Following the war a federal report on the Selective Service Act recorded that "available statistics indicate that up to April, 1945, 21,767 Indians served as enlisted personnel in the Army, 1,910 in the Navy, 723 in the Marine Corps and 121 in the Coast Guard. Many served as officers in various branches of the services."[20]

A new superintendent, William B. Hill, arrived at the Seminole Agency in July 1941, just in time to revise the plans for spending the $20,000 grant from the Rehabilitation Division. A portion of the funds were allocated to Big Cypress and used to purchase 150 head of native cattle which the stockman Fred Montsdeoca had located. This expenditure of $6,500 consumed most of the $9,000 originally earmarked to purchase horses and cattle. Next, Hill sought permission to spend over $13,000 for equipment—including $6,000 on a single diesel tractor— which brought a caution from Commissioner Collier to be more selective in expending the limited funds available. A month later the director of extension for the Indian Office, A. C. Cooley, complained, "It is our feeling that Mr. Hill has never had the complete picture with regard to the Cow Creek development, particularly the commitments on the part of the livestock association to operate this equipment if it had been purchased. We are inclined to think that he is proposing to spend entirely too much money on such things as corrals and stables for the horses and is not securing some of the equipment that is necessary to maintain these ranges after they have been improved. . . . It is our opinion that we must confer with Mr. Hill in the near future, so that a strict understanding may be had with regard to the whole development."[21] Zimmerman sent not one but two letters dated December 11, 1941; both took the superintendent to task, chastising him for everything from poor management skills to poor judgment.[22] Although the CCC-ID funding for FY-42 projects was increased to $34,200, it became increasingly obvious that Hill was having great difficulties administering the work at the Seminole Agency. However, this lack of managerial skills would soon become a moot point, for the CCC-Indian Division programs were about to be scuttled in Washington.

As the nation's war effort moved into high gear during 1942, the Indian Office became one of the federal agencies deemed most expendable; even its office space would be commandeered for more vital war-related agencies. By August 1942 the headquarters and staff had been moved from the nation's capital to rented quarters in Chicago. Reduced appropriations virtually suspended capital investment on the reservations for land acquisition, irrigation, roads, and utilities. The final blow was delivered to the Indian New Deal on July 2, 1942, when an act of Congress provided funds for the liquidation of the Civilian Conservation Corps.[23] Accordingly, work had stopped on all reservations by July 10 of that year. Its passing was treated with official formality in Commissioner Collier's annual report for 1942, which concluded that the original objectives of CCC–Indian Division were to provide employment and vocational training for Indians who were in need of work, but "actual accomplishments far surpassed those initial aims."[24] He then recited the familiar statistical litany: over 75,000 Indians had found employment, and vocational training was provided in 55 different occupations, while approximately 6,500 former enrollees were in the armed forces where their CCC experience would prove of inestimable value to the nation. Collier was less dispassionate in his article in *Indians at Work*. In his own unique style the commissioner recounted that thirty-five years earlier the great William James had published his fundamental work, "The Moral Equivalent of War," and nine years ago the CCC was created not solely as a relief measure but to meet James's challenge. After nine years his assessment was, "Indian CCC, indisputably, has made history. Along with tribal self-government it has altered—has re-oriented—the life of a race."[25] The dismantling of so successful a program was "a heavy and undeserved blow," but Collier was confident that the Indian tribes would reach within their own "racial and individual virtue" to compensate for the loss.

It would fall to Superintendent Hill to oversee the winding down of CCC-ID activities and prepare the Seminole Agency to lie idle for the duration of the hostilities. Even before Congress acted to end this program the Indian Office was preparing to cut back its operations on the reservations. On April 22, Hill received a message from D. E. Murphy stating that "In view of the fact that CCC-ID has been placed on a war basis and work restricted to (a) aid in war work construction, and (b) war resources protection and development of natural resources, it does not appear that you should continue to carry on several types of work that you have heretofore been doing at Seminole." He went on to say that while forest protection fell within the parameters of acceptable projects, it was known that limited forest land existed at Seminole; however, if the superintendent could generate projects that met requirements, he was invited to submit an FY-43 proposal. Otherwise, "if you cannot do this, please arrange to close out your CCC-ID work as soon as possible, advising us of the date on which the work can be stopped and the amount of funds that may be withdrawn if all funds now in your hands are not needed."[26]

Murphy sent a follow-up message confirming that the CCC-ID program for fiscal year 1943 would be restricted primarily to the protection of war resources, with development of natural resources as a secondary priority.[27] Protection of war resources on Indian reservations meant mainly protection from fire. Obviously, such protection could not be maintained on a standby basis, but enrollees could be used for development of natural resources when not actually engaged in fire protection. William B. Hill having relinquished his position to enter military service, the disbursing agent at the Seminole Agency responded that it would be possible to undertake CCC-ID work on the reservations during the next fiscal year in accordance with the directives issued.[28] But the Indian Office must have been aware of the impending legislative action, for on June 9 the field agents were requested to provide an estimate of the funds needed as of July 1 to complete projects under way and provide terminal leave for CCC-ID employees.

Ten days later Chester E. Faris, field representative in charge of the Seminole Agency, notified the Indian Office that $8,000 would be required to close out CCC-ID projects without serious loss—over $2,000 of this going for a shed in which to store the equipment.[29] In estimating the terminal leave for employees, it was suggested that two persons be retained as long as possible to oversee completion of the projects and the proper storage of the equipment. The military services had first call on surplus CCC-ID equipment, and that not claimed was to be retained by the Indian Office; a final accounting at the Seminole Agency showed that property worth $2,903.51 was transferred to the Navy and $1,134.59 to the Indian Office.[30] Thus, when the congressional axe finally fell in July 1942, the Seminole Agency was already terminating its activities. The New Deal for the Seminoles of Florida had come to an end.

It is appropriate to ask here what generalizations can be made about the impact of the Indian New Deal on the Florida Seminoles. Unlike many other tribes, the Seminoles did not have Works Progress Administration or National Youth Administration programs, so the CCC–Indian Division projects became synonymous with the Indian New Deal in Florida. Although the Florida tribe was relatively small, essentially unorganized, and geographically isolated from the western Indians, it received the same type of Indian New Deal assistance offered to other Indian groups—and enjoyed the same mixed results. Certainly the federal employment and direct assistance efforts offered short-term, immediate relief to many Seminole families who otherwise would have been in dire straits. The long-range impact is more difficult to assess. Evidently this remains a general problem in Indian historiography, for a leading chronicler of the Indian New Deal, Donald Parman, has found that "even though the public has always accepted CCC publicity which stressed the program's wholesome effects on the enrollees, we have no conclusive evidence that these assertions are true on a long-range basis. We badly need careful follow-up studies of former enrollees' careers before any accurate assessment can be made about the social effects of the CCC. Such studies might well reveal that the program had much less rehabilitative effect than is commonly believed. In the case of the Indian enrollees, the impact of the CCC is complicated by their minority status in American society. The obstacles faced by Indians made the benefits of CCC—improved morale, better adjustment to changing conditions, and acquisition of work skills—much more important for Indians than for whites. Unfortunately, we do not have sufficient data on the subsequent careers of former Indian enrollees to be able to determine whether service in the CCC greatly benefitted them."[31]

A limited carryover from federal programs such as CCC-ID is certainly indicated in the Florida Indian experience, perhaps owing in part to the fact that from the outset it was a scaled-down program and lacked a unifying CCC-ID camp situation. Funds were never available to employ all the Indians who wanted work, and at first enrollees were limited to twenty hours a week for a maximum of three months. Even so, this work was their only source of cash income, and many displaced Seminole families lived in miserable situations while waiting for their turn to work. The Florida Indians were not brought together in supervised family camps where hygienic living standards were maintained, although some schooling and recreational facilities were provided as needed. Family camps were encouraged on the large western reservations and would have helped ease the transition period for the Seminoles.[32]

The CCC-ID certainly did not generate a broad-based upgrading of Seminole work skills or prepare them to enter the job market outside their reservations. All of the Indian elders interviewed were employed as unskilled laborers, and only a few members of the tribe attained the proficiency to become carpenters, truck drivers, or heavy machinery operators. Then, too, the isolation of the reservations limited the job opportunities available to the Seminoles. The tribal communities were too far removed from urban industrial centers for them to participate on a regular basis in war-related occupations. Equally important, few families were interested in relocating from the reservations, preferring to endure minimal subsistence. Thus, the CCC-ID jobs became a closed circuit providing the Indians a source of primary or supplementary income rather than a preparation for broader participation in an expanding off-reservation economy.

It was an interesting contradiction of the Indian New Deal that while official government policy espoused total Indian cultural and religious self-determination, it was simultaneously fostering programs on the reservations that would lead to their rapid social and economic assimilation.

To a certain extent there was a prevailing sentiment in the Indian Office that the Seminoles should not be pushed too far in the direction of assimilation. No doubt it was engendered by Commissioner Collier's concern, expressed in the article that he wrote for *Indians at Work* in 1935 after returning from the meeting with the Seminoles at West Palm Beach, that whatever programs were introduced should be limited and specific in nature so as not to disrupt the fragile structure of Indian culture in Florida. Only the idealistic Collier could have rationalized educating an elite that would lead the tribe back to primitive conservationism while denying schooling to the others for fear of corrupting them. Of course, when he wrote, he was still enthralled with the Seminoles, perceived by him as a relatively pristine tribal group. It would take another few years before the commissioner and his fellow bureaucrats concluded that the traditionalist and progressive elements of the tribe could be treated differentially; thereafter the Indian Office strongly supported economic development for the Reservation Seminoles, primarily by funding CCC-ID projects and a cattle enterprise.

Although a limited educational program was available at the day school on the Dania Reservation up until 1936, only a few adults availed themselves of the opportunity to improve their English reading and writing skills. Thus they further limited their chances for significant off-reservation employment. Neither would there be any wholesale entry of the Seminoles into the military when World War II began. Even if there had not been stiff resistance to Selective Service registration, it is unlikely that many Seminole inductees would have passed the minimal literacy tests required for active duty. It could not be coincidental that the three Seminoles who volunteered and were accepted for military service had all attended the Cherokee Indian School.

All of this evidence is not meant to imply that there were no positive aspects to the Indian New Deal activities among the Seminoles. When assessing the impact of the Indian New Deal, commentators generally begin by recounting the extensive physical improvements to the reservations, and certainly it was the case in Florida as well. The CCC-ID Work Program proposal for fiscal year 1942, which Gardin submitted in April 1941 shortly before his departure, contained a statistical summary of how the funds had been expended since March 31, 1933, on the Florida Seminole reservation.[33] A total of $178,622.32 had been spent on all projects. The net area of the federal reservation was calculated at 69,475 acres, which meant an average investment in land improvements of $2.55 an acre. The number of Indians on the tribal roll in 1941 was 604, of which 167 were males eligible for work. Evidently more people were moving to the reservations each year, for the tribal enrollment was 586 for the previous year and would rise to 619 in 1942. Nevertheless, throughout the entire existence of the Seminole CCC-ID program, fewer than 100 individual Seminoles had been employed.[34]

Through FY-1941 the largest single expenditure was $59,301.40 for construction and maintenance of 37.2 miles of truck trails. Over 29,800 rods of range were fenced at a cost of $41,606.38, while the revegetation of 2,359 acres of range cost $19,286.89. Over $14,000 was expended for general cleanup—clearing the land of palmettos, and so on. In addition, 11 miles of telephone lines were run, 40 wells were sunk, a 16-acre public campground was developed, and 29 signs and markers were erected. A value of $164,516.52 was fixed for permanent improvements made on the reservations. There were also many other substantial services ranging from forest fire prevention to wildlife protection, all of which generally improved the livability and productivity of the reservations. Still, there was a notable absence of modern dwellings on the rural reservations, even though in 1938 the September issue of *Indians at Work* had singled out the Seminoles (replete with pictures of chikis) as one of the tribes that still lived in substandard housing.[35] However, it is questionable whether the Indians themselves were ready in the 1940s to make the cultural adaptation, in both psychological and physical terms, that a transition from chikis to conventional housing entailed. Even at the Dania Reservation the living area that Glenn had so painstakingly renovated fell into disrepair and some families reverted to living in chikis, especially after the Seminole Agency headquarters was again moved to Fort Myers.

In 1939 an issue of *Indians at Work* had reported—somewhat prematurely, as it turned out—that the Seminole Agency was being returned to its original location at Fort Myers on the west coast of Florida.[36] Fort Myers was not the original site of the agency; it had been moved there from Miami during Captain Spencer's absence at the time of World War I. The rationale for such a move was that it would locate the agency more centrally to serve the newly activated reservations in Glades and Hendry counties, which had become the center of Florida Indian country. Further, the number of Indian families residing at Dania Reservation had dwindled to six, and since the two-story frame structure housing the headquarters was considered "insufficiently storm-resistant," it would not be worthwhile to rebuild it at that site. An additional advantage of being closer to the reservations was the reduced consumption of gasoline and tires, both of which would be tightly rationed during the war. In 1942 these were evidently considered valid arguments for relocation, so the Indian Field Service officer and his clerk occupied a small suite of offices in the federal building at Fort Myers.[37] Not unexpectedly, the relocation of the headquarters was bitterly denounced by Mrs. Stranahan and several of the Indians living at Dania, but to no avail.[38]

Belatedly, the Indian Office had accepted the logic of the recommendations of Roy Nash, D. Graham Copeland, Commissioner Charles J. Rhoads, and others who over a decade earlier advocated relocating the agency closer to the center of Seminole population—though that group clearly would have preferred a location further south near the town of Everglades in Collier County. From Fort Myers, C. E. Faris and his immediate successor, superintendent Kenneth Marmon, would oversee the drastically curtailed operations on the Seminole reservations throughout the remaining years of the war.

The Seminoles had made it through the worst period of the Great Depression with only limited assistance from the Indian New Deal; moreover, they had avoided virtually all of the conflicts generated by Collier's application of the Indian Reorganization Act and enforcement of New Deal policies among the larger tribes. In his work *The Navajos and the New Deal*, Donald Parman points out that among the nation's largest Indian group, "such tribal unity as developed in the 1930s largely grew out of the Navajo opposition to the government. Navajo antagonisms against herd reduction, plus the resistance of traders and missionaries, played a fundamental role in the defeat of the Wheeler-Howard referendum in 1935."[39] At the other corner of the United States there was also discontent, largely because of Commissioner Collier's failure to grasp that all Indian people did not conform to the southwestern cultural paradigm which he had subconsciously accepted. This failure is affirmed by Laurence Hauptman, who found that, "despite his good intentions and significant accomplishments, Collier largely did not understand the Iroquois. Collier especially did not comprehend the Iroquois' overriding concern with legality as well as with the real and symbolic reaffirmation of treaty rights."[40]

In one respect the Florida Indians were beneficiaries of benign neglect: they were so small a tribe, and so far removed from the mainstream of American Indian affairs, that scant attention was paid to them by the Indian Office bureaucracy or the harried Commissioner Collier. Without a tribal governing body in place to be reorganized under the provisions of Wheeler-Howard, and initially lacking either a viable livestock or handicraft industry, there was really nothing to do with—or to— the Seminoles in the early days of the New Deal. As J. L. Glenn had grasped, it was not a matter of reorganizing but *organizing* that had to take place among the Seminoles. Indeed, during the first four years of the Indian New Deal there was a palpable vitality and enthusiasm engendered by the CCC-ID projects, the acquisition of reservation lands by the Resettlement Administration, and the establishment of a beef cattle enterprise. Ironically, though, as the depression worsened and their needs became more acute after 1937, the Seminoles received little attention and limited funding; as the agents noted, Indians were enticed to the reservations in ever increasing numbers, and there was always a greater demand for employment than funds available. As late as 1939, only about one-half of the Florida tribe was living on government lands or receiving assistance. The Seminoles were all but forgotten until the cattle tick controversy and Indian "draft dodging" became national news for a brief period in the early 1940s.

Thus, as was the case with so many American Indian tribes, the impact of the Indian New Deal was neither totally positive nor totally negative; but among the Florida Seminoles it was definitely limited in its scope, and its primary value lay in preparing the way for future change. Over the next decade the close-knit reservation populations, while retaining their own unique qualities of language and life-style, would also forge many common social, economic, and religious bonds. This community of interests allowed the reservation Seminoles to rebuff successfully congressional attempts at terminating federal obligations to the tribe in the 1950s; to prevent it from recurring, they would then organize under provisions of the Indian Reorganization Act as the Seminole Tribe of Florida. It would not be too long thereafter that the Trail Indians themselves saw the potential threat and sought legal recognition as the Miccosukee Tribe of Indians.

9

The Seminole
Depression Babies

The Great Depression of the 1930s marked indelibly a generation of Americans who lived through it—so much so, in fact, that the term *depression babies* was coined to denote their generalized outlook on economic and social issues as a result of having survived those traumatic times. Even though this label is applied to an entire generation, Americans actually displayed a broad range of reactions to the depression. In his article "Living with Hard Times," John Steinbeck recalled, "Sure I remember the Nineteen Thirties, the terrible, troubled, triumphant, surging Thirties. I can't think of any decade in history when so much happened in so many directions. Violent changes took place. Our country was modeled, our lives remodeled, our Government rebuilt, forced to functions, duties and responsibilities it never had before and can never relinquish."[1] Steinbeck, of course, was one of those fortunate depression babies who possessed an intellectual toughness and youthful resiliency that enabled him to see things through and triumph over adversity. But many other citizens, having seen their financial security dissolve and jobs disappear, were less sure of themselves; millions became dependent on the federal government's employment and relief programs for their livelihood. Even when prosperity returned, they did not become risk takers; they still gave lip service to free enterprise but harbored a distrust of the financial and banking systems while looking to the government for a broad range of regulation and entitlements ranging from federal deposit insurance to Social Security. Thus, many social critics have denounced the New Deal as a stultifying influence on personal initiative which undermined self-sufficiency in American life.

Although North American Indian communities were securely enmeshed in a matrix of social and religious traditions that left them relatively immune from rapid value shifts, the Great Depression and New Deal programs were bound to engender change. The Tewa scholar Alfonso Ortiz relates that in his native San Juan Pueblo, the national economic decline had little impact initially, not because the people were so poor but because they were not caught up in a cash economy.[2] In time, though, they became addicted to the whites' foods and funds, thereby creating conflicts that disrupted communal harmony. This possibility was precisely what concerned the anthropologist Alexander Spoehr when he informed Commissioner Collier that reservation employment schemes were making younger Seminoles too dependent on the government for economic survival, echoing the misgivings that Collier voiced after first visiting the Florida Indians.

Certainly the Seminole experience differed from that of the Pueblos in that they had previously engaged in a vigorous cash-based trading relationship; an exceptional few had even operated their own stores. Nevertheless, for most the old values of self-sufficiency and economic independence were sorely tested by a prolonged economic malaise— which, it should be recalled, began for the Florida tribe shortly after 1900. As the depression deepened, an increasing number of Seminoles found it necessary to turn to the federal authorities for assistance, and even those who refused to relocate to the reservations were forced to make adjustments in their life-style. Therefore, it would be interesting to know if the exigencies of this period produced Seminole depression babies, that is, a generation of Indians whose values and patterns of behavior were so modified by the Great Depression and New Deal experience as to be at variance with traditional tribal ways and who presented a unique redefinition of their Indian-ness.

Nearly a decade of depression era economics and Indian New Deal policies provided the crucible in which Seminole culture began to be dramatically, if not immediately, reshaped. Clearly, a large number of the miniscule Florida tribe—which constituted about 0.2 percent of the Indian population nationally[3]—emerged with many old values and behavior patterns either revised or replaced by new ones more befitting their changing status. These changes were typified by a movement to reservations, the adoption of Christianity, and an acceptance of government-sponsored programs such as CCC-ID, cattle herding, education, and medical care. On the other hand, the minority of social and religious traditionalists who clung to the old ways were ultimately able to organize a new tribal entity in which to realize their own goals and values. Yet in both groups there were elements of continuity and change that combined to create a unique life-style that remained identifiably Indian. The cultural melding process that began in the 1930s would be most pronounced among the reservation dwellers, and defined the world view of the Seminole depression babies.

Tribal social organization in the 1930s was marked by a clear delineation between two primary groups of Seminoles: the progressives, who were willing to resettle on federal trust lands known as reservations, where they engaged in a variety of government-sponsored programs, and the traditionalists, who would not resettle on federal lands under any circumstances or acknowledge any basis for governmental intrusion into their affairs. It is noteworthy, also, that this division was not strictly along ethnolinguistic lines, i.e., the Mikasukis in opposition to the Muskogees. With the splitting away in 1937 of a sizable number of Trail Indians who moved to the Big Cypress Reservation, the total on-reservation Seminole population became predominantly Mikasuki-speaking. A small splinter group of Mikasuki-speaking traditionalists was left clinging to their camps on or near the Tamiami Trail. Their political organization dominated by the medicine men and the busk council, as well as an extremely conservative social and religious outlook, further exacerbated their separation from the other Mikasuki-speakers; it also set the agenda that eventually resulted in the organization of an independent Miccosukee Tribe.[4]

Signs of the Seminoles' ability to incorporate new ideas and values had long been evident in the material culture of their camps. Beginning in the intensive trading period in the last quarter of the nineteenth century, they had consistently replaced handcrafted items with manufactured goods. In even the most isolated camps, long before the people considered moving to reservations, it was not uncommon to find a variety of store-bought items such as iron pots and skillets, kerosene lanterns, coffee mills, and hand-powered sewing machines or phonographs. Also, it was not unusual for Indians to have acquired Model T Fords; some stripped the body away to make the vehicle lighter for travel across the marl prairies. By the 1930s there was a clear distinction in dress between the northern Muskogee camps and the Mikasuki-speakers living further south of Lake Okeechobee. The Cow Creek men had adopted white clothing almost exclusively, including cowboy hats, boots, denim work shirts, and trousers—the last sometimes worn with an Indian patchwork shirt and kerchiefs. The Cow Creek women, too, wore cheaper, less elaborately made clothing than their Mikasuki counterparts, perhaps owing to the fact that they did more field labor and the garments took greater abuse than those worn primarily around camp. The abandonment of traditional dress was the most tangible evidence of acculturation among the Seminole depression babies, in that it signaled a psychological validation of other non-Indian modes of behavior as well.

Those Seminoles who opted for reservation life were also the ones most inclined to accept wage-labor employment. For the most part they were families who had been living at the edge of subsistence; they came from marginal ecological regions where the hunting and trapping had played out, and they had no title to the land where they camped and raised meager crops. They were forced therefore to engage in seasonal agricultural labor on farms, ranches, and groves whenever jobs were available. Interestingly, the Indian women tended to make this adaptation earlier and easier than did the men. With the opening of the Dania Reservation in 1926, the local Indian males had their first opportunity for government-subsidized employment, the job of clearing the land. Thus the way was paved for wider tribal participation when programs of the Civil Works Administration (the only project which employed Seminole women) and Indian Emergency Conservation Work were initiated there in 1933. These programs were their first experience with government-guaranteed work at an established rate of pay—which also introduced the expectations of good work habits and reasonable job performance. The Seminoles who adapted to this routine, especially a few who learned to operate heavy equipment such as tractors and road graders, were well on their way to economic assimilation. Others viewed the CCC-ID work only as a stopgap, to tide them over between hunting seasons or give them the means to buy another bottle; they willingly accepted a scaled-back work week and wages of $1.50 a day plus subsistence, and they showed up irregularly. When the CCC-ID placed enrollees on a flat $30 a month for a five-day week,[5] it demanded more regularity in the workplace. As economic conditions continued to degenerate in the late 1930s and the Seminoles became increasingly dependent on the CCC-ID as their sole source of income, there was a greater willingness to conform to this regimen. One hallmark of these progressive Seminole depression babies, then, was their acceptance of distinctly non-Indian, work-related norms such as punctuality, initiative, and reliability, all requirements for retaining steady employment.

Although the bulk of Seminole employment fell into the category of unskilled labor, a few individuals did learn to handle sophisticated equipment, and all received a modest amount of on-the-job instruction from the supervisors. However, it was not until the Indians began to enter the cattle business that there was direct and sustained instruction in skills that would pay future dividends. In this respect the importance of agricultural extension agent Fred Montsdeoca's contribution cannot be overstated. The Seminoles who became cattle owners formed the nucleus of an economic and political elite that received special treatment within the tribe for almost twenty years. The necessity of organizing the cattle program was also one factor moving Seminoles toward elected representative government. When the Brighton people were to select trustees to sign the cattle agreement in 1939, the Indian Office assumed that the Seminoles would elect their leaders; however, selection is not synonymous with election in a consensual Indian society. Although they were instructed on how an election should be conducted, things did not go smoothly; the women voted for everyone (perhaps to avoid friction rather than because they were confused), and one trustee was chosen who formerly had nothing to do with the cattle. There were conflicting claims that the man was elected because he owned a horse, or because the Indians realized that Montsdeoca actually ran the program and did not take the election seriously. Another possibility, however, is that the individual was a consensual leader in the Brighton community. It would take many more years before the Seminoles were ready to totally adopt the whites' process of electing their leadership. Even then, according to R. T. King, the old clan affiliations played an important role in determining who was chosen.[6] Whether that thesis is correct or merely coincidental, it is certain that during the late 1930s and early 1940s the Seminoles were exposed to an increasing number of situations that called for the exercise of democratic procedures in electing trustees and other leaders; thus they became better prepared to adopt the balloting process required when the tribe organized formally at a later date.

Closely related to the trend toward democratic process was a growing interaction with non-Indians during this period. By the 1930s there was a subtle shift in the Indians' willingness to accept assistance and direction from the Seminole agent on such matters as medical assistance, welfare, and CCC-ID employment. While there still remained a great deal of hostility toward the government among the traditionalists, reservation residents increasingly dealt with superintendents, teachers, and other government employees on a daily basis. In interviews with Seminole elders, although the informants were few in number, there were no decidedly negative comments concerning the representatives of the Office of Indian Affairs. This fact cannot be attributed solely to Indian informants' telling historians what they want to hear, since the interviews were conducted in the Indian languages and largely gathered by native speakers. On the contrary, the tendency was for them to recall the agents from Spencer to Gardin as people who had done the best they could to help the Seminole people with the limited resources at their command. The accounts were sprinkled with anecdotes illustrating a good deal of personal interaction on a day-to-day basis between the agents and their charges. Conversely, the agents developed a greater appreciation of the Indians as individuals—though not always condoning their diet, hygiene, or frequent inebriation—and were willing to work with them, as opposed to bossing them on the reservation projects. Certainly the inclusion of Stanley Hanson among the government cadre was a positive move in cementing such relationships, as he had already developed close ties with many Florida Indians. Through this interaction, government functionaries would come to exert great influence in determining the Seminole political consensus.

Away from the reservations, Seminole interaction with non-Indians generally increased during the 1930s and 1940s as they worked on farms and ranches, resided in tourist vilalges or took war-related jobs. The pioneering effort of Mrs. Frank Stranahan was formalized in the Friends of the Seminoles organization at Fort Lauderdale, which became a permanent support group dedicated to improving Seminole living conditions and educational opportunities. Deaconess Harriet Bedell, the Episcopal missionary, who operated her little Glades Cross station near the Tamiami Trail, organized the handicraft industry and greatly improved the income of the Mikasuki-Seminoles in that region. Other individuals such as W. D. Roberts in Immokalee, Albert Devane of Sebring, and Robert Mitchell of Orlando were among the most outspoken advocates of Seminole interests.

The acceptance of Christianity was not just a matter affecting personal salvation; it also had a major influence on tribal politics. The establishment of a Baptist church at Dania Reservation in 1936 was symbolically important, but it directly involved only a small number of old people and children; however, when a number of the Reservation Mikasukis followed the lead of the former medicine man Josie Billie and converted en masse in 1945, their act opened the way for a new type of leadership to emerge which was at variance with traditional Seminole values. Among the Seminoles the cultural norm was passive, nonconfrontational behavior; one did not like to be told what to do and did not presume to tell others what to do. Decisions affecting the entire group were arrived at by consensus after lengthy discussion among spokesmen whose judgment was prized. This pattern was interrupted when a few Indian converts were sent for training at a Baptist-run Bible college in Lakeland, Florida. These Indian lay ministers returned to work among the Seminole people and began to advise their flock on political as well as personal and religious matters, thereby legitimizing the behavior pattern of telling people what to do without reaping the social ostracism of being called a "big shot." Ultimately the Baptist churchmen challenged and surpassed the medicine men and busk councils for political leadership; thus there emerged a new type of social and political consensus based on church membership. By the late 1940s there were Baptist congregations on the Dania and Big Cypress reservations, and the Indian lay ministers became the first elected leaders of the Seminoles' unique organizational structure. The Florida tribe was the only group taking advantage of the Indian Reorganization Act which opted for a tribal council separate from its corporate board of directors.[7] All three of these elements—the growth of the cattle industry, increased influence of government employees and other non-Indians, and the rise of lay ministers as a political force—would combine to make the Seminole depression babies more receptive to the democratic political process and an elected leadership.

It would appear to be overstating the case to claim that an educational elite emerged during the New Deal era, especially since the day school at Dania was closed in 1936 and the Brighton people did not open their school until two years later. Nevertheless, that is exactly what happened— only on a delayed basis. The Seminole youngsters who were sent away to the Cherokee Indian School in North Carolina came from families that had, for a variety of reasons, accepted the idea of having their children educated to compete in the white world away from the reservation. They could foresee a time when Indian youngsters would need to read and write to survive as individuals and to lead their people. This small group of youngsters would be promoted by the Indian Office as representing the future of the tribe. After returning from Cherokee they served as interpreters for tribal leaders in various negotiations, appeared before numerous congressional committees, and generally served as government-approved role models. After the Seminole Tribe was formally organized, many of them assumed leadership positions; one of the first high school graduates, Betty Mae Jumper (née Tiger), later became the first—and so far, the only—woman elected to lead the tribal council.[8] During her term the tribe took great strides toward improving reservation schools as well as encouraging attendance in public schools. So there is evidence that a limited number of young depression babies, at least those who became leaders, were imbued with the idea that schooling was both practical and necessary.

A cadre of informal leaders emerged during the 1930s who embodied most of these traits and thereby became prototypical Seminole depression babies. One such individual was the Muskogee-speaking Sam Tommie, who spearheaded the effort to set aside a reservation. Although he had little formal education, he spoke passable English and came from the family of Annie Tommie which was influential in the affairs at the Dania Reservation. She was a Muskogee-speaker who had married Doctor Tommie, a Mikasuki, and lived at the Pine Island settlement. Her children were raised speaking both languages, so it was easy for her son Sam to marry a Cow Creek woman and be accepted into that band. Sam enjoyed no ascribed leadership status among the Cow Creeks, but, like his brother Tony B. M. Tommie, he aspired to be recognized as a spokesman for his people.[9] Unfortunately, Sam was not politically sophisticated and therefore was occasionally used by newsmen and others interested in debunking the work of the Seminole agents. Soon, though, he learned that more could be accomplished by appealing directly to Commissioner Collier than working with Glenn. Although he never achieved the prominence that he sought, Sam Tommie can certainly be counted among the progressive Seminoles of this era. The same was true of men such as John Josh, Charley Micco, and Willie Gopher, the first cattle trustees, who were placed in the awkward position of directly opposing the medicine men and busk council over accepting federal assistance funds. Among those Mikasukis who moved to Big Cypress Reservation, the former medicine man Josie Billie made perhaps the most dramatic transition from cultural traditionalist to progressive Christian leader involved in agitating for a cattle program.

Seminole women were the major conservators of traditional Indian life-style, so they never moved to the forefront in political and religious change—though they were always consulted for approval before major decisions were made. Theirs was the role of preserving and perpetuating traditions of language, dress, and kinship that marked the boundaries of their social system. Having said that, one can immediately think of dominant female personalities such as Annie Tommie, a respected medicine woman and mother of six prominent sons, who broke with tradition and moved her camp to government land on the Dania Reservation. There was also Ada Tiger who defied the Cow Creek headmen, brought her family from Indiantown, and enrolled her children Betty Mae and Howard in the Dania day school; she encouraged them to attend the Cherokee Indian School until graduation and lived to see her daughter elected to the highest office in the tribe. The families of these two women produced strong leaders for the Seminole Tribe of Florida through its early years of organization. Susie Jim Billie learned healing and spiritual medicine from her parents and brother, Buffalo Jim, a Mikasuki medicine man.[10] She represented one of the last significant links with old ways among the Big Cypress Reservation people and served as a constant reminder of how important it is that the spiritual fires of a people not be allowed to go out.

Throughout the thirties the spiritual fire of the Seminole people was never in danger of being extinguished. It always blazed brightly in the secluded and reclusive Mikasuki camps. It flickered intermittently through the difficult years of transformation when the Indian people were learning to adapt to reservation life, make significant changes in occupation, and experiment with representative government and undergoing a sweeping and profound religious conversion. If some isolated and fragmented groups of Seminoles were in danger of being absorbed into that army of displaced persons spun off by the Great Depression, the opening of the Brighton and Big Cypress reservations and baiting them with Indian New Deal programs reversed the process; the people were brought together again and the flame rekindled. Moreover, they were spared most of the wrenching social and political upheavals that the Indian Reorganization Act and other New Deal programs had wrought among the larger tribes such as the Navajos and Iroquois.

In their safe enclaves the Seminoles began the process of tribal ethnogenesis; the new skills and attitudes embraced by the Seminole depression babies melded easily with existing values and social structures of family camp, clan, and kinship. The slow spread of Christianity was not unduly disruptive and could be integrated into the Seminole cultural pattern; for while the Protestant emphasis on individual salvation and economic success was at variance with traditional Indian communitarianism, it also strengthened the new economic and political structures that were evolving. The resulting amalgam made the Seminoles a stronger and more resilient people, both psychologically and socially better able to withstand the next great threat to their tribal existence that arose in the 1950s when the federal government instituted its termination policy.

Transcending all else was the Seminoles' sense of self, an awareness of belonging to a unique group whose cosmology began beyond the memory of the oldest wise ones. Their belief system was still firmly rooted in the land, in natural phenomena, and in the spirit world. Their time orientation, sense of fatalism, and code of appropriate behavior were generally at variance with the conventions of white society. Thus, there existed an inherent cultural chasm that could never be totally bridged. Indians might take on the material trappings of the white society that had engulfed their land, practice scientific herding and marketing techniques, attend school, and even revise the way they governed themselves, but beneath it all they remained fundamentally Indian. Even the infusion of Christianity initially took place within a context that was essentially Indian, not like the Native American Church, which was a distinct religion, but in much the same manner that Mayan and Catholic beliefs were blended in the Mesoamerican church.

From this point onward the Seminoles would constantly be seeking to achieve and maintain both personal and societal stasis—an equilibrium that would allow them to survive the overwhelming changes of the late

Annie Tommie and her son, Tony Tommie (courtesy Fort Lauderdale Historical Society)

twentieth century. With greater mobility Florida Indians were inevitably drawn into prolonged contact with the dominant culture, and it became increasingly difficult to practice the old folkways or retain traditional values. Intrapersonal conflict increased, and the classic "caught-between-cultures" syndrome emerged to plague successive generations. Ultimately each Seminole would have to find the camp, light the fire, and sing the song—and be Indian in his or her own way.

Notes

Introduction

1. Florida, Department of State, Division of Cultural Affairs, "Four Corners of Earth," a thirty-minute videotape on Seminole women.

Chapter 1

1. Harry A. Kersey, Jr., *Pelts, Plumes, and Hides: White Traders among the Seminole Indians, 1870–1930.*

2. Alfred J. Hanna and Kathryn A. Hanna, *Lake Okeechobee*, 340. See also 31 *Stat.* 187 (1900).

3. U.S. Congress, Senate, *Indian Affairs, Laws and Treaties*, 678–79.

4. James O. Buswell, Review of *Pelts, Plumes, and Hides*, 192–93.

5. U.S. Congress, Senate, *Seminole Indians in Florida*, 5.

6. *Fort Myers Daily Press*, September 22, 1914.

7. U.S. Congress, Senate, *Special Report of the Florida Seminole Agency*, 5.

8. U.S. Congress, Senate, Subcommittee of the Committee on Indian Affairs, *Survey of Conditions of the Indians in the United States*, 7614–15.

9. Interview with Frank Cypress.

10. Interview with Abraham Clay.

11. Interview with Susie Billie.

12. Interview with Jimmie Cypress.

13. Tony B. M. Tommie to C. J. Rhoads, February 5, 21, 1930. File 7453-1930-Seminole-154, Records of the Bureau of Indian Affairs, National Archives, Central Classified Files, cited hereafter as BIACF.

14. *Special Report of the Florida Seminole Agency*, 3.

15. *Annual Report, Seminole Agency, 1926*, 1–2, Records of the Bureau of Indian Affairs, National Archives, Narrative Reports, Seminole, 1926, cited hereafter as NR.

16. William C. Sturtevant, "A Seminole Personal Document," 58.

17. Patsy West, "Seminoles in Broward County: The Pine Island Legacy," 10.

18. Numerous authors have written about Mrs. Stranahan's work among the Seminoles. The most detailed are August Burghard, *Watchie-Esta/Hutrie (Little White Mother), The Remarkable Story of Mrs. Frank Stranahan, Broward County's First School Teacher;* Harry A. Kersey, Jr. and Rochelle Kushin, "Ivy Stranahan and the 'Friends of the Seminoles,' 1899–1971"; Alan K. Craig and David McJunkin, "Stranahan's: Last of the Seminole Trading Posts."

19. A summary of Mrs. Stranahan's work as the Indian welfare chairman for the Florida Federation of Women's Clubs may be found in Senate, *Survey of Conditions of Indians in the United States,* 7603–14.

20. *Annual Report, Seminole Agency, 1927,* 1, NR.

21. *Fort Myers Times,* October 5, 1926.

22. *Annual Report, Seminole Agency, 1927,* 2.

23. *Annual Report, Seminole Agency, 1929,* 14, NR.

24. *Annual Report, Seminole Agency, 1930,* 6, NR.

25. Senate, *Survey of Conditions of the Indians in the United States,* 7618.

26. *Annual Report, Seminole Agency, 1927,* 7.

27. Ibid., 8.

28. *Annual Report, Seminole Agency, 1929,* 10.

29. The Florida Seminoles had no direct impact from the General Allotment Act. For a discussion of this federal program see Wilcomb E. Washburn, *The Assault on Indian Tribalism: The General Allotment Law (Dawes Act) of 1887.*

30. U.S., *Statutes at Large,* 43:253.

31. Brookings Institution, Institute for Government Research, *The Problem of Indian Administration.*

32. Kenneth R. Philp, *John Collier's Crusade for Indian Reform, 1920–1954,* 92–95.

33. John Collier, *From Every Zenith,* 148.

34. Roy Nash, *Survey of the Seminole Indians of Florida.*

35. Charles Curtis to C. J. Rhoads, August 8, 1930, file 41982-1930-Seminole-155, BIACF.

36. C. J. Rhoads to Charles Curtis, August 27, 1930, ibid.

37. C. J. Rhoads to Duncan U. Fletcher, January 2, 1931, file 46579-1930-Seminole-150, BIACF.

38. Nash, *Survey,* 35, 41.

39. Ibid., 83; interview with Frank Cypress.

40. Nash, *Survey,* 76.

41. Vine Deloria, Jr. and Clifford Lytle, *The Nations Within: The Past and Future of American Indian Sovereignty,* 46.

42. Senate, *Survey of Conditions of the Indians in the United States,* 7603–58.

43. Ibid., 7613, 7637, 7638, 7639.

44. Ibid., 7618, 7619.

45. Philp, *John Collier's Crusade,* 96.

46. William C. Sturtevant, "The Medicine Bundles and Busks of the Florida Seminole."

Chapter 2

1. Barron Collier to Charles H. Burke, February 28, 1929, file 11408-1929-Seminole-150, BIACF.

2. James Lafayette Glenn, *My Work among the Florida Seminoles,* 33.

3. Ibid., 74–75.

4. Roy Nash to C. J. Rhoads, December 5, 1930, file 63866-1930-Seminole-162, BIACF.

5. James L. Glenn, "The Saga of the Florida Indians," 331. In 1932 Glenn nearly lost his position but, with the strong backing of Mrs. Stranahan, was retained with the title of financial clerk. See B. J. Gardner to Mrs. Frank Stranahan, August 24, 1932, and James L. Glenn to Mrs. Frank Stranahan, September 6, 1932, box 8, file 1-Indian Federal Agencies 1915–1951, Stranahan Collection, FLHS.

6. Glenn, *My Work,* 11, 14.

7. Ibid., 15–16.

8. Senate, *Survey of Conditions of the Indians in the United States,* 7637.

9. *Annual Report, Seminole Agency, 1932,* 11, NR.

10. *Annual Report, Seminole Agency, 1933,* 10, NR.

11. First Seminole Indian Baptist Church, "Souvenir Brochure, Dedicatory Service . . . May 29, 1949," 3, copy in files of the author.

12. James O. Buswell III, "Florida Seminole Religious Ritual: Resistance and Change," 261–62.

13. Betty Mae Jumper, "'. . . and with the Wagon came God's Word'," 14.

14. Buswell, "Florida Seminole Religious Ritual," 263.

15. Edward Earl Joiner, *A History of Florida Baptists,* 154–55.

16. Glenn, *My Work,* 38–39.

17. Joiner, *Florida Baptists,* 155; Buswell, "Florida Seminole Religious Ritual," 264.

18. *Annual Report, Seminole Agency, 1929,* 4, NR.

19. Interview with Betty Mae Jumper, January 2, 1985.

20. *Annual Report, Seminole Agency, 1933,* 2.

21. Interviews with Albert Billie and Frank Cypress.

22. *Annual Report, Seminole Agency, 1929,* 15–16.

23. Nash, *Survey of the Seminole Indians of Florida,* 38–39.

24. Glenn, *My Work,* 20.

25. Interviews with Susie Billie, Abraham Clay, and Willie Tiger.

26. Interview with Albert Billie.

27. Nash, *Survey,* 21–22.

28. Ibid., 36; interviews with Frank Cypress and Willie Frank.

29. Patsy West, "The Miami Indian Tourist Attractions: A History and Analysis of a Transitional Mikasuki Seminole Environment."

30. Senate, *Survey of the Conditions of the Indians in the United States,* 7622.

31. West, "Miami Indian Tourist Attractions," 204.

32. *Miami Daily News,* June 5, 1926; Glenn, *My Work,* 102. For biographic sketches of Tony Tommie see Bill McGoun, *A Biographic History of Broward County,* 47–49, and Harry A. Kersey, Jr., "The Tony Tommie Letter, 1916: A Transitional Seminole Document."

33. *Annual Report, Seminole Agency, 1935,* 4, NR.

34. West, "Miami Indian Tourist Attractions," 219–20.

35. Interviews with Albert Billie and Buffalo Tiger.

36. *Annual Report, Seminole Agency, 1935,* 4.

37. West, "Miami Indian Tourist Attractions," 203.

38. Ruth Bryan Owen to C. J. Rhoads, September 22, 1930. Subsequently, the first assistant secretary of the Department of the Interior requested an investigation of the Willie Willie affair by the Department of Justice: see Jos. M. Dixon to Attorney General, November 11, 1930, file 46600-1930-Seminole-155, BIACF.

39. U.S. Department of Justice, Bureau of Investigation, *Jax File 70-22, January 23, 1931,* 2. A copy of this report by the FBI special agent who had investigated Lasher's business affairs was included with a letter from the attorney general to C. J. Rhoads, February 2, 1931, file 46600-1930- Seminole-155, BIACF.

40. *Annual Report, Seminole Agency, 1932,* 4; Glenn, *My Work,* 100.

41. *Annual Report, Seminole Agency, 1933,* 9.

42. Photographs of Indian-operated tourist camps during this period are found in Glenn, *My Work,* 107; Charlton W. Tebeau, *Florida's Last Frontier: The History of Collier County,* 67; Frances Densmore, *Seminole Music,* 225, pl. 9.

43. *Annual Report, Seminole Agency, 1933,* 11.

44. Interview with Betty Mae Jumper, January 2, 1985.

45. *Annual Report, Seminole Agency, 1933,* 9.

46. James L. Glenn to John Collier, June 2, 1933, file 24298-1933-Seminole-433, part I, Records of the Bureau of Indian Affairs, Civilian Conservation Corps–Indian Division, cited hereafter as CCC-ID; John Collier to James L. Glenn, June 10, 1933, ibid.; James L. Glenn to John Collier, October 25, 1933, ibid.

Chapter 3

1. Harold L. Ickes, *The Autobiography of a Curmudgeon*, 265, 266.

2. Floyd A. O'Neil, "The Indian New Deal: An Overview," 34.

3. Philp, *John Collier's Crusade for Indian Reform*, 117.

4. Calvin W. Gower, "The CCC Indian Division: Aid for Depressed Americans, 1933–1942," 3; William E. Leuchtenburg, *Franklin D. Roosevelt and the New Deal, 1932–1940*, 41–62.

5. *Annual Report, Seminole Agency, 1934*, 3, NR. See also John Collier to James L. Glenn, November 23, 1933, file-24291-1933-Seminole-162, BIACF.

6. Ibid., 4.

7. Ibid.

8. Ibid., 2

9. Ibid., 4. This work was specifically authorized in John Collier to James L. Glenn, January 18, 20, 23, 1934, file 24298-1933-Seminole-344, part I, CCC-ID.

10. Glenn, *My Work*, 18.

11. Ibid., 16.

12. D. E. Murphy, "Final Report of the Indian Emergency Conservation Work and Civilian Conservation Corps–Indian Division Program, 1933–1942," typescript, CCC-ID.

13. *Annual Report, Seminole Agency, 1934*, 12.

14. Murphy, "Final Report," 24.

15. *Annual Report, Seminole Agency, 1934*, 5.

16. Interviews with Albert Billie, Jimmie Cypress, Willie Tiger, and Abraham Clay.

17. Mrs. Frank Stranahan to A. C. Monahan, June 4, 1934, file-24298-1933-Seminole-344, part I, CCC-ID.

18. *Annual Report, Seminole Agency, 1934*, 5–6.

19. Ibid., 12.

20. Mrs. Frank Stranahan to John Collier, May 1, 1934, file-24298-1933-Seminole-344, part I, CCC-ID.

21. Mrs. Frank Stranahan to Duncan U. Fletcher, May 1, 1934, ibid.

22. A. C. Monahan to Mrs. Frank Stranahan, May 5. 1934, and telegram, John Collier to Mrs. Frank Stranahan, May 5, 1934, ibid.

23. Harry A. Kersey, Jr., "Private Societies and the Maintenance of Seminole Tribal Integrity, 1899–1957," 312–14.

24. Roy Nash to C. J. Rhoads, December 5, 1930, file-63866-1930-Seminole-162, BIACF; Glenn, *My Work,* 56–57, 58.

25. Mrs. Frank Stranahan to John Collier, March 23, 1935, Records of the Bureau of Indian Affairs, box 17, entry 178, Office File of Commissioner John Collier, 1935–45, cited hereafter as COF; see also John Collier Papers, Yale University Library, cited hereafter as Collier Papers.

26. *St. Petersburg Daily News,* February 15, 1927.

27. Cecil R. Warren, "Florida's Seminoles: An Eye-Witness Story of Indian Want and Privation as Published by the *Miami Daily News* with affidavits and accompanying documents." Further references to this source appear in parentheses in the text following quotations.

28. The text of Hanson's report is found in Senate, *Survey of Conditions of the Indians in the United States,* 7654–58.

29. Allen H. Andrews, *A Yank Pioneer in Florida,* especially chap. 37.

30. Glenn, *My Work,* 54.

31. Willie Jumper, Sam Tommie, and Jim Gopher to John Collier, April 19, 1934, and John Collier to Jim Gopher, May 7, 1934, file-12596-1936-Seminole-120, BIACF.

32. Collier to Glenn, May 16, 1934, ibid.

33. Glenn to Collier, November 4, 1934, Collier to Glenn, November 14, 1934, ibid.

34. Glenn to Collier, December 4, 1934, Collier to Glenn, December 12, 1934, ibid.

35. Glenn to Collier, December 15, 1934, Collier to Glenn, December 19, 1934, ibid.

36. Glenn to Collier, March 35, 1935, and Collier to Glenn, April 15, 1935, ibid.

Chapter 4

1. Deloria and Lytle, *The Nations Within,* 136–39.

2. John Collier, "The Red Atlantis," 17–18.

3. Rupert Costo, "Federal Indian Policy, 1933–1945," 48.

4. Deloria and Lytle, *The Nations Within,* 172.

5. John Collier to James L. Glenn, December 24, 1934, file-9735-1936-Seminole-066, BIACF.

6. James L. Glenn to John Collier, December 28, 1934, ibid.

7. J. Mark Wilcox to John Collier, January 3, 1934, file-694-1934-Seminole-150, BIACF.

8. A. C. Monahan to John Collier, January 29, 1934, ibid.

9. Glenn, *My Work,* 32–33.

10. Interview with James L. Glenn.

11. Interview with Glenn.

12. A. C. Monahan to James L. Glenn, March 1, 1935, COF.

13. James L. Glenn to A. C. Monahan, March 2, 1935, ibid.

14. Glenn, "The Florida Seminoles," 282.

15. *New York Times,* March 17, 1935.

16. John Collier to Harold L. Ickes, March 13, 1935, included as Exhibit 8, Indian Law Resource Center, "Report to Congress: Seminole Land Rights in Florida and the Award of the Indian Claims Commission." See also Senate, Select Committee on Indian Affairs, *Distribution of Seminole Judgment Funds,* 147. This memorandum was prepared in response to Ickes's request for advice concerning disposition of a document titled "Petition for Peace Treaty," which a group of Seminole Indians in Florida had addressed to President Roosevelt. It remains unclear who originated the idea for this treaty petition and who drafted it. After specifying particular remedies sought, it ended with the plea, "NOW, THEREFORE, we, the Seminole Indians of Florida on the one hundredth anniversary of the war between our fathers and the Great Government of the United States of America, do hereby petition the United States of America for a treaty of peace and beg that our people be given reparation for the losses that they have sustained." Collier saw no reason why the petition should not be passed on to Roosevelt but noted that by an act of Congress approved March 13, 1871, no Indian nation or tribe could be acknowledged as an independent unit with whom the United States could contract a treaty and that the Indians were now citizens of the United States. Furthermore, he held that the land they were seeking was deemed unsuitable for their use.

17. Petition to Honorable Harold L. Ickes, secretary of the interior, March 20, 1935, box 17, entry 178, COF.

18. James L. Glenn to A. C. Monahan, March 2, 1935, ibid.

19. *Palm Beach Post* and *Fort Lauderdale News,* March 21, 1935.

20. Ibid.

21. Department of the Interior Memorandum for the Press, for release in afternoon papers of Tuesday, April 2, 1935, box 17, entry 178, COF.

22. Ibid.

23. John Collier, "With Secretary Ickes and the Seminoles," 3–4.

24. Ibid., 5.

25. James L. Glenn to John Collier, March 30, 1935, file-9735-1936-Seminole-066, BIACF.

26. James L. Glenn to F. H. Daiker, April 4, 1935, ibid.

27. John Collier to James L. Glenn, April 9, 1935, ibid.

28. William Zimmerman, Jr. to Francis J. Scott, April 22, 1936, ibid.

29. Glenn to Daiker, April 4, 1935, ibid.

30. 48 *Stat.* 987 (1934).

31. W. Stanley Hanson to John Collier, March 21, 1935, box 17, entry 178, COF.

32. O. B. White to J. Mark Wilcox, March 13, 1935, ibid.

33. Harold L. Ickes to O. B. White, March 26, 1935, ibid.

34. John Collier to W. Stanley Hanson, March 26, 1935, ibid.

35. Ibid.

36. Mrs. Frank Stranahan to John Collier, March 23, 1935, ibid.; Louis Capron to John Collier, April 4, 1935, ibid. The position of Ickes and Collier also received strong editorial support in the *Palm Beach Post,* April 5, 1935, file-6975-1934- Seminole-150, BIACF.

37. Harriet Bedell to John Collier, April 12, 1935, Collier Papers.

38. Agnes Fitzgerald to John Collier, April 30, 1935, file-6975-1934-Seminole-150, BIACF.

39. 48 *Stat.* 816 (1934).

40. James W. Covington, "Brighton Reservation, Florida, 1935–1943."

41. Chapter 285.06, *Fla. Stats.* 1985.

42. William C. Sturtevant, "Creek into Seminole," 117–23.

43. John Collier, *From Every Zenith,* 213.

Chapter 5

1. *Palm Beach Post,* March 21, 1935.

2. Sturtevant, "Creek into Seminole," 102–5. See also Kenneth W. Porter, "The Cowkeeper Dynasty of the Seminole Nation."

3. Chapter 285.01, *Fla. Stats.* 1985.

4. Nash, *Survey,* 87–88.

5. *Annual Report, Seminole Agency, 1935,* 6, NR.

6. 48 *Stat.* 816 (1934).

7. Glenn, *My Work,* 6. The boundaries of the Indian Prairie Region are described in South Florida Water Management District, "Water Shortage Plan," fig. 21–8.

8. Paul E. Mertz, *New Deal Policy and Southern Rural Poverty,* 124–26, 162–64.

9. *Annual Report, Seminole Agency, 1935,* 7.

10. E. F. Stumpf to Harold L. Ickes, October 11, 1935. file-24921-1935-Seminole-343, and August Burghard to William Zimmerman, Jr., March 28, 1936, file-6975-1935-Seminole-150, BIACF.

11. James W. Covington, "Trail Indians of Florida," 40–42.

12. Gene Stirling, *Report on the Seminole Indians of Florida*, 2–4.

13. Glenn, *My Work*, 60; interview with Sam Tommie.

14. *Annual Report, Seminole Agency, 1935*, 12.

15. 49 *Stat.* 339 (1935).

16. Chapter 285.04, *Fla. Stats.* 1985.

17. Florida, Trustees Internal Improvement Fund, *Minutes of the Trustees of the Internal Improvement Fund*, 240, 260.

18. Francis J. Scott to John Collier, February 19, 1938, cited in Covington, "Brighton Reservation, Florida," 59. These figures are also found in E. J. Utz to Paul L. Fickinger, September 7, 1955, Land Office Files, Seminole Agency, Hollywood, Florida.

19. "Executive Order 7868," Code of Federal Regulations, April 15, 1938, 3 CFR 395.

20. 70 *Stat.* 581 (1956).

21. Utz to Fickinger, September 7, 1955.

22. *Minutes of Internal Improvement Fund*, 259–63.

23. Chapter 285.06, *Fla. Stats.* 1985.

24. Chapter 285.061, *Fla. Stats.* 1985.

25. 96 *Stat.* 2012 (1982); 101 *Stat.* 1558 (1987).

26. C. R. Roseberry, *Glenn Curtiss: Pioneer of Flight*, 425–26; Barbara B. Darsey, "Brighton Seminole Indian Reservation," typescript, 1939, 1–3, Florida Historical Society, WPA File.

27. Darsey, "Brighton Seminole Reservation," 4; Covington, "Brighton Reservation," 59–60.

28. Glenn, *My Work*, xii; John Collier to Francis J. Scott, January 20, 1936, file-24298-1933-Seminole-344, part I, CCC-ID.

29. Covington, "Brighton Reservation," 60. For a general overview of Seminole economic development see George H. Dacy, *Report on the Seminole Indians of Florida for the National Resources Planning Board*, Department of the Interior, Seminole Agency.

30. *Annual Report, Seminole Agency, 1933*, 10, NR; Glenn, *My Work*, 30.

31. James L. Glenn to John Collier, December 4, 1934, file-24298-1933-Seminole-344, Part I, CCC-ID; Glenn, *My Work*, 30.

32. *Annual Report, Seminole Agency, 1935*, 14.

33. Darsey, "Brighton Seminole Reservation," 1.

34. Merwyn S. Garbarino, *Big Cypress, A Changing Seminole Community*, 106.

35. Ibid., 109; on Montsdeoca, see *Tampa Tribune*, December 15, 1974.

36. "Seminoles Participate in Florida State Fair."

37. R. S. Bristol to William Zimmerman, Jr., August 16, 1939, file-77671-1939-Seminole-155, BIACF.

38. R. T. King, "Clan Affiliation and Leadership among the Twentieth-Century Florida Indians," 146. See also interview with Fred Montsdeoca.

39. "Trust Agreement to Reimburse for Cattle" (copy included in Bristol to Zimmerman, August 16, 1939), 4, 3.

40. Covington, "Brighton Reservation," 61–63.

41. Seminole Agency, Florida, *Conservation Working Plan Report F. Y. 1940* (July 1, 1939–June 30, 1940), file-24298-1933-Seminole-344, part III, CCC-ID.

42. Francis J. Scott to John Collier, Attn: D. E. Murphy and Fred H. Daiker, November 12, 1937, file-24298-1933-Seminole-344, Part II, CCC-ID.

43. Francis J. Scott to William Zimmerman, Jr., May 28, 1938, ibid.

44. Unsigned report titled "The Brighton Reservation," typescript, 1939, WPA File. Sources cited are *Miami Daily News,* October 16, 1938; Associated Press Report, November 16, 1938.

45. *Constitution of the Seminole Crafts Guild of Glades County, August 10, 1940,* enclosure in William D. Boehmer to Carita Doggett Corse, November 20, 1940, WPA File.

46. "Florida Seminole CCC Sponsors Community Celebration." Fechner's visit is reported in Jerrell H. Shofner, "Roosevelt's 'Tree Army': The Civilian Conservation Corps in Florida," 446.

47. Buswell, "Florida Seminole Religious Ritual: Resistance and Change," 267.

48. Alexander Spoehr to John Collier, August 22, 1939, file-63866-1939-Seminole-162, BIACF.

49. John Collier to Alexander Spoehr, September 27, 1939, ibid.

50. John Collier, "Office of Indian Affairs," in U.S. Department of the Interior, *Annual Report of the Secretary of the Interior for the Fiscal Year Ending June 30, 1939,* 34.

51. Deloria and Lytle, *The Nations Within,* 165.

52. Memorandum, "Indian Organization," March 4, 1941, file 9735-1936-Seminole-066, BIACF.

53. Dwight R. Gardin to John Collier, June 24, 1941, file 76081-1941-Seminole-066, Indian Rehabilitation.

54. Dwight R. Gardin to Xavier Vigeant, April 11, 1940, ibid.

55. William Zimmerman, Jr. to Dwight R. Gardin, April 11, 1941, ibid.

Chapter 6

1. Indian Law Resource Center, "Report to Congress: Seminole Land Rights in Florida and the Award of the Indian Claims Commission"; Senate, Select Committee on Indian Affairs, *Distribution of Seminole Judgment Funds,* 85.

2. *Florida Times-Union,* February 23, 1937.

3. David Sholtz to Harold L. Ickes, February 26, 1936, "Report to Congress" and *Distribution of Seminole Judgment Funds,* 194–95.

4. Harold L. Ickes to David Sholtz, March 20, 1936, ibid., 196–97.

5. Francis J. Scott to John Collier, April 4, 1936, ibid., 200.

6. Ernest F. Coe to David Sholtz, February 28, 1936, Sholtz to Coe, April 14, 1936, ibid., 193, 201.

7. Francis J. Scott to John Collier, March 25, 1937, file-87314-1936-Seminole-155, BIACF.

8. Francis J. Scott to John Collier, Attention: D. E. Murphy and Fred H. Daiker, November 12, 1937, file-24298-1933-Seminole-344, Part II, CCC-ID.

9. Ibid.

10. Ethel Cutler Freeman, "We Live with the Seminoles," 228.

11. Robert Greenlee, "Aspects of Social Organization and Material Culture of the Seminole of the Big Cypress Swamp"; Greenlee, "Folktales of the Florida Seminole"; Greenlee, "Medicine and Curing Practices of the Modern Florida Seminoles"; Alexander Spoehr, "Camp, Clan and Kin among the Cow Creek Seminoles of Florida"; Spoehr, "The Florida Seminole Camp"; Louis Capron, "The Medicine Bundles of the Florida Seminole and the Green Corn Dance"; Capron, "Notes on the Hunting Dance of the Cow Creek Seminoles."

12. Sturtevant, "Creek into Seminole," 112.

13. Because few investigators possessed a working knowledge of the Seminole languages and the quality of informants was uneven, there was much misunderstanding of Seminole culture. Thus it should be noted that Greenlee's identification of distinct Tiger and Panther clans is suspect. Sturtevant has pointed out that in the Mikasuki language the term for Tiger, Puma, or Panther is synonymous. Sturtevant, "The Medicine Bundles and Busks of the Florida Seminole," 66.

14. Garbarino, *Big Cypress,* 75. At the time of Garbarino's field work among the Mikasukis on Big Cypress during the 1960s a few members of the Bear clan were reportedly still living, although Greenlee had declared that clan to be extinct.

15. Capron, "Medicine Bundles," 162.

16. Ethel Cutler Freeman, "Culture Stability and Change among the Seminoles of Florida," 251.

17. Buswell, "Seminole Religious Ritual," 270–79.

18. Oscar L. Chapman and John Collier to the Seminole Indians of Florida, April 19, 1938, file-24298-1933-Seminole-344, part II, CCC-ID.

19. Francis J. Scott to John Collier, Attention: William Zimmerman and D. E. Murphy, June 30, 1938, ibid.

20. D. E. Murphy to Francis J. Scott, October 20, 1938, ibid.

21. D. E. Murphy to Francis J. Scott, June 13, 1939, and to Dwight R. Gardin, June 12, 1940, ibid.

22. Francis J. Scott to John Collier, Attention: D. E. Murphy, A. C. Cooley, W. W. Beatty, June 16, 1939, ibid.

23. Francis J. Scott to John Collier, et al., July 24, 1939, file-24298-1933-Seminole-344, part III, CCC-ID.

24. Seminole Agency, Florida, *Conservation Working Plan Report, F.Y. 1940* (July 1, 1939–June 30, 1940), ibid.

25. *Annual Report, Seminole Agency, 1918*, 2, NR.

26. John Collier to Kenneth A. Marmon, January 22, 1944, file-9735-1936-Seminole-066, BIACF.

27. Kenneth R. Philp, "Turmoil at Big Cypress: Seminole Deer and the Florida Cattle Tick Controversy."

28. "Secretary Ickes Upholds Seminoles in Opposing Slaughter of Their Deer," 10.

29. Senate, Committee on Indian Affairs, *Eradicating Cattle Tick, Seminole Indian Reservation, Fla., Hearings*, 70.

30. Philp, "Turmoil," 33.

31. *Senate Hearings Cattle Tick,* 71.

32. John Collier, "The Seminoles Move Forward," 2.

33. Philp, "Turmoil," 41.

34. Ibid., 43, 44.

35. John Collier to Kenneth A. Marmon, January 22, 1944, file-9735-1936-Seminole-066, BIACF.

36. John Collier to Kenneth A. Marmon, January 25, 1944, ibid.

37. Kenneth A. Marmon to John Collier, November 25, 1944, ibid.

38. Garbarino, *Big Cypress,* 106.

Chapter 7

1. Margaret Szasz, *Education and the American Indian: The Road to Self-Determination, 1928–1973*, 30.

2. Ibid., 34.

3. *Annual Report, Seminole Agency, 1927*, 8, NR.

4. *Annual Report, Seminole Agency, 1929*, 10, NR.

5. Ibid., 12.

6. Glenn, *My Work,* 32.

7. *Annual Report, Seminole Agency, 1932*, 7, NR.

8. *Annual Report, Seminole Agency, 1934,* 10, NR.

9. Harry A. Kersey, Jr., "Educating the Seminole Indians of Florida, 1879–1970," 28; interview with Betty Mae Jumper, June 17, 1969.

10. James L. Glenn, "The Saga of the Florida Indians," 371, typescript, Glenn Collection.

11. *Annual Report, Seminole Agency, 1934,* 11.

12. *Annual Report, Seminole Agency, 1933,* 8, NR.

13. Glenn, *My Work,* 33.

14. John Collier, "Indian Education," 4.

15. *Annual Report, Seminole Agency, 1932,* 8.

16. *Annual Report, Seminole Agency, 1934,* 11–12.

17. Ibid., 11.

18. W. Carson Ryan, Jr., " A Trip among the Indian Communities of the Southeast," 41.

19. *Annual Report, Seminole Agency, 1932,* 8.

20. F. J. Scott, "Education for the Florida Seminoles," 46.

21. Willard W. Beatty, "Education for the Whole Community," 28.

22. Ibid., 31.

23. Elsie H. Devol, "Activities at the Seminole Day School, Dania, Florida"; "Activities at the Seminole Day School, Florida."

24. Brookings Institution, *The Problem of Indian Administration,* 36.

25. Harry A. Kersey, Jr., "Federal Schools and Acculturation among the Florida Seminoles, 1927–1954," 171–72.

26. Kersey, "Educating the Florida Seminoles," 30.

27. Ethel Cutler Freeman, "Our Unique Indians, the Seminoles of Florida," 22.

28. Kersey and Kushin, "Ivy Stranahan and the 'Friends of the Seminoles'," 9–10.

29. Interviews with Mary Parker Bowers, Betty Mae Jumper, March 22, 1977, and Dorothy Tucker.

30. Sharlotte Neely, "The Quaker Era of Cherokee Indian Education, 1880–1892."

31. Interview with Betty Mae Jumper, 1977.

32. Szasz, *Education and the American Indian,* 65.

33. Interviews with Mary Parker Bowers and Dorothy Tucker.

34. Interview with Mary Parker Bowers.

35. Kersey, "Private Societies and the Maintenance of Seminole Tribal Integrity," 315. Jumper, "' . . . and with the Wagon came God's Word'," 1–20.

36. Glenn, *My Work,* 27; Alexander Spoehr to John Collier, August 22, 1939, file-62440-1939-Seminole-101, BIACF; Willard W. Beatty to Joe Jennings, October 11, 1939, ibid.

37. Interviews with Mary Parker Bowers and Betty Mae Jumper, 1977 and 1985.

38. Kersey and Kushin, "Ivy Stranahan," 9.

39. Interview with Mary Chiltoskey.

40. Kersey, "Educating the Florida Seminoles," 31.

41. Szasz, *Education and the American Indian,* 76.

42. Alan R. Beals with George and Louise Spindler, *Culture in Process,* 239–247; George and Louise Spindler, *Education and Culture,* 23–28, 34–38.

Chapter 8

1. Dwight R. Gardin to D. E. Murphy, April 15, 1940, file-24298-1933-Seminole-344, part III, CCC-ID.

2. D. E. Murphy to Dwight R. Gardin, June 12, 1940, ibid.

3. Interview with Willie Frank.

4. Ray Ovid Hall to D. E. Murphy, July 23, 1940, file-24298-1933-Seminole-344, part III, CCC-ID.

5. D. E. Murphy to Dwight R. Gardin, August 7, 1940, ibid.

6. Philp, "Turmoil at Big Cypress," 34n. See also John Collier to Dwight R. Gardin, December 2, 1940, March 29, 1941; John Collier to S. G. Grover, March 29, 1941, all in part I, series I, reel 24, Collier Papers.

7. *Senate Hearings Cattle Tick,* 73, 96–107; see also John Collier to Dwight R. Gardin, January 8, 18, December 27, 1940, part I, series I, reel 24, Collier Papers.

8. Dwight R. Gardin to E. J. Armstrong, August 2, 1940, file-24298-1933-Seminole-344, part III, CCC-ID.

9. William Zimmerman, Jr. to Dwight R. Gardin, April 11, 1941, Records of the Bureau of Indian Affairs, Indian Rehabilitation, file-76081-1941-Seminole-066, cited hereafter as IR.

10. James W. Covington, "The Seminoles and Selective Service in World War II."

11. John Collier, "Office of Indian Affairs," in *Annual Report of the Secretary of the Interior 1942,* 237, 239–40.

12. Buswell, "Seminole Religious Ritual," 268.

13. Interview with Susie Billie.

14. Dwight R. Gardin to John Collier, June 24, 1941, and Dwight R. Gardin to Xavier Vigeant through Collier, June 25, 1941, file-76081-1941-066, IR.

15. Covington, "Selective Service," 49.

16. *Florida Times-Union,* March 5, 1943.

17. Interview with Willie Frank; personal communication between Buffalo Tiger and the author, 1986.

18. Department of the Interior, Office of Indian Affairs, *Indian Census Roll,* 45.

19. "Howard Tiger Is First Seminole to Enlist."

20. Selective Service System, *Special Groups,* 8.

21. A. C. Cooley, *Memorandum regarding Seminole Cattle "Cow Creek Group,"* November 26, 1941, file-76081-1941-Seminole-066, IR.

22. William Zimmerman, Jr. to William B. Hill, December 11, 1941 [two items], ibid.

23. D. E. Murphy, "Final Report of the Indian Emergency Conservation Work and Civilian Conservation Corps–Indian Division Program, 1933–1942," typescript, CCC-ID.

24. Collier, "Office of Indian Affairs," 242–43.

25. John Collier, "The Spirit of CCC Will Last Forever."

26. Murphy to William B. Hill, April 22, 1942, file-24298-1933-Seminole-344, part II, CCC-ID.

27. D. E. Murphy to William B. Hill, May 28, 1942, ibid.

28. Luther A. Williams to D. E. Murphy, June 3, 1942, file-24298-1933-Seminole-344, part III, CCC-ID.

29. C. E. Faris to D. E. Murphy, June 19, 1942, ibid.

30. Murphy, "Final Report," 77.

31. Donald L. Parman, "The Indian and the Civilian Conservation Corps," 144.

32. Murphy, "Final Report," 26–28.

33. *CCC-ID Work Program Fiscal Year 1942,* file-24298-1933-Seminole-344, part II, CCC-ID.

34. Murphy, "Final Report," 24.

35. "How Indians Are Housed."

36. "Seminole Agency to Be Moved to Fort Myers, Florida."

37. C. E. Faris to Paul Fickinger, July 15, 1942, Superintendent's Office File, Seminole Agency, Hollywood, Florida.

38. Mrs. Frank Stranahan to John Collier, July 9, 1942, and Ben Tommie, Brown Tommie, and Jimmie Tiger to John Collier, July 9, 1942, box 8, file 1-Indian Federal Agencies 1915-51, Stranahan Collection.

39. Donald L. Parman, *The Navajos and the New Deal,* 291.

40. Laurence M. Hauptman, *The Iroquois and the New Deal,* 29.

Chapter 9

1. John Steinbeck, "Living with Hard Times," 28; reprint of an article from *Esquire* (June 1960) entitled "A Primer on the Thirties."

2. Alfonso Ortiz, "Indian Policy, 1933–1945," 64.

3. John Collier, "Office of Indian Affairs," in *Annual Report of the Secretary of the Interior for the Fiscal Year Ending June 30, 1938*, 261.

4. Sturtevant, "Creek into Seminole," 119–21; Covington, "Trail Indians of Florida."

5. Murphy, "Final Report of Indian Emergency Conservation Work and Civilian Conservation Corps–Indian Division Program, 1933–1942," 21.

6. King, "Clan Affiliation and Leadership among the Twentieth-Century Florida Indians."

7. Department of the Interior, Bureau of Indian Affairs. *Constitution and By-laws of the Seminole Tribe of Florida* and *Corporate Charter of the Seminole Tribe of Florida;* Robert L. Bennett, "Implementing the IRA," 85.

8. Seminole Tribe of Florida, "20th Anniversary of Tribal Organization, 1957–1977"; contains biographical profiles of former chairmen and presidents of the tribal council and board of directors.

9. Kersey, "The Tony Tommie Letter, 1916."

10. Florida, Department of State, Division of Cultural Affairs, *Florida Folk Artists and Apprentices 1984–1985*, 2. See also the division's "Four Corners of Earth," a video on Seminole women.

Bibliography

"Activities at the Seminole Day School, Florida." *Indians at Work* 4 (September 1936): 17–18.

Andrews, Allen H. *A Yank Pioneer in Florida*. Jacksonville: Douglas Printing Co., 1950.

Beals, Alan R. with George Spindler and Louise Spindler. *Culture in Process*. New York: Holt, Rinehart & Winston, 1967.

Beatty, Willard W. "Education for the Whole Community." *Indians at Work* 3 (June 1936): 28–31.

Bennett, Robert L. "Implementing the IRA." In Philp, ed., 83–86, q.v.

Brookings Institution, Institute for Government Research. *The Problem of Indian Administration*, edited by Lewis Meriam. Baltimore: Johns Hopkins Press, 1928.

Burghard, August A. *Watchie-Esta/Hutrie (Little White Mother), The Remarkable Story of Mrs. Frank Stranahan, Broward County's First School Teacher*. Fort Lauderdale: privately published, 1968.

Buswell, James O. III. "Florida Seminole Religious Ritual: Resistance and Change." Ph.D. dissertation, St. Louis University, 1972.

———. Review of *Pelts, Plumes and Hides*. *Florida Historical Quarterly* 55 (1976): 190–93.

Capron, Louis. "The Medicine Bundles of the Florida Seminole and the Green Corn Dance." *Bureau of American Ethnology Bulletin* 151 (December 1953): 155–210.

———. "Notes on the Hunting Dance of the Cow Creek Seminoles." *Florida Anthropologist* 9 (December 1956): 67–78.

Casagrande, Joseph B., ed. *In the Company of Man: Twenty Portraits by Anthropologists*. New York: Harper, 1960.

Cohen, Felix S. *Handbook of Federal Indian Law*. Albuquerque: University of New Mexico Press, 1971.

———. *The Legal Conscience: Selected Papers of Felix S. Cohen*. Edited by Lucy Kramer Cohen. New Haven: Yale University Press, 1960.

Collier, John. *From Every Zenith*. Denver: Sage Books, 1963.

———. "Indian Education." *Indians at Work* 3 (August 1935): 1–7.

———. "The Red Atlantis." *Survey Graphic* 49 (October 1, 1922): 15–20, 63, 66.

———. "The Seminoles Move Forward." *Indians at Work* 7 (February 1940): 1–3.

———. "The Spirit of CCC Will Last Forever." *Indians at Work* 9 (May–June 1942): 35.

———. "With Secretary Ickes and the Seminoles." *Indians at Work* 2 (April 1, 1935): 1–5.

Costo, Rupert. "Federal Indian Policy, 1933–1945." In Philp, ed., 48–54, q.v.

Covington, James W. "Brighton Reservation, Florida, 1935–1943." *Tequesta* 36 (1976): 54–65.

———. "Dania Reservation, 1911–1927." *Florida Anthropologist* 29 (1976): 137–44.

———. "The Seminoles and the Civilian Conservation Corps." *Florida Anthropologist* 34 (1981): 232–37.

———. "The Seminoles and Selective Service in World War II." *Florida Anthropologist* 32 (June 1979): 46–51.

———. "Trail Indians of Florida." *Florida Historical Quarterly* 58 (July 1979): 37–57.

Craig, Alan K., and David McJunkin. "Stranahan's: Last of the Seminole Trading Posts." *Florida Anthropologist* 24 (1971): 45–50.

Dacy, George H. *See* Department of the Interior, Seminole Agency.

Deloria, Vine, Jr., and Clifford Lytle. *The Nations Within: The Past and Future of American Indian Sovereignty*. New York: Pantheon Books, 1984.

Densmore, Frances. *Seminole Music*. New York: Da Capo, 1972.

Devol, Elsie H. "Activities at the Seminole Day School, Dania, Florida." *Indians at Work* 3 (August 1936): 27.

Downs, Dorothy. "Coppinger's Tropical Gardens: The First Commercial Indian Village in Florida." *Florida Anthropologist* 34 (1981): 225–31.

First Seminole Indian Baptist Church. "Souvenir Brochure, Dedicatory Service, First Seminole Indian Baptist Church (Four Miles West of Dania) Dania, Florida, May 29, 1949."

"Florida Seminole CCC Sponsors a Community Celebration." *Indians at Work* 6 (August 1939): 20–22.

Freeman, Ethel Cutler. "Culture Stability and Change among the Seminoles of Florida." In Wallace, ed., 249–54, q.v.

———. "Our Unique Indians, the Seminoles of Florida." *American Indian* 21 (1944–45): 14–28.

———. "The Seminole Woman of the Big Cypress and Her Influence in Modern Life." *American Indigena* 4 (1944): 123–28.

———. "We Live with the Seminoles." *Natural History* 49 (April 1942): 226–36.

Garbarino, Merwyn S. *Big Cypress, A Changing Seminole Community*. New York: Holt, Rinehart & Winston, 1972.

Glenn, James L. "The Florida Seminoles." Typescript, Fort Lauderdale Historical Society.

———. *My Work among the Florida Seminoles*. Edited with an introduction by Harry A. Kersey, Jr. Gainesville: University Presses of Florida, 1982.

———. "The Saga of the Florida Indians." Typescript, Fort Lauderdale Historical Society.

Gower, Calvin W. "The CCC Indian Division: Aid for Depressed Americans, 1933–1942." *Minnesota History* 43 (September 1972): 3–13.

Greenlee, Robert. "Aspects of Social Organization and Material Culture of the Seminole of the Big Cypress Swamp." *Florida Anthropologist* 5 (December 1952): 25–32.

———. "Folktales of the Florida Seminole." *Journal of American Folklore* 58 (April–June 1945): 138–44.

———. "Medicine and Curing Practices of the Modern Florida Seminoles." *American Anthropologist* 46 (July–September 1944): 317–28.

Haas, Theodore H. *Ten Years of Tribal Government under the I.R.A.* Chicago: Haskell Institute Printing Service, 1947.

Hanna, Alfred J., and Kathryn A. Hanna. *Lake Okeechobee*. New York: Bobbs-Merrill, 1948.

Hartley, William, and Ellen A. Hartley. *A Woman Set Apart*. New York: Dodd, Mead, 1963.

Hauptman, Laurence M. *The Iroquois and the New Deal*. Syracuse: Syracuse University Press, 1981.

"How Indians Are Housed." *Indians at Work* 6 (September 1938): 4–5.

"Howard Tiger Is First Seminole to Enlist." *Indians at Work* 9 (September–October 1943): 4–5.

Hundley, Norris, ed. *The American Indian: Essays from Pacific Historical Review*. Santa Barbara: Clio Books, 1974.

Ickes, Harold L. *The Autobiography of a Curmudgeon*. Chicago: Quadrangle Books, 1969.

Indian Law Resource Center. "Report to Congress: Seminole Land Rights in Florida and the Award of the Indian Claims Commission." Washington, D.C., May 9, 1978.

Irons, Peter. *New Deal Lawyers*. Princeton: Princeton University Press, 1982.

Joiner, Edward Earl. *A History of Florida Baptists*. Jacksonville: Convention Press, 1972.

Jumper, Betty Mae. "'. . . and with the Wagon came God's Word'." Hollywood: Seminole Tribe of Florida, 1980.

Kelly, Lawrence C. *The Assault on Assimilation: John Collier and the Origins of Indian Policy Reform*. Albuquerque: University of New Mexico Press, 1983.

Kelly, William H., ed. *Indian Affairs and the Indian Reorganization Act: The Twenty-Year Record*. Tucson: University of Arizona Press, 1954.

Kersey, Harry A., Jr. "A 'New Red Atlantis': John Collier's Encounter with the Florida Seminoles in 1935." *Florida Historical Quarterly* 66 (1987): 131–51.

———. "Educating the Seminole Indians of Florida, 1879–1970." *Florida Historical Quarterly* 49 (1970): 16–35.

———. "Federal Schools and Acculturation among the Florida Seminoles, 1927–1954." *Florida Historical Quarterly* 59 (1980): 165–81.

———. "Florida Seminoles in the Depression and New Deal, 1933–1942: An Indian Perspective." *Florida Historical Quarterly* 65 (1986): 175–95.

———. *Pelts, Plumes and Hides: White Traders among the Seminole Indians, 1870–1930*. Gainesville: University Presses of Florida, 1975.

———. "Private Societies and the Maintenance of Seminole Tribal Integrity, 1899–1957." *Florida Historical Quarterly* 56 (January 1978): 297–316.

———. "The Tony Tommie Letter, 1916: A Transitional Seminole Document." *Florida Historical Quarterly* 64 (January 1986): 301–15.

———, and Rochelle Kushin. "Ivy Stranahan and the 'Friends of the Seminoles,' 1899–1971." *Broward Legacy* 1 (October 1976): 6–11.

King, Robert T. "Clan Affiliation and Leadership among the Twentieth-Century Florida Indians." *Florida Historical Quarterly* 55 (October 1976): 138–52.

———. "The Florida Seminole Polity, 1858–1978." Ph.D. dissertation, University of Florida, 1978.

Leacock, Eleanor B., and Nancy O. Lurie, eds. *North American Indians in Cultural Perspective*. New York: Random House, 1971.

Leuchtenburg, William E. *Franklin D. Roosevelt and the New Deal, 1932–1940*. New York: Harper & Row, 1963.

McGoun, Bill A. *A Biographic History of Broward County*. Miami: *Miami Herald*, 1972.

McNickle, D'Arcy. *Native American Tribalism, Indian Survivals and Renewals*. New York: Oxford University Press, 1973.

Mertz, Paul E. *New Deal Policy and Southern Rural Poverty*. Baton Rouge: Louisiana State University Press, 1978.

Nash, Jay B., Oliver LaFarge, and W. Carson Ryan. *The New Days for the Indians: A Survey of the Working of the Indian Reorganization Act*. New York: Academy Press, 1938.

Nash, Roy. *See* U.S. Congress. Senate. *Survey of the Seminole Indians of Florida*.

Neely, Sharlotte. "The Quaker Era of Cherokee Indian Education, 1880–1892." *Appalachian Journal* 2 (Summer 1975): 314–22.

O'Neil, Floyd A. "The Indian New Deal: An Overview." In Philp, ed., 30–46, q.v..

Ortiz, Alfonso. "Indian Policy, 1933–1945." In Philp, ed., 64–69, q.v.

Parman, Donald L. "The Indian and the Civilian Conservation Corps." In Hundley, ed., 127–45, q.v.

———. *The Navajos and the New Deal*. New Haven: Yale University Press, 1976.

Philp, Kenneth R. *John Collier's Crusade for Indian Reform, 1920–1954*. Tucson: University of Arizona Press, 1977.

———, ed. *Indian Self-Rule*. Salt Lake City: Howe Brothers, 1986.

———. "Turmoil at Big Cypress: Seminole Deer and the Florida Cattle Tick Controversy." *Florida Historical Quarterly* 56 (July 1977): 28–44.

Porter, Kenneth W. "The Cowkeeper Dynasty of the Seminole Nation." *Florida Historical Quarterly* 30 (April 1952): 341–49.

Roseberry, C. R. *Glenn Curtiss: Pioneer of Flight*. New York: Doubleday, 1972.

Ryan, W. Carson, Jr. "A Trip among the Indian Communities of the Southeast." *Indians at Work* 1 (April 1934): 40–41.

Schrader, Robert Fay. *The Indian Arts & Crafts Board: An Aspect of New Deal Indian Policy.* Albuquerque: University of New Mexico Press, 1983.

Scott, F. J. "Education for the Florida Seminoles." *Indians at Work* 4 (May 1937): 45–46.

"Secretary Ickes Upholds Seminoles in Opposing Slaughter of Their Deer." *Indians at Work* 7 (March 1940): 8–11.

"Seminole Agency to Be Moved to Fort Myers, Florida." *Indians at Work* 6 (February 1939): 20.

Seminole Tribe of Florida, and Seminole Tribe of Florida, Inc. "20th Anniversary of Tribal Organization, 1957–1977, Saturday, August 20, 1977." Mimeo.

"Seminoles Participate in Florida State Fair." *Indians at Work* 5 (June 1938): 35.

Shofner, Jerrell H. "Roosevelt's 'Tree Army': The Civilian Conservation Corps in Florida." *Florida Historical Quarterly* 65 (April 1987): 433–56.

Spindler, George, and Louise Spindler. *Education and Culture*. New York: Holt, Rinehart & Winston, 1963.

Spoehr, Alexander. "Camp, Clan and Kin among the Cow Creek Seminoles of Florida." *Anthropological Series Field Museum of Natural History* 33 (1941): 1–27.

———. "The Florida Seminole Camp." *Anthropological Series Field Museum of Natural History* 33 (1944): 121-50.

Steinbeck, John. "Living With Hard Times." *Esquire* (June 1983): 27–32.

Stirling, Gene. *See* U.S. Department of the Interior, Office of Indian Affairs. *Report on the Seminole Indians of Florida.*

Straight, William M. "Josie Billie, Seminole Doctor, Medicine Man, and Baptist Preacher." *Journal of the Florida Medical Association* 57 (1970): 33–40.

Sturtevant, William C. "A Seminole Medicine Maker." In Casagrande, ed., 505–32, q.v.

———. "A Seminole Personal Document." *Tequesta* 16 (1956): 55–75.

———. "Creek into Seminole." In Leacock and Lurie, eds., 92–128, q.v.

———. "The Medicine Bundles and Busks of the Florida Seminole." *Florida Anthropologist* 7 (May 1954): 30–71.

Szasz, Margaret. *Education and the American Indian: The Road to Self-Determination, 1928–1973*. Albuquerque: University of New Mexico Press, 1974.

Taylor, Graham D. *The New Deal and American Indian Tribalism: The Administration of the Indian Reorganization Act, 1934–1945*. Lincoln: University of Nebraska Press, 1980.

Tebeau, Charlton W. *Florida's Last Frontier: The History of Collier County*. Miami: University of Miami Press, 1957.

———. *Story of the Chokoloskee Bay Country*. Miami: University of Miami Press, 1955.

Tyler, S. Lyman. *A History of Indian Policy.* Washington: Bureau of Indian Affairs, 1973.
"Views from Seminole Reservation in Florida." *Indians at Work* 4 (1937): 18.
Wallace, Anthony F. C., ed. *Men and Cultures: Selected Papers of the Fifth International Congress of Anthropological and Ethnological Sciences, Philadelphia, September 1–9, 1956.* Philadelphia: University of Pennsylvania Press, 1960.
Warren, Cecil R. "Florida's Seminoles: An Eye-Witness Story of Indian Want and Privation as Published by the *Miami Daily News* with affidavits and accompanying documents." Miami: *Miami Daily News,* 1934.
Washburn, Wilcomb E. *Red Man's Land–White Man's Law.* New York: Charles Scribner's Sons, 1971.
———. *The Assault on Indian Tribalism: The General Allotment Law (Dawes Act) of 1887.* Philadelphia: J.P. Lippincott, 1975.
———. *The Indian in America.* New York: Harper & Row, 1975.
Weidling, Philip, and August Burghard. *Checkered Sunshine: The History of Fort Lauderdale, 1793–1955.* Gainesville: University of Florida Press, 1966.
West, Patsy. "Seminoles in Broward County: The Pine Island Legacy." *New River News* 23 (Fall 1985): 4–11.
———. "The Miami Indian Tourist Attractions: A History and Analysis of a Transitional Mikasuki Seminole Environment." *Florida Anthropologist* 34 (December 1981): 200–224.
Works Projects Administration, Federal Writers' Program. *Seminole Indians in Florida.* Washington: Government Printing Office, 1941.

NATIONAL ARCHIVES

Records of the Bureau of Indian Affairs. Record Group 75
Central Classified Files, 1907–39 (BIACF)
Civilian Conservation Corps–Indian Division (CCC-ID)
Commissioner's Office File (COF)
Indian Rehabilitation (IR)
Narrative Reports, Seminole, 1913–35 (NR)

OTHER ARCHIVAL SOURCES

Florida Historical Society, University of South Florida, Tampa.
Works Progress Administration Writers' Project of Florida File (WPA File)
Fort Lauderdale Historical Society, Fort Lauderdale, Florida. (FLHS)
Glenn Collection
Stranahan Collection
Yale University Library, New Haven, Connecticut.
John Collier Papers

FEDERAL GOVERNMENT DOCUMENTS

"Executive Order 7868," *Code of Federal Regulations,* Title 3. 1938.
Indians at Work, Vols. I–X. Washington: Office of Indian Affairs, 1933–43.
U.S. Congress. Senate. *Indian Affairs, Laws and Treaties.* 62d Cong., 2d sess., 1913. Vol. 3. S. Doc. 719. Washington, 1913.
———. *Seminole Indians in Florida.* 63d Cong., 1st sess., 1913. S. Doc. 42. Washington, 1913.
———. *Special Report of the Florida Seminole Agency.* 67th Cong., 2d sess., 1921. S. Doc. 102. Washington, 1921.

————. *Survey of the Seminole Indians of Florida* by Roy Nash. 71st Cong., 3d sess., 1931. S. Doc. 314. Washington, 1931.

————. Committee on Indian Affairs. *Eradicating Cattle Tick, Seminole Indian Reservation, Fla. Hearings on S.1476.* 77th Cong., 1st sess., 1941. Washington, 1941.

————. Select Committee on Indian Affairs. *Distribution of Seminole Judgment Funds: Hearing before the United States Senate Select Committee on Indian Affairs, March 2, 1978. Hearings on S.2000 and S.2188.* 95th Cong. Washington, 1978.

————. Subcommittee of the Committee on Indian Affairs. *Survey of Conditions of the Indians in the United States. Hearings Pursuant to Senate Resolution 79 and Senate Resolution 308,* Part. 16. 71st Cong., 3d sess., March 31, 1930. Washington, 1931.

U.S. Department of the Interior. *Annual Report of the Secretary of the Interior for the Fiscal Year Ending June 30, 1938.* Washington, 1938.

————. *Annual Report of the Secretary of the Interior for the Fiscal Year Ending June 30, 1939.* Washington, 1939.

————. *Annual Report of the Secretary of the Interior 1942.* Washington, 1942.

————. Bureau of Indian Affairs. *Constitution and Bylaws of the Seminole Tribe of Florida, Ratified August 21, 1957.* Washington, 1958.

————. Bureau of Indian Affairs. *Corporate Charter of the Seminole Tribe of Florida, Ratified August 21, 1957.* Washington, 1958.

————. Office of Indian Affairs. *Indian Census Roll, Seminoles of Florida, Seminole Agency, January 1, 1942, taken by William B. Hill Superintendent.* Hollywood, Florida: Seminole Agency, Superintendent's Office.

————. Office of Indian Affairs. *Report on the Seminole Indians of Florida* by Gene Stirling (Doc. 126567). Washington: Office of Indian Affairs, Applied Anthropology Unit, 1936. Mimeo.

————. Seminole Agency. *Report on the Seminole Indians of Florida for the National Resources Planning Board* by George H. Dacy. Dania, Florida, 1941. Mimeo.

U.S. Selective Service System. *Special Groups.* Special Monograph Series No. 10, Vol. 1. Washington, 1953.

United States Statutes at Large, Vols. 43, 48, 49, 70, 96, 101.

FLORIDA GOVERNMENT DOCUMENTS

Florida. Department of State. Division of Cultural Affairs. *Florida Folk Artists and Apprentices, 1984–85.* Tallahassee, 1985.

————. Videotape, "Four Corners of Earth." Tallahassee: Bureau of Florida Folklife and WFSU-TV, 1984.

Florida Statutes 285. "Indian Reservations and Affairs." 1985.

Florida. Trustees Internal Improvement Fund. *Minutes of the Trustees of the Internal Improvement Fund,* Vol. 20. Tallahassee, 1936.

South Florida Water Management District. "Water Shortage Plan." In *Rules of the South Florida Water Management District, Chapter 40E–21.* West Palm Beach, 1986.

TAPED INTERVIEWS, University of Florida Oral History Archives

Albert Billie, October 30, 1984. SEM 191A, UFHA.

Susie Billie, May 6, 1984. SEM 187A, UFHA.

Mary Parker Bowers, January 27, 1977. SEM 154A, UFHA.

Mary Chiltoskey, June 6, 1977. SEM 170A, UFHA.

Abraham Clay, May 6, 1984. SEM 193A, UFHA.

Frank Cypress, April 22, 1984. SEM194A, UFHA.
Jimmie Cypress, October 30, 1984. SEM 190A, UFHA.
Willie Frank, May 21, 1984. SEM 192A, UFHA.
James L. Glenn, January 12, 1978. SEM 172A, UFHA.
Betty Mae Jumper, June 17, 1969. SEM 8A, UFHA; March 22, 1977. SEM 156A, UFHA;
    January 2, 1985. SEM 186A, UFHA.
Fred Montsdeoca, December 4, 1972. SEM 76A, UFHA.
Buffalo Tiger, May 3, 1984. SEM 185A, UFHA.
Willie Tiger, October 30, 1984. SEM 188A, UFHA.
Sam Tommie, March 14, 1969. SEM 14A, UFHA.
Dorothy Tucker, February 10, 1977. SEM 155A, UFHA.

Index

Agriculture, U.S. department of, 50, 86, 96, 126, 127, 128
The American Eagle, 64
American Indian Defense Association, 10, 15, 49, 69
American Museum of Natural History, 114
Andrews, Allen H., 64, 65
Arizona, 48, 156
Assimilation, 14, 15, 131–32, 153, 173, 178–79; and Christianity, 33; and economics, 46; and education, 132–51; and Great Depression, 20; and Indian Office, 29, 69, 73, 165–66; and traditional dress, 172; vs. tribalism, 17–18; and World War II, 161. *See also* Education, Indian

Beatty, Willard Walcott, 142, 146, 147, 148, 150
Bedell, Harriet, 58, 75–76, 85, 175
Big Cypress region, 1, 4, 8, 9, 24, 36, 57, 59, 61, 62, 63, 82, 83, 89, 90
Big Cypress Reservation, 107, 108, 130; cattle enterprise at, 100, 118, 124, 125, 129, 154, 160, 162; construction of road at, 124, 153; destruction of deer at, 125–26, 127, 128, 129; draft registration at, 156; language of, 97, 114; Mikasukis at, 112, 118, 120, 172, 177; missionaries at, 6, 121, 122; and New Deal pro-

grams, 102, 105, 113, 178; religious leaders at, 175–76; schools at, 145
Billie, Albert, 35, 54
Billie, Buffalo Jim, 177
Billie, Charley, 62, 63
Billie, Chesnut, 45, 61, 62
Billie, Ingraham, 45, 62, 92, 121
Billie, Josie: and cattle enterprise, 124, 177; conversion to Christianity, 121, 122, 175; and draft registration, 157, 158; and Everglades National Park, 112; and Indian schools, 24; as medicine man, 120, 123, 156
Billie, Susie Jim, 7, 36–37, 157, 177
Boehmer, William, 103, 144–45, 156
Boehmer, Mrs. William, 103
Bowlegs, Billy, 61
Brandon, F. E., 7, 8
Brecht, J. E., 8
Brickell, Bill, 1
Bright, James H., 97
Brighton Reservation, 32, 86, 91, 95–96, 98, 114, 115, 124; acculturation at, 120, 130; cattle enterprise at, 99, 100, 101, 106, 129, 155, 160, 173–74; community life at, 104; draft registration at, 156, 159; economic activities at, 101–2; language of, 97; Mikasukis at, 117; and New Deal programs, 105, 122, 178; organization of, 106, 107; schools at, 102–3, 106, 131, 144, 150, 176. *See also* Cow

Stranahan, Ivy Cromartie (Mrs. Frank), 9–10, 38, 56, 59, 73, 145, 149, 168, 175; and Indian schools, 12; as temperance advocate, 57; testimony of, 19, 144; and West Palm Beach meeting, 85. *See also* Dania Reservation

Sturtevant, William, 86

Summerlin, Clarence, 37

Sun Dance, 76

Survey of Conditions of the Indians in the United States (U.S. Senate; 1928), 18

Survey of the Seminole Indians of Florida (U.S. Senate; 1931), 15, 16, 17, 25, 110

Szasz, Margaret, 133, 146

Taft, William H., 3–4

Tallahassee, 25, 95

Tamiami Trail, 61, 76, 79, 82, 94, 175; camps on, 45, 58, 59, 63, 86, 109, 111, 112, 113, 117, 118, 141, 159, 172; effect on Indian culture, 24. *See also* Trail Indians

Tampa, 58, 102

Teapot Dome Scandal, 14

Thomas, Senator Elmer, 18, 20, 70

Tiger, Ada, 161, 177

Tiger, Betty Mae (Mrs. Moses Jumper), 145, 147, 149, 160, 161, 176, 177

Tiger, Brown, 62

Tiger, Cuffney, 113, 120

Tiger, Frank, 62, 160

Tiger, Howard, 143, 145, 149, 161, 177

Tiger, John, 160

Tiger, Lena, 160

Tiger, Naha, 19, 61

Tiger, William Buffalo, 37, 41, 43, 54, 109, 160

Tommie, Annie, 9, 10, 38, 60, 176, 177, 179

Tommie, Jack, 61

Tommie, Mary, 143

Tommie, Sam, 60, 61, 63, 66, 77, 83, 93, 176–77

Tommie, Tony, 7, 9, 10, 11, 12, 38, 59, 60, 62, 179; as spokesman, 177; wedding of, 40

Tourist villages, commercial, 21, 38, 41, 43, 76, 117, 118, 126, 152; demoralizing effect of, 17, 36, 40, 44–45, 123

Tractors, use of, 52, 53, 54

Trading posts, 1–2, 4, 10, 17

Trail Indians, 92, 112, 117, 120, 169, 172. *See also* Miccosukee Tribe; Tamiami Trail

Trapping, 1–3, 4–5, 23, 37, 88, 90. *See also* Hunting

Tribalism, 14, 15, 17–18, 131. *See also* Assimilation; Culture, Indian

Tugwell, Rexford G., 91

Villa, Pancho, 7

Wallace, Henry A., 127

Warren, Cecil R., 59–60, 61, 62, 63, 64

Weltner, Dr. Philip, 99

West, Patsy, 41

West Palm Beach, meeting at, 75–78, 82–87, 91–92, 106, 109, 110, 111, 166

Wheeler, Senator Burton K., 70, 153

Wheeler-Howard Act. *See* Indian Reorganization Act

Whiskey Bay Reservation (Michigan), 6

White, O. B., 83, 84, 109

Wickard, Claude, 128, 129

Wilcox, Congressman J. Mark, 73, 84

Willie, Charlie, 43

Willie, Elizabeth Willie, 44

Willie, Willie, 41–43, 44

Wirtz, A. J., 127

Women, Seminole, 29, 33, 35; adaptability of, 119, 173; as agricultural laborers, 36, 173; and child bearing, 116; as conservators of cultural tradition, 118–19, 177; and CWA, 52; and drinking, 118; and handicrafts, 103, 104; and matrilocal marriage, 116; and schooling, 147, 149; status of,